The
BEGINNING
of the
GOSPEL

Probings of Mark in Context

ADELA YARBRO COLLINS

Fortress Press   Minneapolis

THE BEGINNING OF THE GOSPEL
Probings of Mark in Context

Library of Congress Cataloging-in-Publication Data

Collins, Adela Yarbro.
    The beginning of the Gospel : probings of Mark in context / Adela
Yarbro Collins.
        p.   cm.
    Includes bibliographical references and indexes.
    ISBN 0-8006-2622-2 (alk. paper) :
    1. Bible.   N. T.   Mark—Criticism, interpretation, etc.   2. Bible.
N.T.   Mark—Theology.   I. Title.
BS2585.2.C569   1992
226.3'06—dc20   92-32115
                                                               CIP

The paper used in this publication meets the minimum requirements of American National Standard for Information Sciences—Permanence of Paper for Printed Library Materials, ANSI Z329.48-1984.   ∞™

Manufactured in the U.S.A.   AF 1-2622
  96   95   94   93   92   1   2   3   4   5   6   7   8   9   10

This volume is dedicated
to the memory of
Robert T. Voelkel
former Vice President and Dean of Pomona College
and the William M. Keck Distinguished Professor of Religion
Mentor and Friend

CONTENTS

CONTENTS

PREFACE

FOR CENTURIES THE GOSPEL OF MARK was relatively neglected since it was regarded as a mere summary of Matthew. In the nineteenth century a new consensus emerged that Mark is the earliest of the four canonical Gospels. It was simply assumed for a time that "early" meant "historically accurate and reliable." Confidence in the historical reliability of Mark was shaken by the works of Wilhelm Wrede (*Das Messiasgeheimnis in den Evangelien*, 1901) and K. L. Schmidt (*Der Rahmen der Geschichte Jesu*, 1919). Scholarly attention then turned to the smaller forms behind the Gospels (form criticism). In 1956, Willi Marxsen inaugurated a new approach to Mark, known as redaction criticism (*Mark the Evangelist*). In the 1970s, an aesthetic-literary approach to Mark was developed (Robert Tannehill, "The Disciples in Mark: The Function of a Narrative Role," *JR* 57 [1977] 384–405). Since then a daunting number of redaction-critical and literary studies on Mark have appeared. The current situation is characterized by a conflict of methods. Should scholars and students focus on the "story world" of Mark or on the relation between the text and its social and historical context? What should the relationship be between study of the Gospel in its present form and study of the process through which the Gospel came into being?

I believe that more attention should be paid to Mark in its historical context and to the process through which the Gospel came into being. Literary methods are essential, since we are dealing with a text. But for those of us interested in origins and historical development, it is important to ask which literary questions, methods, and comparisons are appropriate to a first-century text with Mark's specific literary features.

The essays in this volume are programmatic studies, written between 1988 and 1991, for the Hermeneia commentary on Mark that I am preparing. They have been informed by literary approaches to Mark, but use primarily the methods of the history of religion and tradition history. It is my hope that they will shed some light on both the meaning and the significance of Mark.

The essay "Suffering and Healing in the Gospel of Mark" was presented at the Theology Institute of Villanova University in 1989. I would like to thank Francis Eigo and his colleagues at Villanova for inviting me to participate in the Institute and Susan Ross and William M. Thompson, my respondents, for their colleagueship and suggestions. The essay "Is Mark's Gospel a Life of Jesus?" was the 1989 Père Marquette Lecture in Theology. I am grateful to John J. Schmitt and his colleagues in the Department of Theology at Marquette for their hospitality and encouragement. The essay "The Empty Tomb and Resurrection according to Mark" was presented at a conference on "Philosophical Theology and Biblical Studies," sponsored by the Center for Philosophy of Religion at the University of Notre Dame in 1990. I would like to thank the organizers of the conference, Thomas Flint and Eleonore Stump, for their invitation to participate, and Stephen Davis and Normann Kretzmann for their comments on the paper. Versions of the paper were also presented at the Divinity School of the University of Chicago and the Central States Regional meeting of the SBL/AAR/ASOR in 1991. On both occasions, the conversation was very encouraging and helpful. I would also like to thank my former colleage at McCormick Theological Seminary, David Reeves, for stimulating conversations about the resurrection. The essay "Mark 13: An Apocalyptic Discourse" was presented to the Seminar on Apocalyptic in the New Testament at the general meeting of the Studiorum Novi Testamenti Societas in Bethel-bei-Bielefeld in 1991. I am grateful to Charles Homer Giblin and Traugott Holtz for inviting me to give the paper and to the members of the seminar for their comments. The essay "The Passion Narrative of Mark" was presented to a seminar working on the history of the tradition related to Jesus that met at the University of Alberta in Edmonton in 1991. I would like to thank Robert

Funk, Stephen Patterson, and Philip Sellew for inviting me to participate and all the members of the seminar for a very helpful and stimulating discussion.

Marshall Johnson, Editorial Director of Fortress Press, and Charles Puskas, Jr., Academic Editor, have been very helpful, both in getting this project under way and seeing it through to its completion.

I would also like to express my thanks to the Association of Theological Schools for the Theological Scholarship and Research Grant that was awarded to me for the academic year 1991–92 and to the Divinity School of the University of Chicago for granting me a study leave during the fall quarter, 1991. The grant and the leave provided time for writing the essay "The Passion Narrative of Mark" and for revising the other essays in the preparation of this volume. I am grateful to Walter Wilson for preparing the bibliography and to Gary Lee for copyediting the manuscript and compiling the indexes.

Translations from the New Testament are my own unless otherwise noted.

Adela Yarbro Collins
December 1991

ACKNOWLEDGMENTS

The author thanks the original publishers for permission to republish her essays in this book:

1. *Is Mark's Gospel a Life of Jesus? The Question of Genre*. The Père Marquette Lecture in Theology 1989. Milwaukee, Wis.: Marquette Univ. Press, 1990.

2. " 'Remove This Cup': Suffering and Healing in the Gospel of Mark." In *Suffering and Healing in Our Day*. Ed. Francis A. Eigo, O.S.A. Proceedings of the Theology Institute of Villanova University 22. Villanova, Pa.: Villanova Univ. Press, 1990. Pp. 29–61.

3. "The Eschatological Discourse of Mark 13." In *The Four Gospels 1992: Festschrift for Frans Neirynck*. Ed. C. M. Tuckett, F. Van Segbroeck, G. Van Belle, J. Verheyden. Bibliotheca ephemeridum theologicarum lovaniensium. Gembloux: Duculot/ Leuven Univ. Press, 1992.

4. "The Composition of the Passion Narrative in Mark," *Sewanee Theological Review* (Dec. 1992).

5. "The Empty Tomb in the Gospel according to Mark." In *Hermes and Athena: Biblical Exegesis and Philosophical Theology*. Ed. Thomas Flint and Eleanore Stump. Notre Dame, Ind.: Univ. of Notre Dame Press, 1992.

ABBREVIATIONS

ANET	*Ancient Near Eastern Texts Relating to the Old Testament.* Ed. J. B. Pritchard. 3d ed. Princeton: Princeton Univ. Press, 1969.
BEvT	Beiträge zur evangelischen Theologie
CBQ	*Catholic Biblical Quarterly*
CBQMS	Catholic Biblical Quarterly Monograph Series
ET	English translation
ExpTim	*Expository Times*
FRLANT	Forschungen zur Religion und Literatur des Alten und Neuen Testaments
HSCP	*Harvard Studies in Classical Philology*
HTKNT	Herders theologischer Kommentar zum Neuen Testament
HTR	*Harvard Theological Review*
ICC	International Critical Commentary
IDB	*Interpreter's Dictionary of the Bible.* Ed. G. A. Buttrick. 4 vols. Nashville: Abingdon, 1962.
IDBSup	Supplementary volume to *IDB.* Ed. K. Crim, 1976.
JBL	*Journal of Biblical Literature*
JBLMS	Journal of Biblical Literature Monograph Series (name has been changed to SBLMS)
JR	*Journal of Religion*
JSOT	*Journal for the Study of the Old Testament*
JTS	*Journal of Theological Studies*

LCL	Loeb Classical Library
LXX	Septuagint
MT	Masoretic Text
NovT	*Novum Testamentum*
NovTSup	Novum Testamentum, Supplements
NRSV	New Revised Standard Version
NTS	*New Testament Studies*
OCD	*Oxford Classical Dictionary*. Ed. M. Cary et al. Oxford: Clarendon, 1949.
OTP	*Old Testament Pseudepigrapha*. Ed. James H. Charlesworth. 2 vols. Garden City, N.Y.: Doubleday, 1983–85.
RSV	Revised Standard Version
SANT	Studien zum Alten und Neuen Testament
SBL	Society of Biblical Literature
SBLMS	Society of Biblical Literature Monograph Series
SBT	Studies in Biblical Theology
TU	Texte und Untersuchungen zur Geschichte der altchristlichen Literatur
WUNT	Wissenschaftliche Untersuchungen zum Neuen Testament
ZNW	*Zeitschrift für die neutestamentliche Wissenschaft*

Chapter One

IS MARK'S GOSPEL
A LIFE OF JESUS?
THE QUESTION OF GENRE

WHEN WE READ A TEXT such as the Gospel of Mark, composed nearly two thousand years ago, we often rely unconsciously on the work of many people who have made our access to that text possible. If we read it in Greek, we rely on the paleographers and textual critics who have prepared, for example, the twenty-sixth edition of the Nestle text, the most widely used critical edition of the Greek New Testament.[1] If we read it in English, we rely not only on those scholars but also on a translator, often a committee of translators, who stand on the shoulders of a long line of translators before them.[2] Once we remind ourselves of these matters, it is easy to see how we are dependent on transmitters, editors, and translators of texts. The role that notions of genre play in the process of reading a text is more subtle but equally important.[3]

1. *Novum Testamentum Graece* (ed. Eberhard Nestle, Erwin Nestle, Kurt Aland et al.; 26th ed.; Stuttgart: Deutsche Bibelgesellschaft, 1979).
2. For example, the RSV is a revision of the King James (Authorized) Version. In other words, its authors were dependent on the work of those who produced the King James Version and ultimately upon William Tyndale, on whom the authors of the King James Version were dependent. See "English Versions of the Bible," *The New Oxford Annotated Bible with the Apocrypha, Expanded Edition, Revised Standard Version* (ed. Herbert G. May and Bruce M. Metzger; New York: Oxford Univ. Press, 1977) 1551–57; and Gerald Hammond, "English Translations of the Bible," *The Literary Guide to the Bible* (ed. Robert Alter and Frank Kermode; Cambridge: Harvard Univ. Press, 1987) 647–66.
3. W. G. Doty, "The Concept of Genre in Literary Analysis," *The Genre of the Gospels: Studies in Methodology, Comparative Research and Compositional Analysis* (Missoula, Mont.: SBL,1972) 29–64; H. Dubrow, *Genre* (New York: Methuen, 1982); A. Fowler, *Kinds of Literature: An Introduction to the Theory of Genres and Modes* (Cambridge: Harvard Univ. Press, 1982).

Whenever we read a text, we bring to it (or form very quickly) an idea about what kind of text it is. Understanding depends on a notion of genre or "kind" of text, a notion that includes expectations about literary form and style, content, and function. The basic options with regard to the "kind" of text Mark is include "gospel," "history," and "life" or "biography."[4] The decision about the genre of Mark is not merely a matter of taxonomy or academic scholarship. One's assumptions about the literary form of Mark affect the way this work is allowed to function in the lives of readers, in the life of the church, and in society.

The judgment that Mark is a "gospel," a unique Christian literary form, sets it aside as a "holy" text, as an instance of Scripture, a book unlike other books. This point of view implies that Mark belongs to the church and has little to say to society in a secular or pluralistic world. The judgment that Mark is a life of Jesus implies that it is a record of an individual who serves as a model for others. People in modern and ancient times have read biography to find out what another person was like and to compare oneself with him or her.[5] Although people are born into different circumstances, each person has to do the best one can with the hand one has been dealt. Virtue and vice are primary categories of biography. So even if Jesus is viewed as unique, this understanding of Mark implies that it presents Jesus as a model to be imitated. The work has significance primarily for the ethics and piety of the individual.

The judgment that Mark belongs in the category of history implies that the work has significance not only for the individual but also for a wider group. Some histories, of course, are sectarian, but Mark clearly has a universal perspective—"And the gospel must first be preached to all the nations" (13:10). Even if the point of view of Mark is that the world must be converted or reformed, at least it takes seriously

4. The term *biographia* ("biography") appears first in fragments of a text composed in the fifth century C.E., Damascius's *Life of Isidorus*, and preserved by a ninth-century writer, Photius. The usual term for an account of a person's life in the Greco-Roman period was "life," *bios* in Greek and *vita* in Latin (Arnaldo Momigliano, *The Development of Greek Biography* [Cambridge: Harvard Univ. Press, 1971] 12).

5. Momigliano cited Mark Longaker with approval to the effect that "The present day reader most often goes to biography because he is interested in himself." Momigliano suggests that the earliest Greek readers of biography turned to it for vicarious excitement, but he admitted that later Greek readers saw biography as a mirror of human nature (*Development*, 21–22).

the entire created world. The cosmic perspective of chapter 13 is unmistakable. Thus if we think that Mark is history with a universal perspective, we allow its significance to extend beyond personal piety to the situation of the human race in the world.

Most of us would not be comfortable, however, with a determination of genre based on the desired effects. A persuasive case for the definition of the genre of Mark must be made on the basis of analysis and comparison with other texts.

THE ORDER OF THE GOSPELS

The first issue that must be addressed, however briefly, is the order of composition of the Gospels according to Matthew, Mark, and Luke.[6] Most questions of interpretation are affected by the interpreter's presupposition regarding which is the earliest Gospel. The question of literary form or genre is no exception. The Gospels of Matthew and Luke are more similar than Mark to the ancient literary form called the "life," a predecessor of the modern genre "biography." Like many ancient biographies, Matthew and Luke discuss Jesus' ancestry, birth, and early life. Luke also includes an incident that illustrates Jesus' precocious wisdom (2:41-51). Such illustrations are typical of ancient biography.[7] Mark has nothing like this at the beginning of the Gospel. Jesus' immediate family are later mentioned in passing.[8] The Gospel

6. Augustine thought that the Gospels were written in the order in which they appear in the canon. He considered the author of Mark to have been the "slave and epitomist" of Matthew (Werner G. Kümmel, *Introduction to the New Testament* [trans. H. C. Kee; rev. and expanded English ed. Nashville: Abingdon, 1975] 45). Augustine thought that Luke was dependent on both Matthew and Mark. In 1789 J. J. Griesbach argued that Mark was a summary of both Matthew and Luke (ibid., 47). William Farmer has recently revived a form of this hypothesis. A minority of New Testament scholars now hold some form of the so-called Griesbach hypothesis (ibid., 48). The majority opinion is the Two-Source Theory. See n. 10 below.

7. For example, see the *Life of Homer* (*Vita Herodotea*) section 5 (*Vitae Homeri et Hesiodi* [ed. Ulrich von Wilamowitz-Moellendorff; Kleine Texte 137; Berlin: de Gruyter, 1929] 5); ET: *The Lives of the Greek Poets* (trans. Mary R. Lefkowitz; Baltimore: Johns Hopkins Univ. Press, 1981). Quintilian advocates the use of the same technique in the related genre, "encomium," a speech in praise of a person (*Institutes* 3.7.15).

8. In Mark 3:21 his family is mentioned generally, without indicating relationships or names; in 3:31-35, his mother and brothers are mentioned, but again without names; in 6:3, the names of Jesus' mother and brothers are given; his sisters are mentioned but no names are given for them. It is disputed whether the second Mary mentioned in 15:40 is the mother of Jesus. The point of contention is whether "James the younger" mentioned in 15:40 is the same person as the "James" mentioned in chap. 6 as the

3

of Luke is sometimes defined as a historical monograph, rather than a biography, because it is part of a two-volume work (Luke-Acts). Since Acts fits the genre "history" and it is thought that the two volumes must share the same genre, some conclude that Luke is also a historical monograph.[9]

The relationship of the Gospel of Mark to the literary form "biography" appears in a different light to those who believe it was composed prior to Matthew and Luke than it does to those who think it was composed later, especially in dependence on them. If Mark was written first, its literary form may have little to do with ancient "lives." If Matthew and Luke used Mark as a source, the authors of the two later Gospels, or at least the author of Matthew, may have transformed the genre of Mark into a life of Jesus. If Mark is a summary of Matthew or Luke, however, it makes more sense to understand Mark as an example of the literary form "biography."

In what follows, I assume that Mark is the earliest Gospel. This presupposition is based on my acceptance of the Two-Source Theory as the best solution available to the Synoptic problem. As is well known, this theory represents the majority opinion among New Testament scholars today.[10] From this point of view, the author of Mark was a pioneer among early Christian writers; his work constitutes a remarkable achievement. He was the first to gather the various oral forms, and perhaps short written collections and discourses, of the tradition about Jesus into an extended narrative.[11]

MARK AS "GOSPEL"

The question of the genre of the Gospel of Mark is usually answered in one of two ways. One position is that the term *gospel* adequately

---

brother of Jesus and whether the "Joses" mentioned in 15:40 is the "Joses" mentioned in chap. 6 as the brother of Jesus. If the Mary mentioned in 15:40 is intended to be the mother of Jesus, it is odd that she is not described as such in that passage.

9. For example, David E. Aune, *The New Testament in Its Literary Environment* (Philadelphia: Westminster, 1987) 77–157.

10. This theory holds that Mark is the earliest Gospel and that Matthew and Luke were composed independently, though each was dependent on the same two sources. These sources were the Gospel of Mark and a hypothetical document called the Synoptic Sayings Source, usually abbreviated as "Q" (from the German word for "source," *Quelle*). See Kümmel, *Introduction*, 48.

11. Whether there was a pre-Markan passion narrative is disputed. See chap. 4, "The Passion Narrative of Mark."

defines its literary form and reflects the fact that a new genre emerged in early Christian literature: an account of the "good news" that centers on the life, death, and resurrection of Jesus Christ. The use of this term in the opening statement of Mark is not a self-designation of literary form, but it represents an important stage in the development of the new genre.

The process envisaged by those who hold this position is analogous to the relationship of the book of Revelation to the genre "apocalypse." Prior to the writing of the book of Revelation, the term *apocalypse* was used to mean the process or content of revelation, or simply a "secret." It was not used to designate a literary form. The word *apocalypse* is used in the opening statement of the book of Revelation to characterize the content of the work as a whole and to indicate the means by which it had been made known. Later, and in dependence on the book of Revelation, the term came to be used for a type of literature.[12]

This analogy does not hold on one point. Although the term *apocalypse* had not been used to designate literary works prior to the composition of the book of Revelation, there had been works similar to Revelation in literary form, such as the book of Daniel. But those who hold that "gospel" is a new Christian literary creation de-emphasize the similarities between Mark and other, non-Christian texts.

The other position is that the term *gospel* is used in early Christian writings for a variety of literary forms, so its use does not determine the genre of Mark. The four canonical Gospels are in the mode of realistic narrative. The *Gospel of Thomas*, preserved in Greek fragments and in Coptic, is best understood as an instruction or some other type of wisdom book.[13] The *Gospel of Truth* is a homily or meditation.[14] In the light of this diversity of usage in the first two centuries, one must compare the earliest Gospel with other writings

12. Morton Smith, "On the History of *apokalyptō* and *apokalypsis*," *Apocalypticism in the Mediterranean World and the Near East* (ed. David Hellholm; Tübingen: Mohr/Siebeck, 1983) 9–20.

13. James M. Robinson, "LOGOI SOPHON: On the Gattung of Q," in James M. Robinson and Helmut Koester, *Trajectories through Early Christianity* (Philadelphia: Fortress, 1971) 75–80; John S. Kloppenborg, *The Formation of Q* (Philadelphia: Fortress, 1987) 27–34, 327–28.

14. Harold Attridge, "The Gospel of Truth as an Exoteric Text," *Nag Hammadi, Gnosticism, and Early Christianity* (ed. Charles W. Hedrick and Robert Hodgson, Jr.; Peabody, Mass.: Hendrickson, 1986) 241.

from the time to clarify the literary tradition in which it stands and thus its meaning and function.

Closely related to the question of literary form is the issue of cultural context. Although the old simplistic distinction between "Jewish" and "Hellenistic" is untenable, it is still worth asking in what cultural context the most influential literary models for Mark had their home. Since the Gospel of Mark appears to have been composed in Greek, these models were most likely documents written in Greek, although works composed in other languages may also have had an indirect effect. Some scholars look to the literature of Hellenistic Judaism for the raw materials, if not the prototypes, of Mark, whereas others look to non-Jewish Greek literary, philosophical, and religious works. Another point of view is that the author of Mark deliberately conflated Jewish traditions with traditions from Greco-Roman culture.[15] Such conflation had already been accomplished by Greek-speaking Jews, such as Philo and Josephus.

The notion that the genre of Mark is best described as "gospel," a newly created early Christian genre, is closely tied to the form-critical view of the origin of Mark.[16] This view was articulated most fully by Rudolf Bultmann and restated more recently by Philipp Vielhauer.[17] The root metaphors of this view are organic growth and evolutionary development. The starting point is the fact that the term *gospel* is used in two different ways in early Christianity. The first is as a designation of the early Christian message. This usage is typical of the writings that were eventually collected and known as the New Testament. Although the term *gospel* appears with this meaning in such writings, its origin was in the oral proclamation of early Christian missionaries.

15. For example, Aune, *New Testament*, 46; Vernon K. Robbins, *Jesus the Teacher: A Socio-Rhetorical Interpretation of Mark* (Philadelphia: Fortress, 1984) 68.

16. For a criticism of the view that "gospel" is a unique, Christian genre, see Aune, *New Testament*, 23–25 and Hubert Cancik, "Die Gattung Evangelium: Das Evangelium des Markus im Rahmen der antiken Historiographie," *Markus-Philologie: Historische, literargeschichtliche und stilistische Untersuchungen zum zweiten Evangelium* (ed. Hubert Cancik; WUNT 33; Tübingen: Mohr/Siebeck, 1984) 87–92.

17. Philipp Vielhauer, *Geschichte der urchristlichen Literatur* (New York: de Gruyter, 1975) 252–58, 348–55. Besides Bultmann, Karl Ludwig Schmidt has been an important influence on those who take this position ("Die Stellung der Evangelien in der allgemeinen Literaturgeschichte," *EUCHARISTERION: Studien zur Religion und Literatur des Alten und Neuen Testaments Hermann Gunkel zum 60. Geburtstag . . . dargebracht* [ed. Hans Schmidt; 2 vols. FRLANT, n.f. 19; Göttingen: Vandenhoeck & Ruprecht, 1923] 2.50–134).

An example of this usage is Rom 1:1-7. "Gospel" in this sense is never used in the plural.

The term *gospel* is also used for a book that reports about Jesus' life, death, and resurrection. This usage does not appear in the writings that eventually became the New Testament, except for the titles that were secondarily attached to the works attributed to Matthew, Mark, Luke, and John. The earliest datable instance of this use of "gospel" as a literary term is in the writings of Justin Martyr.[18] The starting point for this literary use was apparently the opening statement of Mark that equates the story of Jesus' activity with the proclamation of salvation. This incipient literary usage is not taken up by the authors of Matthew and Luke, perhaps because they did not perceive it as a literary term but as a description of the content of the work. As many had announced the good news in oral form, it was now to be recorded in written form. In the extracanonical "apostolic" literature, the term *gospel* seems to refer at times to the (oral) teaching of Jesus and at times to a written document. Even when "gospel" seems to refer to a document (e.g., *Did.* 15:3-4 and 2 *Clem.* 8:5), the reference seems to be to content rather than to a literary form.[19]

According to Vielhauer, following Bultmann, the collection of the tradition about Jesus and the process of writing it down in historical-biographical form constituted a natural development.[20] Nevertheless, he discussed four theories regarding the origin of Mark: (1) Mark is a composition following the model of the Hellenistic "life"; (2) Mark is the expansion of a previously existing "frame" or summary of the gospel, that is, the oral proclamation of early Christians; (3) Mark is the result of an immanent development of the tradition about Jesus; (4) Mark is an original literary creation.[21]

Vielhauer rejected the theory of immanent development because such development seems to have led only to collections of units of the same form. Small collections of controversy stories, parables, and miracles have been discerned as sources used by the author of Mark. Documents such as the *Gospel of Thomas* (a collection of sayings of

18. It is disputed whether the references to "his [the Lord's] gospel" and to "the gospel" in the *Didache* refer to oral tradition or a written text (*Did.* 8:2, 15:3).
19. Vielhauer, *Geschichte*, 253–54.
20. Ibid., 349.
21. Ibid. In enumerating these four theories, Vielhauer follows Gerd Theissen.

Jesus) and the infancy gospels may also be seen as products of such an immanent development.

Vielhauer also rejected the theory that Mark was composed on the model of the Greco-Roman "life," at least as argued by S. Schulz.[22] His reasons were that the examples cited by Schulz, the *Life of Apollonius of Tyana* by Philostratus and the lives of Alexander of Abonoteichos and Peregrinus by Lucian, are later than Mark. A further argument is that those writings are on a higher literary level than Mark; in particular, that they are less episodic.

The theory that Mark is an original literary creation was put forward in a weak form by Willi Marxsen, since he presupposed that the author made use of sources, such as a preexistent passion narrative and certain collections. Vielhauer had no great objection to the weak form of this theory. E. Güttgemanns presented a strong form, arguing that Mark must be understood in, by, and for itself. The creation of the gospel form and the fixing of the tradition about Jesus in writing were one and the same event. Vielhauer rejected this theory as nonexplanatory and because it is refuted by the evidence for pre-Markan Christian writings. It is not clear whether Vielhauer had in mind here primarily the letters of Paul and the hypothetical Sayings Source (Q), whose date is in any case uncertain, or sources used by Mark, assuming that they were sources already fixed in writing.[23]

The theory positing an already existing "frame" or "summary" used by the author of Mark was advocated by Martin Dibelius, Bultmann, and C. H. Dodd. The main evidence is provided by the summaries of the early Christian message in the book of Acts. The problem is that it is by no means certain that these summaries are older than Mark.[24] To avoid this problem, Vielhauer adopted a simpler version of this theory by agreeing with Bultmann that the proclamation of the death and resurrection of Jesus constitutes the seed from which Mark was cultivated and that other material was added because of various needs of the community.[25] The letters of Paul attest the early emphasis on the death and resurrection of Jesus.

22. S. Schulz, "Die Bedeutung des Mk für die Theologiegeschichte des Urchristentums," in *Second International Congress on New Testament Studies at Christ Church, Oxford*, ed. F. L. Cross; Studia Evangelica 2–3; TU 87 (1964)143–44; cited by Vielhauer, *Geschichte*, 330, 350.

23. Vielhauer, *Geschichte*, 350; cf. 353.

24. Aune argues in addition that Mark and the reconstructed oral kerygma differ significantly in form, content, and function (*New Testament*, 24–25, 43).

25. Vielhauer, *Geschichte*, 350.

Thus Vielhauer's position is that Mark was formed neither by a free creative act nor by mechanically adding together previously composed material. The author of Mark received traditional material *and* limits to that material in the form of a chronological framework. This framework was bounded at the end by the death and resurrection of Jesus and at the beginning by the activity of John the Baptist. The death of Jesus is the more significant of the two as the chronological end of a life. Although Vielhauer was aware that some ancient biographies were not organized chronologically, he considered chronological organization to be the most natural. Further, he viewed the death of Jesus as the origin of the whole tradition about Jesus, since early Christians universally viewed it as a salvific event.[26]

Since the evidence for a preexisting "frame" or "summary" of the life, death, and resurrection of Jesus is not strong, Vielhauer argued for a framing consciousness rather than a literary frame. The individual forms in the tradition about Jesus—parables, miracle stories, and so on—show that centrifugal forces were at work in the tradition and that there were different Christologies. But Vielhauer did not conclude that the opposing centripetal forces were created by the author of Mark. Rather, they were already in the tradition. Behind the formation and transmission of every unit of tradition is the consciousness of the identity of the earthly and exalted Jesus. For Vielhauer, the awareness of this identity implied a consciousness of the meaning of Jesus' death and resurrection, a consciousness that the author of Mark made explicit. Therefore, the composition of Mark brings nothing new in principle, but completes what began with the earliest oral tradition.

It is certainly correct to say that every unit of the tradition presupposes that the crucifixion of Jesus was not counterevidence to the claim that he was the agent of God. It is not clear, however, that every unit is based on the assumption that Jesus had been "exalted." Further, it seems impossible to defend the hypothesis that each unit originates in the conviction that Jesus' death was a saving event. For example, the hypothetical Sayings Source (Q) treats Jesus' death as a typical instance of the suffering of a prophet.[27] The miracle stories do not necessarily imply that Jesus' death was salvific. For them it may simply

26. Ibid., 352–53.
27. See Luke 11:47-51/Matt 23:29-36 and Luke 13:34-35/Matt 23:37-39.

be irrelevant. The later controversies over views labeled "docetic" show that such an attitude was conceivable.[28] If Jesus' death as a saving event was not the source of all the tradition, then the composition of Mark seems to be much less a natural outgrowth of the tradition.

Another argument expressed by Vielhauer seems stronger. He concluded that Mark is not an example of a Greco-Roman "life" because, unlike the typical ancient biography, it shows no interest in the origins, education, and inner development of Jesus.[29] According to Vielhauer, this lack is due to the character of the gospel as proclamation. The smaller forms within the Gospel are borrowed from the surrounding culture, but the gospel form itself is something new.

The lack of accounts in Mark of Jesus' genealogy, family, and birth is striking in comparison with many ancient accounts of lives and is surely significant. The lack of interest in the inner development of Jesus is a somewhat different matter. A psychological interest is characteristic of modern biography.[30] Interest in the inner life of historical figures was relatively much less in antiquity, though not entirely lacking. This argument, if used at all, must be used with caution.

MARK AS BIOGRAPHY

The other major position on the genre of Mark is that "gospel" is not an adequate literary designation. The so-called Gospels have certain unique features, but one must study them in relation to other literature of the time to determine their literary nature or genre. The comparative study of the Gospels and Greco-Roman biographies was initiated in this century by Clyde W. Votaw in two essays published in the *American Journal of Theology* 19 (1915).[31] In 1965 Moses Hadas and Morton Smith published a book in which they argued that the Gospels, es-

28. For example, Ignatius criticized those who argued that the suffering of Jesus was only a semblance (*Trall.* 10).

29. Vielhauer, *Geschichte*, 354; Cancik argued that Lucian's *Life of Demonax* also lacks these characteristics ("Bios und Logos: Formengeschichtliche Untersuchungen zu Lukians 'Demonax,' " *Markus-Philologie*, 129; cf. idem, "Die Gattung Evangelium," ibid., 94–96.

30. See, for example, Momigliano, *Development*, 1, 6; Aune, *New Testament*, 28.

31. These essays were reprinted as Clyde W. Votaw, *The Gospels and Contemporary Biographies in the Greco-Roman World* (Facets Books, Biblical Series 27; Philadelphia: Fortress, 1970).

pecially Luke, belong to a subtype of ancient biography. They characterized this subtype as "spiritual biographies" and adopted the ancient term *aretalogy* to define it. The aretalogical tradition developed in works praising the achievements of heroes (e.g., Dionysus, Herakles, and Theseus), the inspiration of poets (e.g., Hesiod and Pindar), and the attainments of teachers or philosophers (e.g., Orpheus, Empedocles, and Socrates). The influence of the aretalogical tradition is clear, according to Hadas and Smith, in the *Life of Pythagoras* by Porphyry, *On the Life of Moses* by Philo, the Gospel according to Luke, and *The Life of Apollonius of Tyana* by Philostratus.[32] Subsequently, several scholars used the term *aretalogy* in a narrower sense to indicate a pre-gospel form, namely, a collection of miracle stories presenting Jesus as a "divine man."[33] Howard C. Kee has criticized this definition of the genre of the Gospels or a pre-gospel form, primarily on the grounds that the ancients did not recognize a *genre* "aretalogy" and that the notion was in any case linked to gods, not to human beings.[34] Patricia Cox argued that there was no need for a synthesized genre "aretalogy."[35] Although the comparative study of the Gospels and traditions about human wonder-workers in antiquity needs greater terminological precision, these traditions are very important for understanding the portrait of Jesus in the Gospels and should not be ignored.

David Aune has recently reformulated the argument that Mark belongs to the genre of Greco-Roman biography.[36] In response to criticisms of this position, such as Vielhauer's, regarding the relatively

32. Moses Hadas and Morton Smith, *Heroes and Gods: Spiritual Biographies in Antiquity* (New York: Harper & Row, 1965).
33. For example, James M. Robinson, "On the Gattung of Mark (and John)," *Jesus and Man's Hope* (ed. D. G. Buttrick; 2 vols.; Pittsburgh: Pittsburgh Theological Seminary, 1970/71) 1.99–129; for summaries and discussions of this trend, see M. Jack Suggs, "Gospel, Genre," *IDBSup*, 370–72; Robert H. Gundry, "Recent Investigations into the Literary Genre 'Gospel,' " *New Dimensions in New Testament Study* (ed. R. N. Longenecker and M. C. Tenney; Grand Rapids, Mich.: Zondervan, 1974) 97–114; Willem S. Vorster, "Der Ort der Gattung Evangelium in der Literaturgeschichte," *Verkündigung und Forschung: Wissenschaft vom Neuen Testament, Beihefte zu Evangelische Theologie* 29 (1984) 2–25.
34. Howard Clark Kee, "Aretalogy and Gospel," *JBL* 92 (1973) 402–22; idem, *Community of the New Age* (2d ed.; Macon, Ga.: Macon Univ. Press, 1984).
35. Patricia Cox, *Biography in Late Antiquity: A Quest for the Holy Man* (Berkeley: Univ. of California Press, 1983). See also the approving review by Eugene V. Gallagher in *JBL* 104 (1985) 373–75.
36. Aune, *New Testament*, 46–76. See also the work of Charles Talbert, *What Is a Gospel?* (Philadelphia: Fortress, 1977); "The Gospel and the Gospels," *Interpretation*

higher literary level of Greco-Roman "lives," Aune has defined a sub-type characterized as popular, chronologically (not topically) structured biography.[37]

Vernon Robbins has studied "rhetorical forms" and patterns of thought in Mark. He concluded that the author of Mark has conflated Jewish prophetic traditions with traditions about teachers, such as Socrates, in Greco-Roman culture. He proposed that Xenophon's *Memorabilia* is the best model for understanding the genre of Mark.[38]

The Nature of Ancient Biography

In order to ascertain the relationship of Mark to ancient biography, it is well to have some notion of the characteristics of ancient biography. David Aune has proposed a clear and distinct definition: "Biography may be defined as a discrete prose narrative devoted exclusively to the portrayal of the whole life of a particular individual perceived as historical."[39] The late Arnaldo Momigliano wittily pointed out some of the ambiguities in studying ancient biography. Since the sixteenth century, the majority of scholars have considered biography to be a subtype of history. In the Hellenistic period, however, the two were sharply distinguished.[40] Momigliano proposed a brief and flexible definition: "An account of the life of a man from birth to death."[41]

This definition brings to our awareness the fact that the Greeks and the Romans did not write biographies of women. Accounts of the lives of women were sometimes included in other works. For example,

33 (1979) 351–62; and "Once Again: Gospel Genre," *Genre, Narrativity and Theology* (ed. Mary Gerhart and James G. Williams; *Semeia* 43; Atlanta: Scholars Press, 1988) 53–73. Marius Reiser, with reference to P. Wendland, has argued that the closest analogies in Greco-Roman literature to the literary form "Gospel" are the lives of Homer, the Aesop novel, and the Alexander novel ("Der Alexanderroman und das Markusevangelium," *Markus-Philologie*, 161).

37. Aune, *New Testament*, 63–64. See also idem, "Greco-Roman Biography," *Greco-Roman Literature and the New Testament* (ed. David E. Aune; Atlanta: Scholars Press, 1988) 107–26. This essay includes a translation of the *Life of Secundus the Silent Philosopher*.

38. Robbins, *Jesus the Teacher*, 53–55, 68. Cancik argued that Mark would have been read as a prophetic book by Jewish readers familiar with the LXX and as a Greco-Roman "life" of Jesus by Greek and Roman readers ("Die Gattung Evangelium," 94–98, 110).

39. Aune, *New Testament*, 29.

40. Momigliano, *Development*, 1–7.

41. Ibid., 11.

Berossus included an account about Semiramis in his Babylonian history, written about 290 B.C.E. and dedicated to Antiochus I. Plutarch wrote an account of Cleopatra in his *Life of Antony* and a separate work "On the Bravery of Women." But it was not until the fifth century C.E. that discrete lives of women began to appear.[42]

Momigliano pointed out that Greeks and Romans wrote about gods and heroes who were born but did not die, or at least who died a death that was only the beginning of a new period of activity. The modern critical historian may wish to exclude these "lives," such as the "Life" of Herakles, from the category of biography since they are accounts of nonexistent beings. But one must recognize that biographies of gods and heroes probably preceded and influenced biographies of men in antiquity.[43]

The Origin and Development of Greco-Roman Biography

Greek biography apparently originated in the fifth century B.C.E., but discrete biographies from that century have been lost.[44] Herodotus's *History* contains several biographies.[45] The book(s) of Samuel in the Hebrew Bible and its Greek versions may be seen as an analogy. It too is a historical work that contains biographical material, particularly about Samuel, and to some extent about Saul and David as well. Curiosity seems to have been a major factor in the origin of Greek biography. The Greek reader wanted to hear about heroes, poets, and unusual men, such as kings and tyrants. To some degree then, early Greek biography was vicarious travel.[46] Comparison of Herodotus and Thucydides suggests that interest in biographical details was more alive in Asia Minor than in Athens in the fifth century B.C.E. The reason may be the influence of ancient Near Eastern tales with a strong

42. For example, the *Life of Olympias* and the *Life of Saint Pelagia the Harlot*; see Ross S. Kraemer, *Maenads, Martyrs, Matrons, Monastics: A Sourcebook on Women's Religions in the Greco-Roman World* (Philadelphia: Fortress, 1988) 195–204, 316–24.

43. Momigliano, *Development*, 11–12.

44. Ibid., 8. The most important lost works are a life of Heraclides, the tyrant of Mylasa in Asia Minor, by his contemporary, Skylax of Caryanda; a proto-autobiography by Skylax; and a life of the pre-Socratic philosopher Empedocles by Xanthus of Lydia (ibid., 29–31).

45. Ibid., 12.

46. Ibid., 21–22.

biographical flavor. The story of Ahiqar influenced the Greek *Life of Aesop*. Autobiography was a well-cultivated genre in various countries of the Persian Empire from Egypt to Assyria. An analogy with the Bible again presents itself. Nehemiah wrote an autobiography under the Persians at about the same time that Ion was writing his autobiographical memoirs in Chios (fifth century B.C.E.). Both were novelties within their cultures.[47]

Socrates died at the beginning of the fourth century. None of his followers wrote his life. In fact no full "life" or biography seems to have been written in the fourth century. Several works, however, have biographical characteristics. Isocrates and Xenophon wrote prose encomia, Isocrates for Evagoras, a ruler of Cyprus, and Xenophon for Agesilaus, a king of Sparta.[48] Of greatest interest for the student of the New Testament are two works inspired by Socrates, the *Memorabilia* or *Apomnemoneumata* by Xenophon, and the *Apology of Socrates* by Plato. Xenophon's *Memorabilia* is a new genre that combines a judicial defense (the apology of Socrates) with recollections (a collection of philosophical conversations). Plato's *Apology of Socrates* is simply a judicial speech, but one that gives a great deal of biographical detail. The striking thing about these innovations, especially the *Memorabilia* of Xenophon, is that a new biographical genre was devised to write what the modern critical historian must characterize as fiction! The Socratics experimented in biographical writing, attempting to capture the *potential* rather than the *actual* Socrates.[49] Similarly, the authors of Matthew, Mark, Luke, and John wished to create not a portrait of the critically reconstructed historical Jesus but a narrative that expressed the significance of Jesus for his actual and potential followers.

Although his work has been lost, the evidence suggests that Aristoxenus gave Hellenistic biography its distinctive shape. He seems to have been the first biographer among the followers of Aristotle and the first of any tradition to suggest that a good biography is one that is full of anecdotes. From Aristoxenus onward, Hellenistic biography

47. Ibid., 35–36.
48. Ibid., 8, 49–51.
49. Momigliano makes this point, contrasting the *potential* with the *real* Socrates (ibid., 46). He also discusses Xenophon's *Cyropaedia* and calls it "a philosophic novel" with biographical interests (ibid., 8, 56).

was characterized by erudition, scholarly zeal, realism of details, and gossip. What was now called a "life" was a detached, slightly humorous account of events and opinions characterizing an individual. If the individual was a king or politician, biography remained close to political history. Otherwise it served the double purpose of characterizing an individual philosopher, poet, or artist and the teaching and values of the school to which he belonged.[50] The only biographer of the Hellenistic period whose work has survived is Satyrus. In the third century B.C.E. he wrote a life of Euripides, a fragment of which was recovered on a papyrus from Oxyrhynchus in 1912. This "life" was in the form of a dialogue. Biographical details were deduced from the texts of Euripides' plays. Such deduction was standard Peripatetic method.[51]

The oldest collection of biographies that has survived at all is that by Cornelius Nepos, a contemporary of Cicero who wrote in Latin. His work was entitled *De Viris Illustribus* and consisted of at least sixteen books. In it he compared Greeks and Romans and used the categories of generals, historians, kings, poets, and probably orators. He seems to have included a few Carthaginians and Persians. The work was eulogistic and had an ethical aim. The only section fully preserved is that on foreign generals. Nepos introduced a more international and humane type of biography, thereby helping to create a cosmopolitan civilization. He was a major influence on Plutarch.[52]

The only period of ancient biography that we know from the works themselves is that of the Roman Empire. The best-known works are those of Plutarch, Suetonius, Diogenes Laertius, and Philostratus. Some biography of this period was in the service of imperial propaganda. For example, Nicolaus of Damascus wrote a panegyrical biography of Augustus's youth. Nicolaus himself was of a distinguished Greek family and was the court historian and advisor of Herod the Great. His life of Augustus may be characterized as dynastic biography, since it emphasized the devotion of Octavian to his adoptive father, Julius Caesar.[53] Other writers, such as Plutarch, Tacitus, and Suetonius, refused to yield

50. Ibid., 76, 103.
51. Ibid., 5, 8, 80.
52. Ibid., 9, 97–98, 104. See also John C. Rolfe, "Cornelius (2) Nepos," *OCD*, 236.
53. Momigliano, *Development*, 9, 86; Alexander H. McDonald, "Nicolaus of Damascus," *OCD*, 607.

to the temptation to let biography become an instrument of imperial propaganda.[54] Diogenes Laertius wrote a lengthy work entitled *The Lives and Opinions of Eminent Philosophers*. The aim of this work was to trace two "successions" of philosophers (we would say "schools"), the Ionian in the East and the Italian in the West. Anaximander, a pupil of Thales, founded the Ionian succession of philosophers, and Pythagoras, a student of Pherecydes, founded the Italian (1.13–14). Commissioned by the emperor Caracalla's mother, Julia Domna, Philostratus in about 218 C.E. wrote a life of Apollonius of Tyana, an itinerant and wonder-working philosopher who lived in the second half of the first century C.E.[55]

Types of Greco-Roman Biography

Friedrich Leo argued in 1901 that there were two types of Greco-Roman biography. His thesis is still very influential today. He spoke of a Suetonian type of biography as one that combines a tale in chronological order with a systematic characterization of an individual and his achievements. The other is the Plutarchean type, a straightforward chronological account of events. These two types are due to the Greek distinction between history (*historia*) and erudition (*archaeologia* or *philologia*, translated by the Romans as *antiquitates*; note the use of the second term by Josephus in the title of his history of the Jewish people). History was defined as an account of political and military events in chronological order. Erudition involved explanation and discussion of personal names, religious ceremonies, and other topics in systematic arrangement. Suetonius was influenced by an antiquarian approach to biography, whereas Plutarch was nearer to political historiography.[56]

For example, Suetonius began his life of Augustus with a brief chronological account.[57] This account was followed by a systematic treatment of various topics.[58] Similarly, his life of Julius Caesar began with

54. Momigliano, *Development*, 99–100.
55. For an introduction to this work, translations of parts of it, and summaries of the rest, see David R. Cartlidge and David L. Dungan, *Documents for the Study of the Gospels* (Philadelphia: Fortress, 1980) 205–42.
56. Momigliano, *Development*, 14, 18–19.
57. Suetonius, *The Twelve Caesars*, *Augustus* 1–8.
58. Note the transition in ibid., 9.

a more extended chronological account of Caesar's life and achievements.[59] He interrupted this account to give descriptions of Caesar's "appearance, personal habits, dress, character, and conduct in peace and war."[60] After a long discussion of these topics, Suetonius returned to the chronological account. The transition was made by showing how certain aspects of his character and conduct provoked his assassination.[61] In like manner, the first twenty-one sections of the life of Gaius Caligula treat "Caligula the Emperor," whereas most of the rest (sections 22–55) are devoted to "Caligula the Monster."[62] Like the life of Caesar, the last part of the life of Gaius Caligula describes the assassination of the emperor (sections 56–60).

Is Mark a Biography of Jesus?

From the point of view of structure, the Gospel of Mark may be seen as a chronological presentation of Jesus' public career. There is little topical or systematic presentation of Jesus' words or deeds or of his appearance or character. It is clearly not a "life" of the Suetonian type. On the other hand, Mark does not have the clear and coherent chronological narrative quality that characterizes the lives written by Plutarch. Nevertheless, the author chose to maintain at least the appearance of a chronologically ordered narrative.[63]

Most ancient biographies begin with an account of the ancestry of the subject, including details especially about his parents. Information about the birth usually follows; then a description of his childhood and education. Mark begins with the activity of John the Baptist and the baptism of Jesus. David Aune has argued that this starting point is appropriate in a biography. The baptismal scene provides divine legitimation for Jesus' identity as Son of God or Messiah. According to Aune, this scene takes the place and has the function of the discussion of ancestry, birth, and education in Greco-Roman biography.[64]

59. Suetonius, *Twelve Caesars, Julius Caesar* 1–44.
60. The quotation is from the end of section 44; the translation is from Suetonius, *The Twelve Caesars* (trans. Robert Graves; New York: Penguin, 1957) 29.
61. The systematic discussion is contained in Suetonius *Julius Caesar* 45–78. The chronological account resumes in section 79.
62. *Gaius Caligula* 22; quotation from Suetonius, *Twelve Caesars* (trans. Graves) 159.
63. Aune, *New Testament*, 47.
64. Ibid., 48.

Aune's most important argument in favor of defining Mark as a biography of Jesus that relates to the opening of the work involves the use of the term *archē* in 1:1: "[The] beginning [*archē*] of the good news [*euangelion*] of Jesus Christ." Aune argues that the term *archē* is virtually a technical term in historical and biographical writing. Its use expresses the notion that a complete explanation of a historical phenomenon must be based on its origins.[65]

Aune's remarks about the term *archē* certainly apply to ancient historiography. Herodotus, the first Greek historian, wrote an account of the conflict between Greece and Persia. To treat this theme adequately, he was required to go back to its origins and to treat the earlier struggles between the Ionian Greeks and the kingdom of Lydia.[66] It is not clear, however, that *archē* was virtually a technical term in Greco-Roman biography. The examples cited by Aune are all passages from historical writings—Polybius's *Universal History*, Tacitus's *Histories*, and Dionysius of Halicarnassus's *Roman Antiquities*.[67] The use of this term as the opening word in Mark suggests that it is intended to be a historical work, not a life of Jesus, unless *archē* in Mark 1:1 simply means something like "the narrative begins here."[68]

It should be noted that the account of the activity of John the Baptist does not follow immediately upon the incipit of Mark.[69] Prior to the appearance of John the Baptist is a citation from Scripture, introduced by the formula "As it is written in the book of Isaiah the prophet."[70] Just as the voice from heaven legitimates Jesus at the moment of his baptism as son of God (1:11), so the citation of Scripture legitimates John the Baptist. The passage from Scripture speaks of "one crying out in the wilderness" (1:3). John is presented as "in the wilderness" and

65. Ibid.
66. Oswyn Murray, "Greek Historians," *The Oxford History of the Classical World* (ed. John Boardman et al.; New York: Oxford Univ. Press, 1986) 188–89. In his preface, however, Herodotus used the term *aitia* (cause) rather than *archē* (origin, source).
67. Polybius 5.31.1–2; Tacitus *Histories* 1.1.1; Dionysius of Halicarnassus 1.8.4; Polybius 1.5.1; cited by Aune, *New Testament*, 48.
68. M. Eugene Boring discusses this possibility in his essay, "Mark 1:1-15 and the Beginning of the Gospel," *Semeia* 52 (1991) 52. Such a meaning is assumed by Günther Zuntz ("Ein Heide las das Markusevangelium," *Markus-Philologie*, 205).
69. On the possibility that the Gospel of Mark begins with an incipit, i.e., a brief opening less formal than the preface or dramatic prologue, see Dennis Smith, "Narrative Beginnings in Ancient Literature and Theory," *Semeia* 52, 4–6.
70. As is well known, the citation is actually a combination of a passage from the prophet Malachi (3:1) and one from Isaiah (40:3).

"proclaiming" (1:4). These and other links between the citation and the account of the activity of John the Baptist make clear that the reader is expected to infer that John's activity is the fulfillment of prophecy and that he is an agent of God. Scripture and the voice from heaven have a legitimating function, but that legitimation is not necessarily of a biographical type.

Rather than a significant social role, such as king, military commander, philosopher, poet, or artist, as in Greco-Roman biography, the role of Jesus in Mark is a charismatic role, like charismatic figures in older biblical narratives, such as Moses, Elijah, and Elisha. According to Aune, the role into which Jesus is typecast in Mark is an amalgam of eschatological prophet and messianic king.[71] If the role of Jesus in Mark may be designated as "prophet-king," this argument may support the conclusion that Mark is a life of Jesus, since Philo had characterized Moses as priest, prophet, king, and lawgiver in his work *On the Life of Moses*.[72]

Whereas the biblical books that contain the narratives involving Moses are not biographies, Philo's work on Moses, based on those books and on oral tradition (1.4), is a discrete Greco-Roman biography, although a Jewish example of the genre. Book 1 describes the ancestry and parents of Moses, the circumstances of his birth and infancy, how he came to be reared at the Egyptian court, his education, and the main facts of his work as leader or king of the Hebrew people. This first book is arranged chronologically. Book 2 is arranged topically, treating Moses' character under the headings of lawgiver, priest, and prophet. Thus, the form of the work is similar to the biographies of Suetonius, the type of biography influenced by the genre *archaeologia* or *antiquitates*. As we have noted, Mark does not combine chronological narrative with topical or systematic treatment of Jesus' character or roles. In fact, the role of Jesus in Mark is not limited to an amalgam of prophet and king. Another equally important designation of Jesus in Mark, perhaps more important since it is presented as a self-designation, is "Son of Man." This designation is not a typical social

71. Aune, *New Testament*, 54.
72. For an analysis of the biographical works of Philo (*On Abraham, On Joseph,* and *On the Life of Moses*) in comparison with Greco-Roman biography, see Anton Priessnig, "Die literarische Form der Patriarchenbiographien des Philon von Alexandrien," *Monatschrift für Geschichte und Wissenschaft des Judentums* 37 (1929) 143–55.

role in Greco-Roman biography. It does not fit easily into the category "social role" at all. The use of the term in Mark has exegetical elements, alluding to Dan 7:13.[73] These observations, like those on the beginning of Mark, call into question the definition of Mark as a biography of Jesus.

Greco-Roman biographies contain sayings and anecdotes that serve to characterize the subject. Aune remarks that the miracle stories, sayings, and anecdotes in Mark support the appropriateness of the role assigned to Jesus, but admits that they do not function primarily as revelations of *character*.[74] This admission undercuts the argument that Mark is a biography. If they do not function to reveal Jesus' character, their purpose may be to reveal Jesus' mission as an agent of God in history. This point of view on the miracle stories, sayings, and anecdotes suggests that Mark is historical narrative. We shall take up this suggestion later.

As noted earlier, Aune has argued that Mark belongs to a subtype of the genre "Greco-Roman biography," characterized as popular and chronologically (not topically) structured. Examples of this subtype include the *Life of Aesop*, the *Life of Homer*, the *Life of Secundus the Silent Philosopher*, the "Life" of Herakles, and the Jewish or Christian *Lives of the Prophets*. The similarity in the level of literary sophistication and even of style between some of these works and Mark is indeed striking. The argument that Greco-Roman lives are of too high a literary level to have been models for Mark does not hold. As noted earlier, Vielhauer argued that most Greco-Roman biographies cited as models for Mark were later than the first Gospel. The works discussed by Aune are earlier than those cited by Schulz, whom Vielhauer criticized. The "Life" of Herakles (the account in Apollodorus *Library* 2.4.6–2.7.8), the *Life of Aesop*, and the *Life of Homer* attributed to Herodotus are most likely to be earlier than Mark. The version of the "Life" of Herakles in Apollodorus dates somewhere between the mid-first century B.C.E. and the second century C.E.[75] The oldest extant *Life*

73. The allusion to Dan 7:13 is most obvious in Mark 14:62. On the likelihood that the historical Jesus used the term in alluding to Daniel 7, see Adela Yarbro Collins, "The Origin of the Designation of Jesus as 'Son of Man,'" *HTR* 80 (1987) 391–407.
74. Aune, *New Testament*, 57.
75. James G. Frazer determined the mid-first century B.C.E. as the *terminus post quem* for Apollodorus's *Library* (*Apollodorus: The Library* [trans. James G. Frazer; LCL; Cambridge: Harvard Univ. Press, 1961] xi); John F. Lockwood dated it to the first or second century C.E. ("Apollodorus [6]," *OCD*, 69).

of Aesop was written between 30 B.C.E. and 100 C.E.[76] The *Life of Homer* attributed to Herodotus was dated by Wilamowitz-Moellendorff to the end of the Hellenistic period.[77] Thomas W. Allen, however, dated it to the time of Hadrian.[78] The tradition it contains, and perhaps elements of its style and its basic literary form, may go back to the fifth century B.C.E.[79] The *Lives of the Prophets*, although not very similar to Mark in form in any case, is usually dated to the first century C.E.[80]

Although the form and style of most of these lives is similar to Mark, their content and function are very different. Aune admits the major difference in content.[81] He claims, however, that Mark and these biographies are similar in function. He understands the function of "the Gospels" to be "the legitimation of the present beliefs and practices of Christians by appealing to the paradigmatic role of the founder, just as the cultural values of the Hellenistic world were exemplified by the subjects of Greco-Roman biographies."[82] This generalization has some merit. Whether one accepts it as decisive depends upon the level of abstraction one deems appropriate. Aune's definition of function is very abstract.

A further issue is whether one should accept Aune's radical distinction between form and content. In an important way, content and function are inseparable. When one views content and function as a unity, a different picture emerges. As a narrative account of the beginning of the fulfillment of the promises, the Gospel of Mark implies that the life of Jesus is a key part of the history of salvation. The motif of the fulfillment of prophecy, explicit in the introduction of John the Baptist and implicit throughout, makes this clear.[83] The story of Jesus as agent of God claims that the events described have changed the

76. Ben Perry, *Aesopica* (Urbana, Ill.: Univ. of Illinois Press, 1952) 22.
77. Wilamowitz-Moellendorff, *Vitae Homeri et Hesiodi*, 3.
78. Thomas W. Allen, *Homer: The Origins and the Transmission* (Oxford: Clarendon, 1924) 17–18.
79. Momigliano, *Development*, 25–26, 28.
80. Charles C. Torrey, *The Lives of the Prophets: Greek Text and Translation* (JBLMS 1; Philadelphia: Society of Biblical Literature and Exegesis, 1946) 11; D. R. A. Hare, "The Lives of the Prophets," *OTP*, 2.380–81.
81. Aune, "Greco-Roman Biography," 122.
82. Ibid.; see also idem, *New Testament*, 59–63.
83. James M. Robinson argued "that Mark finds meaning and divine action in history, and therefore intends to be recording history" (*The Problem of History in Mark: And Other Marcan Studies* [Philadelphia: Fortress, 1982] 60; see also 72–77; expanded reprint of *The Problem of History in Mark* [London: SCM, 1957]).

world. In the Greco-Roman biographies, the subjects are presented as models for the ways in which the readers should appropriate qualities and ways of life that are presumed to be already available, part of the nature of things. The founder is someone who has acquired insight into the way things are. None of these writings implies that the founder has changed the nature of things. Such is, however, the claim of Mark. The Son of Man came to give his life as a ransom for many (10:45). This statement implies that the death of Jesus has changed reality. The point is not only that Jesus made insight available into the possibilities of human existence in the world, but that his life and death have made new possibilities available. This impression is reinforced by the implicit theme of fulfillment of prophecy in the account of Jesus' death.[84] Jesus' death is presented as a cosmic event that was prepared and prophesied beforehand. Similarly, the discourse of Jesus in chapter 13 speaks of an "end" that has a quite definitive tone to it, at least for those who will be gathered from the four winds, from the ends of the earth (13:27).

As already noted, Vernon Robbins has concluded that the author of Mark conflated Jewish prophetic traditions with traditions about teachers, such as Socrates in Greco-Roman culture. Whereas Aune sees the Jesus of Mark as an amalgam of prophet and king, Robbins sees him as a conflation of prophet and teacher. There is much that is illuminating in Robbins's book, and the parallels he points out between the Jesus of Mark and the disciple-gathering teacher in Greco-Roman literature are worth noting. But the argument that these similarities mean that Mark and the *Memorabilia* of Xenophon belong to the same genre is not compelling. Once again I would argue that similarities in form do not outweigh differences in content. Jesus the teacher in Mark is introduced as an exorcist. The authority of Jesus' teaching is demonstrated by his ability to cast out an unclean spirit (1:21-28). If Jesus in Mark is an amalgam of prophet and teacher, the prophetic element seems dominant. Or, if one prefers a Greco-Roman analogy, he is more like Empedocles than Socrates.[85] There is no claim that Socrates has changed the nature of things. For example, Socrates taught that a

84. For example, the casting of lots for Jesus' garments was "foretold" by Ps 22:18. See chap. 4, "The Passion Narrative of Mark."
85. See the *Life of Empedocles* in Diogenes Laertius *Lives of Eminent Philosophers*, 8.51–77, especially the poems cited in 59 and 62.

blessed afterlife is the hope of the good person, that is, any person who has discerned the right priorities and lived in accordance with them. The Jesus of Mark, however, teaches that eternal life has recently been made available; it will be granted to the one who loses one's life for the sake of Jesus and the gospel (8:35).

MARK AS HISTORY

A recurring issue in the analysis of biblical narratives from the point of view of genre has been the tension between myth and history. The miraculous and supernatural elements in biblical narratives, including Mark, have led modern critical historians to deny that these narratives may be defined as historical narratives. One problem involved in this judgment is that Mark, for example, was read as history for centuries and continues to be read as such.

Myth and History

History may be seen as one type of a larger mode of expression, namely, narrative. Myth is also a narrative genre. The distinction between myth and history is not an easy one to make. Both seem to be highly perspectival and relative terms. Originally, the Greek word *mythos* meant simply a word or speech, like *logos*, without any distinction of truth or falsehood. As early as the fifth century B.C.E., some writers, such as Pindar, began to use *mythos* in the sense of fiction as opposed to historical truth, for which the term *logos* was then reserved.[86] The underlying questions, of course, are what is real and what is true.

Another issue is the status of fiction. One point of view is that fiction is less true and real than history. Others argue that fiction simply has different kinds of truth and reality, indeed, more important kinds than those of many trivial facts. In the nineteenth century, the ideal of history writing was to reconstruct and write an account of what actually happened. In the twentieth century, historians and their critics are becoming increasingly aware that no historical account can reproduce a full picture of the past and that a complete picture is even undesirable. The very choice of historical subject matter involves bias. When data is abundant, the selection of data involves bias. Interpretation involves

---

86. Pindar *Olympian Odes* 1.29; *Nemean Odes* 7.23.

personal preferences and the writing of a historical account has some important similarities to writing fiction.

It is clear that individuals and intellectual traditions have disagreed over what is *mythos* (fiction, legend, myth) and what is *logos* (historical or ontological truth or fact). How the distinction is made depends on the worldview, range of experiences, and cultural context of the individual or intellectual tradition involved. Some intellectual traditions and individuals, ancient and modern, will include some elements under the rubric of history that other individuals and intellectual traditions, ancient and modern, would consider to be mythic. Thus in categorizing ancient texts as myth or history the modern interpreter must be very careful to keep point of view in mind. The presence of elements in a text that a particular modern interpreter would call mythic does not exclude the possibility that the author of the text intended to write history.

History and Biography

As noted previously, the Greeks distinguished history and biography. Charles Talbert has attempted to elucidate that distinction: "whereas [ancient] history focuses on the distinguished and significant acts of great men in the political and social spheres, biography is concerned with the essence of the individual."[87] In a very helpful way, Talbert has highlighted the variety in ancient "lives," pointing out that they do not always describe the subject's entire life from birth to death, are not always in chronological order, as we have already seen, may or may not use myth (reference to the divine or supernatural world and extraordinary deeds, i.e., miracles), and may have any one of a variety of social functions.[88]

Talbert concluded that some of the Christian Gospels either belong to the genre ancient biography or at least are very similar to it, namely, the four canonical Gospels, the *Gospel of Peter*, and the *Childhood* or *Infancy Gospel of Thomas*. The basis for his conclusion is the judgment that their aim is to set forth the essence of their subject, a significant person, Jesus Christ. All employ myth as do some of the

87. Talbert, "Gospel Genre," 55.
88. See also Cancik, "Die Gattung Evangelium," 95–96; and "Bios und Logos," 120–21, 124–26, 129.

24

non-Christian lives. The reason for the use of myth in both the Christian and non-Christian texts is, according to Talbert, that the subject is a hero or founder. Myth is used to characterize the events that brought the community into being as occurring in sacred time.

With regard to the Gospel of Mark at least, one may question whether the *main* purpose of the work is to depict the essence or character of Jesus Christ. The theme of the identity of Jesus and the proper understanding of that identity is a major theme in the Gospel. But it is doubtful that it is the primary or controlling aim of the work as a whole. Similarly, the Jesus of Mark, as one who suffers and dies, may be seen as a model for the implied readers who are threatened with persecution. But this literary or social function can hardly be said to explain fully the significance of Mark even for the first generation of actual readers.

As previously noted, biographies of philosophers, poets, or artists had the double purpose of characterizing an individual and the teaching and values of the school to which he belonged. Such biographies may be called didactic biographies. Philo's *On Abraham* and *On the Life of Moses* are Jewish examples of this type.[89] Some didactic biographies in antiquity seem to have had the purpose of indicating where the true tradition is in the present.[90] Some of the lives in the collection by Diogenes Laertius had this function. Talbert has argued that the anonymous *Life of Pachomius* and Hilary of Arles's *Sermon on the Life of St. Honoratus* are Christian examples of this type of biography.[91]

The theme of the true tradition seems to be implicitly present in Mark. The true followers of Jesus are those who perceive his identity correctly. These are they who know, along with Peter as a character in the narrative, that Jesus is the Messiah, but who also appreciate the significance of his self-designation as Son of Man. The true followers are also implicitly characterized as those who understand the parables of chapter 4 properly and who have the proper understanding of the end time, as elucidated by Jesus' prophecy in chapter 13. Once again, however, it seems inappropriate to claim that this theme expresses the primary purpose of Mark.

89. Priessnig, "Die literarische Form," 148, 155.
90. Talbert, "Gospel Genre," 58, following E. Bickermann.
91. Talbert, "Gospel Genre," 59.

This discussion leads to the question why the author of Mark utilized the narrative mode in producing his text. In answering this question, Talbert does not draw upon the particular characteristics of *biographical* narrative. He concludes that "the canonical Gospels were written to give a controlling context to individual Jesus traditions so they could not be misinterpreted as easily as was possible without such a context."[92] He elaborates this point by arguing that the canonical Gospels were written in connection with a sort of synthetic compromise to resolve the diversity among early Christians, some of whom emphasized the presence of God in Jesus as miracle-worker, others as teacher of morality, and so on. The canonical Gospels in his view then are not so much kerygma as the result of a conscious and deliberate attempt to gather up the various insights into the presence of God in Jesus and into discipleship in a comprehensive and balanced composition, including miracles, teaching, and death on the cross. Since the major aim of the evangelists was to avoid misunderstanding and reductionism in the presentation of the significance of Jesus, no great theological weight should be placed on the choice of genre, according to Talbert.[93]

This thesis is plausible to the extent that it accurately reflects the fact that the genre of the canonical Gospels is complex. If "parable," "miracle story," "pronouncement story," "aphorism," and "passion narrative" are genres, then the Gospel of Mark as a whole is a kind of "host genre" or "macro-genre" into which smaller literary forms may be incorporated.[94] The thesis of synthetic compromise also credibly describes one of a number of functions of the canonical Gospels. But once again it may be doubted that this thesis describes the primary or most fundamental purpose of Mark.

The *fundamental* purpose of Mark does not then seem to be to depict the essence or character of Jesus Christ, to present Jesus as a model, to indicate who possesses the true tradition at the time the

92. In this conclusion, Talbert agrees with Paul Achtemeier (ibid., 63–64). John Dominic Crossan makes a similar case ("Aphorism in Discourse and Narrative," *Genre, Narrativity, and Theology* [ed. Mary Gerhart and James G. Williams; *Semeia* 43; Atlanta: Scholars Press, 1988] 121–36).
93. Talbert, "Gospel Genre," 67.
94. On the notion of a "host genre," see David Aune, "The Apocalypse of John and the Problem of Genre," *Early Christian Apocalypticism: Genre and Social Setting* (ed. Adela Yarbro Collins; *Semeia* 36; Atlanta: Scholars Press, 1986) 80.

Gospel was written, or to synthesize the various literary forms taken by the tradition about Jesus and their theologies. I suggest that the primary intention of the author of Mark was to write history. One could object that Mark is not history because Jesus was not generally recognized as a great man in the first century C.E. In *Mimesis*, however, E. Auerbach has shown that part of the novelty of the Gospel of Mark is that it writes of ordinary (i.e., non-elite) people as if they were great (i.e., of high social standing and influence) and thus fit subjects of literature.[95] The presence of miracles and other mythic elements in the narrative do not refute the hypothesis, since for the author of Mark these elements were simply true and real. In other words, they were compatible with his worldview.

The most obvious difficulty for the hypothesis that Mark is a historical monograph is its focus on the person of Jesus.[96] In the light of that focus, it is instructive to review what Talbert and others have said about works in which history and biography approach one another. In Sallust's *Catiline*, for example, the aim is not to set forth the character of Catiline but to narrate political events with which he was associated. This work belongs to the genre "history" even though it concentrates on an individual.[97] My hypothesis is that Mark is analogous. Mark focuses on Jesus and his identity not in the interest of establishing his character or essence but in order to write a particular kind of history. This type of history may be defined as a narration of the course of the eschatological events. These events began with the appearance of John the Baptist, continued with the baptism of Jesus and with his activity of teaching, healing, and exorcising, came to a climax with his arrest and crucifixion, continued with his resurrection, and at the time of writing are yet to be completed. The presupposition that the eschatological events are yet to be completed explains the open-endedness of the ending of the Gospel.[98]

Apocalypse and History
To support the hypothesis that Mark is an apocalyptic historical monograph I need to show that there were precedents for this subtype of

95. E. Auerbach, *Mimesis: The Representation of Reality in Western Literature* (Princeton: Princeton Univ. Press, 1953).

96. Unlike Momigliano (see pp. 2, 10–16, 21), Cancik does not distinguish sharply between Hellenistic historiography and biography; he describes Mark both as a "historical monograph" and as a "life" of Jesus ("Die Gattung Evangelium," 93, 110).

97. Talbert, "Gospel Genre," 55.

98. I am assuming that the Gospel originally ended with 16:8.

the genre "history." Let me address the question of Israelite-Jewish historiography first. Baruch Halpern has recently made a case for viewing the authors of the corpus extending from Deuteronomy to Kings as the first historians in the Israelite-Jewish tradition. He points out that these Israelite historians had ancient Near Eastern predecessors and contemporaries.[99] His work implicitly calls into question the Western consensus that Herodotus is the father of history.[100] Other canonical examples of historiography include Chronicles, Ezra, and Nehemiah. Deuterocanonical works include 1 Esdras, 1 Maccabees, and 2 Maccabees. The most important extracanonical ancient Jewish histories are *The Jewish War* and the *Antiquities of the Jews* by Josephus.

According to Paul Hanson, the "dawn of apocalyptic" may be discerned in prophetic oracles from the early postexilic period (e.g., the collection distinguished as "Third Isaiah"). The oldest datable apocalypses are two works composed in the third century B.C.E. and attributed to Enoch. They have been preserved as parts of the composite work known to specialists as *1 Enoch* or *Ethiopic Enoch*. One of these contains revelation about the movements of heavenly bodies and is concerned with fixing the calendar to guide the observance of holy days and festivals.[101] The other is itself a composite work that includes an elaborate version of the story of "the sons of God" and "the daughters of humans" found in Gen 6:1-4. It also includes accounts of Enoch's ascent to the throne of God and his journey to normally hidden regions, guided by angels.[102] Neither of these works belongs to the genre "history."

Another part of *1 Enoch*, however, which may have once been an independent document, can be seen as history in an apocalyptic mode. This work is usually referred to as the Apocalypse of Weeks.[103] The text is cast in the form of an address of Enoch to his children. The address may be characterized as prophecy (in its fictional, literary

99. Baruch Halpern, *The First Historians: The Hebrew Bible and History* (San Francisco: Harper & Row, 1988) 7, 200, 213, 219, 230–31, 270–71.
100. For a reaffirmation of the consensus, see Murray, "Greek Historians," 188. Halpern does note that Herodotus made important innovations (*First Historians*, 231).
101. *1 Enoch* 72–82; on this document (often called "The Book of the Heavenly Luminaries"), see John J. Collins, *The Apocalyptic Imagination* (New York: Crossroad, 1984) 46–49.
102. *1 Enoch* 1–36; on this document (often called "The Book of the Watchers"), see Collins, *Apocalyptic Imagination*, 36–46.
103. *1 Enoch* 93:1-10; 91:11-17; see Collins, *Apocalyptic Imagination*, 49–52.

context). Its content is a summary of history from the time of Enoch until the end. All of history is organized into periods of metaphorical "weeks," ten in number. Enoch is born in the first "week" and the end will occur in the tenth "week." The events of the first six weeks constitute a veiled summary of biblical history. It is veiled in the sense that no names and ordinary dates are given. The manner of reference is general and rather abstract. The time of writing was apparently during the seventh "week," since the correlation with events otherwise known ends during that period and the eschatological events begin. This apocalypse was probably written in the early second century B.C.E. In this work we certainly do not have detailed, realistic historical narrative with antiquarian interests. But the text does combine a way of recounting history, however brief and stylized, with eschatological expectation.

Somewhat similar to the Apocalypse of Weeks is the account of Enoch's second vision in the Book of Dreams. This second vision is usually called the Animal Apocalypse.[104] The literary form of this passage is an account of a dream-vision that Enoch tells to his son Methuselah. The content, however, is a review of history in symbolic or allegorical form. This summary begins with Adam, who is symbolized by a white bull. Chapters 85:3—89:14 summarize the story of the book of Genesis. Chapter 89:15-38 summarizes the biblical story roughly from the beginning of Exodus to the end of Deuteronomy, the death of Moses. Chapter 89:39-53 summarizes the story selectively from Joshua to 2 Kings 2, the ascent of Elijah. Chapter 89:54-56 alludes to events recorded in 2 Kings and the prophetic books, especially Isaiah and Jeremiah. Chapters 89:57—90:5 offer a distinctive interpretation of the post-exilic period, involving seventy "shepherds" (i.e., angels), who are given charge of Israel (symbolized by sheep) but abuse that trust. Chapter 90:6-17 alludes to events related to the rise of the Maccabees. The remark that "a big horn grew on one of those sheep" (v 9) is probably an allusion to Judas Maccabee. The summary of actual history seems to end at 90:17. Chapter 90:18-38 describes the eschatological events that were expected to occur at the close of history. The account of history in this document is indirect, like that in the

---

104. The Book of Dreams is contained in *1 Enoch* 83–91; the Animal Apocalypse occurs in chaps. 85–91; see Collins, *Apocalyptic Imagination*, 53–56.

Apocalypse of Weeks. It is ostensibly more veiled due to the symbolic language employed, but the main references are transparent. This account is much more detailed than the Apocalypse of Weeks. It is apocalyptic in perspective in two ways. Classical apocalypticism involves both a horizontal and a vertical dimension; that is, the apocalyptic mentality includes a perspective on history, especially regarding the destiny of the individual and the world, as well as the notion that earthly events are controlled by heavenly or spiritual powers. This notion of supernatural causation is excluded from modern critical historiography and historical analysis. It was, however, of the essence of the apocalyptic view of history.

A similar apocalyptic view of history is expressed in the book of Daniel. The genre of Daniel as a whole is difficult to ascertain. The beginning of the book, "In the third year of the reign of King Jehoiakim of Judah," sounds like the standard introduction to a prophetic book meant to locate the collection of oracles in time in relation to the rule of a particular king or kings.[105] But the text does not go on to mention Daniel and his activity. Rather, it continues, "King Nebuchadnezzar of Babylon came to Jerusalem and besieged it." This portion of 1:1 and verse 2 sound like historical reporting. Even if verses 1 and 2 contain historical inaccuracies, these do not necessarily imply that the author did not intend to write history.[106] The reference to Ashpenaz, the chief eunuch in Babylon, in verse 3 continues to make the impression of historiography. But beginning in verse 4 the text seems to develop, at least in the eyes of the modern critical reader, in the direction of fiction. One factor in this critical conclusion is doubt over the historicity of the character Daniel. Perhaps the best designation of chapters 1–6 is historical romance or historical fiction. Many commentators refer to these chapters individually and collectively as "tales" or "wisdom tales."

It is generally agreed that chapters 7–12 are different in genre from chapters 1–6. Daniel 7–12, and sometimes Daniel as a whole, is referred to as the oldest canonical apocalypse. Chapters 7, 8, 9, and chapters

---

105. Robert C. Tannehill, *The Narrative Unity of Luke-Acts: A Literary Interpretation*, vol. 1, *The Gospel According to Luke* (Philadelphia: Fortress, 1986) 47.

106. R. H. Charles, *A Critical and Exegetical Commentary on the Book of Daniel* (ICC; Oxford: Clarendon, 1929) 1, 4–5, 7–8.

10–12 as a unit may also be characterized individually as vision accounts. One of the tales, chapter 2, focuses on a dream of Nebuchadnezzar and its interpretation by Daniel. The dream involves a statue made of four metals. Daniel interprets it in terms of four kingdoms. This dream and its interpretation have much in common with the vision of the four beasts from the sea in chapter 7. Both passages describe in symbolic form a period of history from the Neo-Babylonian empire to the Hellenistic kingdoms of the successors of Alexander the Great. In both cases, the eschatological kingdom of God, related to the eschatological sovereignty of Israel over other nations, is depicted as the power that will overcome and succeed the Hellenistic kingdoms.

Chapter 8 centers on a vision of a ram with two horns and a he-goat with one great horn, in which the he-goat overcomes the ram. The interpretation indicates that the ram is the Medo-Persian Empire. The he-goat with the one horn represents the Macedonian kingdom and its leader Alexander the Great, who conquered the Medes and the Persians. In the vision, the single horn of the he-goat is broken off and four horns arise in its place. These are clearly the successors of Alexander. Out of one of them comes a little horn that represents Antiochus IV Epiphanes, the Seleucid king ruling the land of Israel at the time of writing. It is "predicted" that he will cause much destruction, but will be destroyed by no human hand. Here again we find a symbolic account of history. The reviews of history in Daniel differ from those in the apocalypses attributed to Enoch in that they do not begin with the antediluvian period. They begin rather with the Neo-Babylonian empire. In other words, the destruction of Jerusalem and the exile constitute the starting point of historical reflection. The example of Daniel indicates that apocalyptic history does not always begin with primordial history.

Chapter 9 begins with an indication of the setting that includes the date and the fact that Daniel was pondering a prophecy in Jeremiah that the exile would last seventy years (vv 1-2). There follows a brief mention of Daniel's ascetic practices and a long account of his prayer (vv 3-19).[107] The prayer involves confession of sin and a request that the people be restored. The implicit problem seems to be that a true

107. On practices mentioned in apocalyptic literature that may have been designed to evoke visions and other ecstatic experience, see Daniel Merkur, "The Visionary Practices of Jewish Apocalyptists," *Psychoanalytic Study of Society* 14 (1989) 119–48.

restoration has not yet occurred, from the point of view of the text's author, and thus the prophecy of Jeremiah seems problematic. This prayer is answered by an epiphany of Gabriel, who reveals that the prophecy of Jeremiah should be understood as "seventy weeks of years" (v 24, RSV). This key to the prophecy of Jeremiah introduces a "prophecy" of history revealed by Gabriel to Daniel (vv 24-27). The review of history begins with "the going forth of the word to restore and build Jerusalem" (v 25, RSV). This is presumably an allusion to the decree of Cyrus also alluded to in Second Isaiah. The review nears its end with an allusion to the blasphemous deeds of Antiochus and concludes with a prophecy of his "decreed end" (v 27). This historical survey is general, like that of the Apocalypse of Weeks, but it is not allegorical like the dream of Daniel 2 and the visions of chapters 7 and 8. Like the other passages in Daniel, it begins with the exile rather than with primordial history.

The last major unit of Daniel, chapters 10–12, is the one most similar to canonical and extracanonical Jewish histories, like 1 and 2 Maccabees and Josephus's *Jewish War*. Like chapter 9, it involves a verbal revelation to Daniel by an angelic being. Most of chapter 10 is taken up with the description of the setting, the ascetic activities of Daniel, the epiphany of the angel Gabriel, and the angel's introductory remarks. For our purposes, one important element in this introductory material is the expression of the apocalyptic view of history in which heavenly powers or realities control earthly events. The earthly events involving the interaction of Persia and Israel are explained as the results of the interaction of angelic beings in the spiritual world (10:13). Likewise, the rule of the Macedonians over Israel reflects the attack of the angelic prince of Greece on the angelic patrons of Israel, Gabriel and Michael (10:20—11:1).

The verbal revelation given by Gabriel to Daniel (based on what is written in the "book of truth") extends from 11:2 to 12:4. This account contains a slightly veiled historical narrative from the Persian king following Cyrus to the exploits of Antiochus IV Epiphanes (11:2-31). The account is not symbolic or metaphorical. The kingdoms of Persia and Greece are mentioned explicitly. The Ptolemies are referred to as the "kings of the south" and the Seleucids as the "kings of the north." Antiochus IV is not named directly but is recognizable. Following the narrative of Antiochus's activities are remarks concerning the varied reactions among the Jewish people (11:32-35). Some collaborate and some resist. The latter receive "a little help" (v 34); this remark is often taken to be an allusion to the Maccabees. The persecution is expected to last until "the time of the end" (v 35).

The section on the reactions of the Jewish people is followed by a passage that offers a general assessment of Antiochus's character and deeds (11:36-39). Then the account departs from history as otherwise known, though it continues to be historylike. It is likely that the remainder of the account was intended to be prophesied history. The passage in 11:40-45 is written in the same style as the rest of chapter 11 and describes further activities of Antiochus followed by his death. These last exploits of the Seleucid king were expected to occur "at the time of the end" and to be followed by a great time of trouble and the resurrection of "many" of the dead (12:1-4). The historical narrative as a whole (11:2—12:4), including both the past and the future, is presented as "revealed history," a category that can also be applied to the work of Josephus.[108]

The community at Qumran did not produce historical works. Among the works they did produce are commentaries (*pesharim*). Fragments of commentaries on Isaiah, Hosea, Micah, Nahum, Habakkuk, Zephaniah, and Psalms 37, 45, 68, and 127 have been published. The interpretations offered show that the community considered these works to be prophecies of the history of their group, including the eschatological period of judgment and renewal. For example, a portion of Isa 54:11, "And I will lay your foundations with sapphires," is commented on as follows: "Interpreted, this concerns the Priest and the people who laid the foundations of the Council of the Community... the congregation of His elect (shall sparkle) like a sapphire among stones."[109] The consciousness of living in the last days is expressed in the commentary on Habakkuk. The comment on Hab 2:1-2 is as follows: "and God told Habakkuk to write down that which would happen to the final generation, but He did not make known to him when time

108. See Robert G. Hall, *Revealed Histories: Techniques for Ancient Jewish and Christian Historiography* (Journal for the Study of the Pseudepigrapha Supplement Series 6; Sheffield: JSOT Press, 1991) 11–30, 89–91.

109. 4QpIsa[d] fragment 1, lines 1-3; translation from Geza Vermes, *The Dead Sea Scrolls in English* (2d ed.; New York: Penguin, 1975) 228–29; see also Maurya Horgan, *Pesharim: Qumran Interpretations of Biblical Books* (CBQMS 8; Washington, D.C.: Catholic Biblical Association, 1979) 126.

would come to an end. And as for that which he said *That he who reads may read it speedily*, interpreted this concerns the Teacher of Righteousness, to whom God made known all the mysteries of the words of His servants the Prophets."[110]

The histories of Josephus are at times silent and at times strongly critical of the eschatological expectations current in the land of Israel in the first century C.E. Nevertheless, Josephus expresses a type of eschatology. He apparently genuinely believed that the messianic prophecies of Israel were fulfilled in Vespasian. Although he may appear self-seeking in this judgment to some, the precedent of Second Isaiah and Cyrus should be kept in mind. Josephus shares another characteristic with the apocalyptists: he apparently considered himself to be an inspired writer of history.[111]

The Gospel of Mark combines realistic historical narrative with an eschatological perspective. The notion that the work of John the Baptist and the activity of Jesus inaugurated the last days is expressed in the summary of Jesus' teaching given in 1:15, "The time is fulfilled and the kingdom of God has drawn near; repent and believe in the good news."

The apocalyptic view of history, that earthly events are controlled by heavenly powers, is reflected in the descent of the Spirit upon Jesus and in the remark that the Spirit drove Jesus out into the wilderness (1:10, 12). The heavenly voice that speaks at the moment of Jesus' baptism by John not only legitimates Jesus but also suggests that he is the agent of God. The voice acknowledges Jesus as "my son" (1:11). The implication is that this God-man bridges heaven and earth; he makes the power of God active on earth.

The apocalyptic view of history is also reflected in the way that Satan is presented as the antagonist of Jesus. When the Spirit drives Jesus out into the wilderness, he is tested by Satan (1:13). In the Gospel of Mark, Satan does not appear primarily as the accuser in the heavenly court. He appears as the tester or tempter of human beings, not only in the wilderness scene at the beginning, but also in the interpretation of the parable of the Sower (4:15) and in the scene in which Peter rebukes Jesus for foretelling his suffering and death (8:33).

110. 1QpHab 7:1-5; translation from Vermes, *Dead Sea Scrolls*, 239; cf. Horgan, *Pesharim*, 16.
111. Hall, *Revealed Histories*, 24–30.

The other major narrative role that Satan plays in Mark is the leader of demons or unclean spirits. If Beelzebul is another name for Satan, as the context implies, then Satan in Mark is "the ruler of demons" (3:22). Satan is said, metaphorically at least, to have a "kingdom" or "kingly power" (3:23-24). Jesus' activity of exorcism is portrayed as an assault on the kingdom of Satan (3:27). Jesus as the agent of God, as the "stronger one" predicted by John the Baptist (1:7), leads the battle of the kingdom of God against the kingdom of Satan. The War Scroll of the Qumran community speaks of the eschatological battle in more traditional warlike language. In Mark the kingship of Jesus and the victory of the kingdom of God manifest themselves in the deliverance of the bodies, minds, and souls of individual human beings from the bondage of Satan (cf. 10:45).

Some apocalypses have a clear and sometimes explicit interest in what we would call politics—kings, lesser rulers, kingdoms, battles, and, of course, persecution. The Animal Apocalypse and especially Daniel have such an interest. Others, like the Apocalypse of Weeks, are interested not so much in relationships and struggles related to political power as in the tension between justice and wickedness. In the Apocalypse of Weeks, the first week is characterized as the time when justice still held sway. The second week is the time when "great wickedness will arise" (*1 Enoch* 93:4). At the end of the third week, a man will be chosen as the "plant of righteous judgment" (93:5). The sixth week will be a time of impiety and the seventh a time of apostasy. But at the end of the seventh week the righteous will be given a sevenfold teaching. Then the wicked will be destroyed by the sword (91:11). The eighth will be a time in which righteous judgment will be executed. In the ninth righteous judgment will be revealed to the whole world, the deeds of the impious will vanish, and all people will look to the paths of uprightness. In the new age, "many weeks without number forever," all will live in goodness and righteousness and sin will never again be mentioned (91:17). The vision of the final state expressed in the Qumran War Scroll is similar, though expressed in more political terms (1QM 17:4-9).

The overt political interest in Mark is limited. The name of the unclean spirits possessing the Gerasene, "legion," may be a veiled allusion to Roman political and economic oppression (5:9). Chapter 6 gives an account of King Herod's execution of John the Baptist, but the motivation attributed to him is much less political than that described by Josephus (*Ant.* 18.116–19). The pronouncement story regarding tribute to Caesar is ambiguous, but is more easily taken as accommodating or apolitical than as critical or resistant (12:13-17). Finally, the account of the trial, mocking, and crucifixion of Jesus is an ironic portrait of Jesus as King of the Jews. Again, the narrative is ambiguous. On the one hand, it may be taken as a claim that Jesus is truly king and that those who brought about his death were ignorant of that reality. On the other hand, it may be read as a parody of the very idea of earthly political kingship. Jesus was much more, or even other than, that.

The Gospel of Mark is then less politically oriented than the Animal Apocalypse and Daniel. Not all apocalypses, even those with an interest in history, are politically oriented, as the example of the Apocalypse of Weeks shows. Mark is somewhat more politically oriented than that work.

Mark is certainly not "revealed history" in the explicit way that the historiographical portions of the apocalypses just discussed are. Further, neither the author nor the narrator claims divine inspiration in an explicit way. Nevertheless, the perspective of the narrative is similar to those "revealed" and "inspired" histories and to the commentaries from Qumran. The use of Scripture in Mark implies that the events narrated are fulfillments of prophecy. It is unlikely that the author and first readers of Mark considered that this insight was achieved by human effort through exegetical study after the resurrection of Jesus. Rather, the interpretation of the events narrated was probably thought to have been revealed by Jesus, the risen Christ, the Holy Spirit, or by all of these. Jesus is portrayed as revealing to his disciples the true significance of John the Baptist in 9:11-13, a significance that involves the fulfillment of prophetic Scripture. In chapter 13, Jesus prophesies what will happen to the disciples after his death, a time during which the Spirit will direct them (13:11). The Gospel also implies that Jesus could not be understood properly until after the resurrection (9:9).

CONCLUSION

The "Gospel" of Mark (1:1) is not only "the good news that God was present in Jesus for our salvation";[112] it is the good news that God has

112. Talbert, "Gospel Genre," 66–67.

acted and is acting in history to fulfill the promises of Scripture and to inaugurate the new age. The Gospel begins with a reference to "Jesus Christ" not out of interest in his character but to present him as God's agent. His message is "the good news of God" (1:14). In the opening statement of the Gospel, "Christ" is not used as a proper name but expresses the affirmation that Jesus is the anointed of God, the Messiah. This interpretation is supported by the presentation of the activity of John the Baptist as the fulfillment of prophecy (1:2-4).[113] Although the Gospel of Mark is not history in the rational, empirical sense of Thucydides or in the modern critical sense, it seems to be history in an eschatological or apocalyptic sense.

Thus Mark was written not only to avoid reductionism or to provide a controlling context for the tradition about Jesus but to place the various genres of that tradition into a historical framework. The genres of this tradition were integrated into a historical narrative of a particular type that became a host genre to those smaller forms. The result was that the various insights into "the presence of God in Jesus" were incorporated into a vision of the significance of God's activity in Jesus for history and for the world.

John Dominic Crossan has suggested that the narrative setting of the aphorism inhibits further and diverse interpretations, whereas the discourse setting fosters the growth of variants and new interpretations.[114] If this hypothesis is correct, he conjectures, it may explain why "the catholic tradition" granted authority only to narrative gospels. The representatives of this tradition wished to control what they saw as the excessive hermeneutical freedom of the "gnostic tradition's" gospels in discourse form. Now if the hypothesis put forward here is valid, that Mark is a historical monograph, it may be that the representatives of "the catholic tradition" shared with the author of this work the conviction that Christian faith is deeply rooted in history and that the discourse gospels were perceived as lacking that root.

If the author of Mark intended to write a historical work, this intention is rightly perceived by those who today continue to read Mark as history. The problem of interpretation is acute, however, for those who are self-conscious about the fact that they do not share the world-view presupposed by Mark. What meaning can the hypothesis that

113. See pp. 18–19 for a discussion of this point.
114. Crossan, "Aphorism," 122–23.

Mark is history have for such people? The theological significance of the hypothesis is the implication that a modern interpretation of Mark ought to aim at achieving the broad scope of the vision of the Gospel that is expressed in the choice of the historical genre in its apocalyptic mode.

It has become fashionable to focus on an aesthetic experience of reading Mark as "parabolic narrative."[115] The social and cosmic scope of the vision of Mark may be retrieved by such a reading if the implications of the "parable" are conceived broadly in keeping with the roots of narrativity. Stephen Crites has suggested that "narrativity has its roots in the fact that the individual self has a developmental history, that the individual is part of multiple communities that have histories, and that both individuals and communities are intertwined with an environment that also has a developmental history."[116]

Norman Perrin accepted the idea that the author of Mark invented a new Christian genre, the "gospel."[117] At the same time, he viewed Mark as a Gospel in the apocalyptic mode.[118] Standing in the Bultmannian intellectual tradition, Perrin believed that the Gospel of Mark, "like all apocalyptic," needs to be demythologized. Perrin thought that the Son of Man coming on the clouds was probably already a symbol for the author of Mark, but in any case must be viewed as a symbol by modern interpreters. This Son of Man, as well as the Gospel as a whole, is "a symbol of the realities and the possibilities for meaning of human existence in the world."[119] Such an approach will not do justice to Mark if "human existence in the world" is conceived as the history and hopes of one ethnic group or class, of one gender, or as a matter of private faith and morality. Only a resymbolization of Mark in terms of a message and purpose of cosmic and universal significance can do justice to the original. In other words, the apocalyptic-historical vision of Mark is best expressed through a theological perspective that attempts to embrace the universe as God's creation with a "developmental history" and a destiny.

---

115. See, e.g., Werner H. Kelber, "Narrative and Disclosure: Mechanisms of Concealing, Revealing, and Reveiling," *Genre, Narrativity, and Theology*, 1–20.
116. Paraphrased by Talbert, "Gospel Genre," 67.
117. Norman Perrin and Dennis C. Duling, *The New Testament: An Introduction* (2d ed.; New York: Harcourt Brace Jovanovich, 1982) 233.
118. Ibid., 238–39.
119. Ibid., 260.

Chapter Two

SUFFERING AND
HEALING IN THE
GOSPEL OF MARK

How can a mortal be just before God? . . . If it is a contest of strength,
he is the strong one! If it is a matter of justice, who can summon him? . . .
I am blameless; I do not know myself; I loathe my life. It is all one;
therefore I say, he destroys both the blameless and the wicked.

(Job 9:2, 19, 21-22)

WITHIN THE BIBLICAL CANON the book of Job poses the problem
of suffering in the starkest and most uncompromising terms. This book
assumes without question the omnipotence of God. The problem is
thus the justice of God. It is on this typically biblical way of posing
the problem of suffering that the theological term for it is based—the
problem of theodicy, how to justify God in the light of the existence
of suffering and evil.

The Greek philosophers put the problem differently. They had no
unanimity on the omnipotence of God. The Epicureans began with a
set of propositions that covered all possibilities. They said either God
"wishes to take away evils and is unable; or He is able, and is unwilling;
or He is neither willing nor able, or He is both willing and able."[1] The
Epicureans rejected the proposition that God is willing but unable,

1. This is the position of Epicurus, according to Lactantius *A Treatise on the Anger
of God* 13; the quotation is from the translation by A. Cleveland Cox, *Fathers of the
Third and Fourth Centuries*, vol. 7 of *The Ante-Nicene Fathers* (ed. Alexander Roberts
and James Donaldson; 10 vols.; c. 1886; reprint, Grand Rapids, Mich.: Eerdmans, 1985)
271.

for this implied that God is feeble, a quality not in keeping with the nature of God. They also rejected the assertion that God is able but unwilling to take away evils. Such an assertion implied that God is envious, a quality likewise incompatible with the character of God. The only remaining possibility is that God is both willing and able to take away evils. The Epicureans explained the fact that God does not take away evils by the argument that God takes no interest in anything.

Philosophers in the Platonic tradition argued that God achieves only those results that are possible given the limitations of the material with which God works, namely, nature. Thus events and the things that exist are not ideal but are the best possible under the circumstances.[2] The physician Galen, writing about 170 C.E. and influenced by both Plato and Aristotle, argued that some things are impossible by nature and that God does not undertake these things.[3] The Stoics and the Neo-Pythagoreans, however, affirmed divine omnipotence.[4]

The Gospel of Mark affirms God's omnipotence. This conviction is stated explicitly in the prayer of Jesus in Gethsemane, "Abba, Father, all things are possible for you" (Mark 14:36). That Jesus shares the omnipotence of God is suggested by the miracle stories. This notion is expressed in the disciples' reaction to the stilling of the storm, "Who then is this, that both wind and sea obey him?" (4:41). It is also through the miracles that Jesus, as God's agent, responds to human suffering by eliminating it with compassion.[5] Further, by portraying Jesus in the context of a miracle story as saying, "All things are possible for the believer" (9:23), the Gospel implies that ordinary humans may share the omnipotence of God.[6] In the Gospel of Mark, however, there is a sharp tension—one could say a paradox—between the God who gives

2. Plato *Timaeus* 47E–48A.
3. Galen *De usu partium* 11.14; text and translation given by R. Walzer, *Galen on Jews and Christians* (London: Oxford Univ. Press, 1949) 11–13.
4. See the discussion by Sharyn Echols Dowd, *Prayer, Power, and the Problem of Suffering: Mark 11:22-25 in the Context of Markan Theology* (Atlanta: Scholars Press, 1988) 83–87.
5. The term *paschō* ("to suffer") is used of a character seeking healing in Mark 5:26. It is used there specifically of the treatments received from physicians by the woman with a flow of blood. Although the term is not used, suffering is clearly described in several accounts, such as the Gerasene demoniac and the possessed boy in chap. 9. The compassion of Jesus is mentioned in relation to the leper (1:41; a textual variant indicates that the text may have referred originally to Jesus' anger rather than compassion). The father of the possessed boy appeals to Jesus' compassion (9:22).
6. Compare the teaching on prayer in Mark 11:22-25.

Jesus power to heal and exorcize and power over the forces of nature and the God who wills that the Son of man suffer and die. The same tension or paradox is evident between the promise that nothing is impossible for those who believe and the teaching that discipleship involves suffering and even death (e.g., 8:34-38). This essay explores each of the poles of this paradox and attempts to show how they fit together.

MIRACLES, CHRISTIAN FAITH,
AND SCHOLARSHIP

The miracles have been a problem for Christian faith and Christian relations to outsiders almost from the beginning.[7] Irenaeus claimed that the Gnostics were involved in magic and that they were more like Simon the magician than Jesus. He claimed that true disciples, however, apparently still in his own time, drive out devils, heal the sick, and even raise the dead, not by magic but by prayer in the name of Jesus Christ.[8] For modern Christians, it is primarily the Enlightenment's critique of miracles that has made the miracle stories of the Bible problematic. For example, David Hume argued that "A wise man . . . proportions his belief to the evidence."[9] The normative evidence for Hume is the evidence of one's own sensory experience. If, with regard to a particular issue, one's experience is consistent or, as he put it, "infallible," one has "proof" with regard to that particular matter of fact. Hume defined miracle as "a violation of the laws of nature." Since "firm and unalterable experience has established these laws, the proof against a miracle, from the very nature of the fact, is as entire as any argument from experience can possibly be imagined."[10] Another argument brought to bear by Hume is that testimony to miracles must be rejected because such supernatural and miraculous events "are observed chiefly to abound among ignorant and barbarous nations; or

7. For a discussion of the evidence that the miracle tradition became problematic very early, see Anton Fridrichsen, *The Problem of Miracle in Primitive Christianity* (trans. R. A. Harrisville and J. S. Hanson; Minneapolis: Augsburg, 1972).

8. Irenaeus *Against Heresies* 3.32.3–5. Origen also distinguishes Christian exorcism from magic (*Against Celsus* 7.4).

9. David Hume, *An Enquiry concerning Human Understanding*, in *The English Philosophers from Bacon to Mill* (ed. Edwin A. Burtt; New York: Modern Library, 1939) 653.

10. Ibid., 656.

if a civilized people has ever given admission to any of them, that people will be found to have received them from ignorant and barbarous ancestors, who transmitted them with that inviolable sanction and authority, which always attend received opinions."[11] In this connection, he observed that the first histories of nations are full of miracles and prodigies, whereas later histories explain things by natural causes. It was with regard to those early histories that Hume made one of his most memorable remarks, "*It is strange*, a judicious reader is apt to say, upon the perusal of these wonderful historians, *that such prodigious events never happen in our days.*"[12]

An early attempt to reconcile the modern philosophical perspective with the biblical accounts of miracles was the "rationalist" or "naturalist" approach. This point of view was popular in the nineteenth century and still has adherents today. In essence, this approach involves accepting the biblical accounts with regard to *what* happened, but rejecting the biblical explanation of *how* the event happened. For example, the Israelites really did cross the Red Sea on more or less dry ground, but God did not intervene directly to divide the sea. Rather, the sea became very shallow for the people of Israel because of natural conditions, for example, a tidal wave. The conditions then changed, and the water rushed back and destroyed the Egyptians as they pursued. An example from the New Testament is the rationalist explanation of the multiplication of the loaves. With regard to the incident in Mark 6, five thousand men did actually have enough to eat. But Jesus did not multiply five loaves and two fish into enough food for that multitude. Rather, the teaching and example of Jesus inspired the people present to share with one another the food that they had brought, and thus all were satisfied. The miracle was not that the laws of nature were broken, but that human beings were taught to love and share. Such explanations attempt to save the relationship of the text to historical fact, but in doing so destroy the significance that the text claims to find in that fact.

Another attempt to solve the dilemma involved the use of the term *myth*. In the early nineteenth century, David Strauss argued that the simple historical framework of the life of Jesus had been elaborated

11. Ibid., 659.
12. Ibid., 660.

42

in the Gospels through pious reflections and fantasies. What David Hume had dismissed as lying, Strauss tried to understand as a process of legendary glorification. He rejected the natural explanations of the rationalists as foreign to the text. But he equally decisively rejected the supernatural claims of the text on philosophical grounds. The appropriate category for interpretation is "myth," which he understood as the concrete formulation of the new Christian ideas in pictures and stories, a kind of "unintentionally poeticizing saga" that looked very much like history. Whereas the rationalists had sacrificed "the essence to the form," Strauss claimed that the essence of the Christian faith is independent of criticism. Although doubts may be cast on the supernatural birth of Christ, his miracles, his resurrection, and his ascension as historical facts, they remain eternal truths.[13]

The miracles are still a problem for New Testament scholars in the second half of the twentieth century. Many scholars are content to ignore the miracle stories in the Synoptic Gospels and concentrate on reconstructing the teaching of Jesus. For those who do take the miracle stories into account, two problems have seemed intractable. One is whether and how the inference of miracle-working activity from miracle stories can be warranted. The other is articulating the import of miracle-working activity in the case of Jesus.[14]

In the early 1970s, John M. Hull investigated the similarities between Hellenistic magic and the Synoptic tradition.[15] He did not attempt to clarify the relationship of the historical Jesus to the magical tradition in any detail. Although he doubted that Jesus thought of himself as a magician, he found evidence that Jesus "entered without reserve into the central conflict of the magician's art, the struggle with evil powers directly confronted in the persons of the possessed," and that Jesus was remembered as using folk remedies.[16] Hull concluded that the Gospel of Mark was deeply influenced by magical beliefs. Besides being a natural development of certain characteristics of the life of Jesus, this influence resulted from the attempt to present the

13. David F. Strauss, *The Life of Jesus Critically Examined* (trans. of 4th Germ. ed.; 3 vols.; London: Chapman Brothers, 1846) 1.1–95.

14. See Burton Mack's formulation of these problems in *A Myth of Innocence: Mark and Christian Origins* (Philadelphia: Fortress, 1988) 209–10.

15. John M. Hull, *Hellenistic Magic and the Synoptic Tradition* (Naperville, Ill.: Allenson, 1974).

16. Ibid., 143–45.

Gospel in terms suitable to the needs and expectations of the audience.[17]

Morton Smith has also investigated the relations between the Synoptic Gospels and the Greco-Roman magical tradition.[18] He reconstructed a picture of the historical Jesus and compared it with various types of ancient magicians, ranging from the deceiver type (*goēs*) to the divine-man type (*theios anēr*). He did not say whether he thought the historical Jesus was a deceiver, but he did imply that Jesus was an ordinary magician.[19]

In the same year that Hull published his book on magic and the Synoptic tradition, the German scholar Gerd Theissen published a major work on the miracle stories.[20] Theissen's book is an essay in hermeneutics in which he hoped to overcome the dichotomy between those who read the accounts of miracles as reports of supernatural events and those who see them as psychological projections of need.[21] Instead of focusing on the question regarding what happened or did not happen, Theissen explored the miracle stories as collective symbolic acts in which a new form of life is disclosed.[22]

The historical issue surfaced once again in an essay by Paul Achtemeier, published in 1975.[23] He focused on the narrative of Jesus' exorcism of a boy recounted in Mark 9:14-29. By form-critical and redaction-critical analysis, Achtemeier reconstructed two miracle stories that had been used in the composition of this narrative. He concluded that these stories circulated without specific theological interpretation of Jesus' exorcistic activity. He then turned to the question whether the historical Jesus actually engaged in exorcistic activity. In

17. Ibid., 144.
18. Morton Smith, "Prolegomena to a Discussion of Aretalogies, Divine Men, the Gospels and Jesus," *JBL* 90 (1971) 174–99; idem, *Jesus the Magician* (San Francisco: Harper & Row, 1978).
19. So Mack, *Myth of Innocence*, 210. One reviewer, Sean Freyne, inferred that Smith probably did favor the conclusion that Jesus was a deceiver (review of *Jesus the Magician*, *CBQ* 41 [1979] 660–61).
20. Gerd Theissen, *Urchristliche Wundergeschichten: Ein Beitrag zur formgeschichtlichen Erforschung der synoptischen Evangelien* (Gütersloh: Mohn, 1974); ET: *The Miracle Stories of the Early Christian Tradition* (trans. Francis McDonagh; Philadelphia: Fortress, 1983).
21. Theissen, *Wundergeschichten*, 45–51 = *Miracle Stories*, 34–40; see also the review by David Tiede, *JBL* 95 (1976) 483–84.
22. Theissen, *Wundergeschichten*, 261 = *Miracle Stories*, 264.
23. Paul Achtemeier, "Miracles and the Historical Jesus: A Study of Mark 9:14-29," *CBQ* 37 (1975) 471–91.

his discussion of the issue, Achtemeier rejected the philosophical position that miracles are impossible on a priori grounds and its corollary
that miracle stories are therefore historically unreliable. This view is
based on a modern construct of reality, which is itself based on the
perceptions of reality that the natural sciences credit as real. In contrast,
many people in the Greco-Roman world perceived divinations, au-
guries, and exorcisms as real. In other words, such events functioned
as reality in that historical era. Impressed by studies in the sociology
of knowledge and the intentionality of perception, Achtemeier has
concluded that there is no transhistorical guarantee that the modern
construct of reality is more real than the Greco-Roman construct.[24]

Achtemeier's position is similar to Strauss's on the relation of historical fact and dogma: it is not permissible to warrant the conclusion
that Jesus performed miracles with doctrines that the tradition has
used the miracle stories to support. In other words, the theological
truth of doctrines may not be used to support the historical truth of
the miracles. As we have seen, he differs from Strauss in his acceptance
of at least the functional reality of miracles in the ancient world. The
issue is complicated by the existence of miracle stories, similar to
those told about Jesus, concerning other heroes of the ancient world.
Achtemeier argued that the same criteria must be used to determine
the historicity of the miracle stories associated with Jesus and those
associated with other heroes. Either one ought to reject the historical
reliability of all miracle stories or, if one concludes that Jesus engaged
in miracle-working activity, one must allow that others engaged in
such activity as well. Such an allowance is, of course, made in the
Synoptic tradition itself.[25] In addition, Achtemeier pointed out that
according to the Synoptic tradition the miracles did not necessarily
lead to faith and that conclusions about Jesus' significance were drawn
also from other evidence, such as his teaching and death on the cross.
He concluded nevertheless that Jesus did heal at least one person in
a way identified in his world as an exorcism and warned that any
reconstruction of the historical Jesus that does not take his activity as
exorcist into account is a distortion.[26]

24. Ibid., 488–89.
25. Ibid., 489–90.
26. Ibid., 490–91.

THE BEGINNING OF THE GOSPEL

A number of scholars conclude that the tradition of miracle stories is rooted in the life of the historical Jesus.[27] Burton Mack has recently challenged this position, claiming that the earliest miracle stories were not reports of the miracle-working activity of Jesus. Mack takes the same position as Strauss in seeing these stories as mythical. He tries to show that they were composed in sets or collections by one of the early Jesus movements. They functioned as a myth of origins for a group who saw themselves as the new "congregation of Israel" and Jesus as their founder.[28]

The primary concern of this essay is how the miracle stories in Mark relate to the issues of human suffering and the justice of God. This concern, however, cannot be separated from the question of the historical Jesus. What we conclude about the role exorcism and healing played or did not play in the life and social setting of Jesus has a great impact on how we understand the significance of these activities as portrayed in the Gospel of Mark. I agree with Paul Achtemeier and other scholars who conclude that the historical Jesus engaged in activities that may be called "exorcising" and "healing." In the next section, I attempt to place these activities in their ancient social context.

EXORCISM AND HEALING
IN ANTIQUITY

Julian Jaynes has pointed to a remarkable cultural change in Mesopotamia that took place sometime between 1700 and 1250 B.C.E. For the first time in human history, evidence appears in art and literature for the experience of the absence of the gods. At about the same time, belief in demons or malevolent spirits arises, or at least increases. Some of these hostile spirits were associated with natural phenomena, such as sandstorms, fire, and wind. Others threatened human beings in lonely places or at crucial times like childbirth. Others were connected with various illnesses. One way in which humans sought to protect themselves from these demons was the wearing of prophylactic amulets.

---

27. Rudolf Bultmann allows this possibility in *The History of the Synoptic Tradition* (trans. John Marsh; rev. ed.; New York: Harper & Row, 1968) 228; cf. Helmut Koester, *Introduction to the New Testament*, vol. 2, *History and Literature of Early Christianity*, (Philadelphia: Fortress, 1982) 78–79.
28. Mack, *Myth of Innocence*, 215.

Many of these have been found in Mesopotamia, dating from about 1000 B.C.E. onward. Since virtually all health problems were ascribed to the influence of demons, medicine became exorcism. Thousands of tablets from the library of Ashurbanipal at Nineveh, collected around 630 B.C.E., describe exorcisms and other antidemoniac practices.[29]

In the history of religions, the malevolent influence of evil spirits has been experienced in two main ways. One type is external. The evil spirit appears to, attacks, or harasses the victim from outside. Such a spirit is sometimes called an "obsessing" spirit. The other type is internal. This type is related to the general phenomenon of "possession." This phenomenon may be defined as the complete domination of a human being and his or her speech by a spirit or god. After the period of possession, the possessed person does not remember what occurred or what he or she has said. The possessed person's ordinary consciousness is replaced by a new and different consciousness.[30] Sometimes possession is a positive and even constructive experience, as in the ancient oracles and in modern spiritualists and channelers. In these cases, genetic endowment seems to be a factor, and the technique can be taught, learned, and controlled in a ritual context.

There is another form of possession, however, that cannot be controlled and is usually not induced, unless through a curse or some form of "black magic." This type may be called demonic possession.[31] It is experienced as a misfortune or illness. The traditional religious explanation is that an evil spirit or demon has entered into and is controlling and using the person involved. A recent psychological explanation is that it is a spontaneous change in the structure and function of an individual's brain in response to stress.[32] Cases of demonic possession in the nineteenth and early twentieth centuries

29. Julian Jaynes, *The Origin of Consciousness in the Breakdown of the Bicameral Mind* (Boston: Houghton Mifflin, 1976) 223–33. Jaynes has a psychological theory to explain these developments; whether or not one accepts his hypothesis, one must recognize the importance of the phenomena he discusses. His sources for these are texts published by W. G. Lambert, *Babylonian Wisdom Literature* (Oxford: Clarendon, 1960); H. W. F. Saggs, *The Greatness That Was Babylon* (New York: Mentor, 1962); and others. E. A. Wallis Budge discusses amulets from Mesopotamia that he believes were made before 2500 B.C.E. (*Amulets and Superstitions* [London: Oxford Univ. Press, 1930; repr., New York: Dover, 1978] 82–86).

30. The term *possession* and the definition given reflect the religious naming and explanation of the phenomenon. A naturalist, psychological explanation may also be given; see, e.g., Jaynes, *Origin of Consciousness*, 349.

31. Jaynes calls it "negatory possession" (ibid., 347).

32. Ibid.

described in the scholarly psychological literature have important similarities to the mental illness called schizophrenia. They both begin with some kind of hallucination, usually a castigating voice that is heard after a stressful period of life. Unlike schizophrenia, in the case of "demonic possession" the voice develops into a secondary system of personality, probably because of the "possessed person's" belief that another being has taken control of his or her body. The possessed person periodically loses control and enters into a trance state in which ordinary consciousness is lost and the "demon" side of the personality takes over. The people experiencing possession usually have little education. The manifestation of the "demonic" personality is usually confined to speech, although the trance state is often accompanied by twisting and writhing and a distorted voice, often guttural. The "demon" may be interested in negotiating contracts with the observers. The cure involves the command of an authoritative person, often following a ritual. Since the Middle Ages, the overwhelming majority of persons experiencing possession have been women.[33]

The Scripture as known to Jesus and other Jews of his time implied on the whole that healing was a divine monopoly. Geza Vermes has summed up the evidence well: "to refer certain matters of health to a priest was a duty; to seek the help of a prophet was an act of [piety]; and to visit the doctor was an act of impiety."[34] It seems that the wisdom tradition was more open than other parts of Scripture to the practice of medicine and to pragmatic attempts to heal or cure. Sirach, a wisdom book written in the second century B.C.E., attempted to synthesize the various ways of seeking healing by advising the sick to repent, pray, and offer sacrifice first—then to see a doctor. The physician's skill and insight are God-given. Likewise, the Lord created medicines from the earth and a sensible person will not despise them.

33. Ibid., 348–53. Jaynes is summarizing the literature, e.g., J. L. Nevius, *Demon Possession and Allied Themes* (Chicago: Revell, 1986); and Traugott K. Oesterreich, *Possession, Demoniacal and Other: Among Primitive Races in Antiquity, the Middle Ages, and Modern Times* (trans. D. Ibberson; London: Kegan Paul, 1930). The German edition of Oesterreich's work appeared under the title *Die Besessenheit* (Langensalza: Wendt & Klauwell, 1921).

34. Geza Vermes, *Jesus the Jew: A Historian's Reading of the Gospels* (Philadelphia: Fortress, 1973) 59–60. According to 2 Chr 16:12, Asa king of Judah consulted physicians rather than seeking the Lord. In the original of the quotation given above, Vermes speaks of seeking the help of a prophet as "an act of religion."

The physician should begin diagnosis and treatment with prayer (Sir 38:1-15).

The book of Tobit gives a glimpse of popular Jewish beliefs regarding demons in the second temple period.[35] A Jewish woman, Sarah, living in Ecbatana in Media, was plagued by an evil demon named Asmodeus ("Destroyer"). This demon had slain Sarah's seven husbands before each had been with her as wife (Tob 3:7-15), apparently on the night of the wedding (6:13). Tobias, the son of Tobit, was able to drive the demon away by following the advice of the angel Raphael to burn the heart and liver of a fish (Tob 6:1—8:3).

According to the pseudepigraphical book of *Jubilees*, composed in the second century B.C.E., unclean demons began to plague the sons of Noah after the flood. When Noah prayed to God for the deliverance of his sons, God ordered the angels to bind all the unclean spirits. But when their leader Mastema petitioned God, God agreed to allow one-tenth of the demons to remain free as agents of punishment. The angels explained to Noah the remedies for the diseases caused by these unclean demons, how to heal them with herbs. Thus the evil spirits were prevented from harming Noah's sons. According to this work, Noah wrote down the angels' instruction in a book that he later gave to Shem, his eldest son (*Jub.* 10:1-14). According to Genesis 10 and *Jub.* 8:12-21, Shem is the ancestor of the Semitic peoples, including Israel.

In popular Jewish religion, Solomon was revered as the source of exorcistic expertise. According to Josephus, "God granted him knowledge of the art used against demons for the benefit and healing of men. He also composed incantations by which illnesses are relieved, and left behind forms of exorcisms with which those possessed by demons drive them out, never to return." Josephus goes on to claim that this art of healing was flourishing among Jews in his own day. In support of this assertion, he states that he himself has witnessed the exorcism of more than one person in the presence of the emperor Vespasian, his sons, tribunes, and a number of other soldiers. These

35. This book, like Sirach (= Ecclesiasticus) is included in the Catholic canon of the Old Testament. The Protestant churches consider it to be deuterocanonical or apocryphal. It is dated variously, sometimes to the fifth or fourth centuries B.C.E., sometimes to the second. It was probably composed in Hebrew or Aramaic, but survives only in Greek, Latin, and other versions.

exorcisms were performed by a Jew named Eleazar. Josephus describes the manner of the cure:

> He put to the nose of the possessed man a ring which had under its seal one of the roots prescribed by Solomon, and then, as the man smelled it, drew out the demon through his nostrils, and, when the man at once fell down, adjured the demon never to come back into him, speaking Solomon's name and reciting the incantations which he had composed. Then, wishing to convince the bystanders and prove to them that he had this power, Eleazar placed a cup or footbasin full of water a little way off and commanded the demon, as it went out of the man, to overturn it and make known to the spectators that he had left the man.[36]

Another text from the Greco-Roman world that describes an exorcism is a passage in a satirical dialogue by Lucian of Samosata, a philosopher and man of letters from Syria who wrote in Greek and lived in the second century C.E. The dialogue is called *The Lover of Lies*. The author's dialogue partner, Ion, describes an otherwise unknown Syrian exorcist from Palestine, who was able to heal "those who were moonstruck and rolled their eyes and filled their mouths with foam." He sent them away healthy in return for a large fee. Ion describes his technique:

> When he stands by them as they lie there, he asks (the demons) from whence they came into the body. The sick man is silent, but the demon answers in Greek or some barbarian tongue, or in the language of the country from which he comes, how and from whence he came into the man. The Syrian then levels oaths at him (to drive him out), but if the demon is not persuaded, he threatens [even worse punishments] and expels the demon. I actually saw one coming out, black and smoky in color.[37]

---

36. Josephus *Ant.* 8.42–48. Translation cited is from *Josephus*, vol. 5, *Jewish Antiquities, Books V–VIII* (trans. H. St. J. Thackeray and Ralph Marcus; LCL; Cambridge: Harvard Univ. Press, 1934, repr., 1977) 593–97. The link between Solomon and exorcism is also attested by a work entitled *The Testament of Solomon*. In the form in which it has been preserved, it is Christian, but it is probably based on an originally Jewish work. See the introduction to and translation of this work by Dennis C. Duling in *OTP*, 1.935–87.

37. Lucian, *The Lover of Lies* 16; translation is from David R. Cartlidge and David L. Dungan, *Documents for the Study of the Gospels* (Philadelphia: Fortress, 1980) 157.

Lucian himself mocks this claim, but Ion's remarks at least reflect the beliefs of many in the second century C.E.

The English words *exorcism* and *exorcist* derive from the Greek verb *exorkizō* and the Greek noun *exorkistēs*. The basic meaning of the verb is "to administer an oath to someone."[38] The verb is used in the sense of "entreat solemnly by an oath" in the Old Greek translation of Gen 24:3 (Abraham adjuring his servant concerning the marriage of Isaac). In the magical papyri, this verb is used to mean "to conjure," or "to summon a demon, spirit, or god."[39] The only occurrence of the verb in the New Testament is in Matt 26:63, in which the high priest adjures Jesus by the living God to say whether he claims to be the Messiah.[40]

The use of the verb *exorkizō* to mean "cast out a demon," "exorcise," is rarely attested. Liddell, Scott and Jones list only one example, a spell or charm inscribed on a tablet that was found on the site of ancient Carthage. But the verb here does not mean "cast out a demon." Rather, it has the more common meaning "to conjure" or "to adjure."[41] The scarce attestation for this meaning in pre-Christian Greek may indicate that the term was indeed rarely used in pre-Christian contexts, or that its usage was popular and oral and thus it does not appear frequently in writing.

The Greek noun *exorkistēs*, meaning one who expels demons or evil spirits by means of a specific technique, is a rare word. As far as I know, it occurs only three times in non-Christian Greek.[42] In the

38. In this meaning, it is equivalent to the older verb *exorkoō*; see Henry G. Liddell, Robert Scott, and Henry S. Jones, eds., *A Greek-English Lexicon* (9th ed.; Oxford: Clarendon, 1940, repr. 1966) 598. Hereafter this work is cited as LSJ.

39. For example, PGM IV.1239; for the text, see Karl Preisendanz, ed., *Papyri Graecae Magicae: Die griechischen Zauberpapyri* (rev. ed. by Albert Henrichs; Stuttgart: Teubner, 1973) 1.114; an English translation by Marvin Meyer may be found in *The Greek Magical Papyri in Translation: Including the Demotic Spells*, vol. 1, *Texts* (ed. H. D. Betz; Chicago: Univ. of Chicago Press, 1986) 1.62. This use of the verb appears in a rite for driving out demons that dates to the fourth century C.E.

40. The verb also appears in textual variants of Acts 19:13-14.

41. The spell was originally published by Molinier in *Mémoires de la Société nationale des Antiquaires de France* 58 (1899); it was also published by R. Wünsch in *Rheinisches Museum für Philologie*, n.f. 55 (1896) 248–59.

42. Lucian *Epigrammata* 23 = *Anthologia Palatina* 11.427 (the epigram is as follows: *Daimona polla lalōn ozostomos exorkistēs exebal', ouch horkōn, alla koprōn dynamei*, "an exorcist cast out a demon by speaking many things with foul breath, not binding it with an oath, but by the power of filth"); *Tetrabiblos* 182 (a work attributed to Ptolemy of Alexandria, the mathematician of the second century C.E. = Claudius

New Testament it occurs only in Acts 19:13 of itinerant Jewish exorcists, identified as sons of a high priest (v 14).

Although the technical terms for exorcisms and exorcists are relatively rare, it is clear that the ideas and practices were well known and widespread in the time of Jesus. The passages from Tobit and Josephus are evidence for the use of particular substances to expel or drive away demons. The passage from Josephus provides evidence also for the use of verbal formulas. Two texts discovered at Qumran describe Jewish heroes as exorcists; such descriptions suggest that exorcism was being practiced among those who read the texts and perhaps more widely in Jewish culture. The *Genesis Apocryphon* (1QapGen) retells the story of Genesis 12. In this later version of the story, Pharaoh is prevented from defiling Sarah by an evil spirit sent by God to scourge him and all his household. Later, Abraham expels the spirit from the king by praying and laying his hands on him.[43] In the *Prayer of Nabonidus* (4QPrNab), the last king of Babylon gives thanks for the healing and forgiveness of sins that he received through a Jewish exorcist.[44]

MIRACLES AND THE HISTORICAL JESUS

As David Strauss argued in the nineteenth century and as Burton Mack is arguing today, it is conceivable that the stories about healings and exorcisms performed by Jesus are legendary formulations or foundation myths created by followers of Jesus after his death. The stories as we have them in the canonical Gospels are certainly shaped by post-resurrection views of Jesus, as Bultmann pointed out.[45] Mack is right to insist that these stories are determined by the meaning and function they had for the Jesus movement after his death, even when they do

Ptolemaeus; this work was edited by J. Camerarius and published in Nürnberg in 1535; it is cited by page number of the repr. published in Basel in 1553 with a Latin translation by P. Melanchthon); Ptolemaeus *Apotelesmatica astrol.* 4.4.10 (ed. F. Boll and A. Boer, 1940). (This last reference is from Walter Bauer, William F. Arndt, and F. Wilbur Gingrich, eds., *A Greek-English Lexicon of the New Testament and Other Early Christian Literature* [2d ed. revised and augmented by F. Wilbur Gingrich and Frederick W. Danker; Chicago: Univ. of Chicago Press, 1979] xxv and 277).

43. An English translation of the text may be found in Geza Vermes, *The Dead Sea Scrolls in English* (2d ed.; New York: Penguin Books, 1975) 218–20.

44. Ibid., 229.

45. Bultmann, *History*, 228.

not contain explicit theological interpretive language.[46] I am not confident that it is possible to strip away theological, legendary, and mythical elements in any story of Jesus' healing or exorcism and end up with an accurate historical report. Nevertheless, it is more plausible historically that these stories have some basis in the life of Jesus than that they are entirely fictional. The miracle tradition is strong and widespread. The two oldest Christian documents, Mark and the hypothetical Synoptic Sayings Source (often referred to as Q), both contain miracle stories.[47] The emphasis on extraordinary deeds among the Christians in the Pauline congregations is evidence for the early tradition of analogous activity in the life of Jesus. The gift of the Spirit after the resurrection of Jesus was understood as making the believers like Jesus.[48] Given the overall picture of Jesus as a charismatic leader from a village in Galilee who apparently identified with the non-elite, it seems likely that he did extraordinary deeds involving healing and exorcism that gave rise to the miracle tradition.[49]

There is no compelling philosophical reason to reject the tradition that Jesus was a healer and exorcist. I agree with Paul Achtemeier that the philosophical position that defines miracles as impossible ought to be rejected. My reasons are somewhat different from his, though related. First, the natural sciences have changed a great deal since Hume's time. The sciences of astrophysics and subatomic physics focus on phenomena that are not directly and simply available to human sensory perception. According to the Newtonian mechanics of Hume's time, if sufficiently accurate measurements were made, predictions of the future behavior of a system, such as the solar system, could be made with great accuracy. In the quantum mechanics of the twentieth century, precise prediction of future behavior is usually impossible. More importantly, at present there is no unified scientific description of reality. Although quantum mechanics is the most successful theory of physical phenomena yet devised by the human mind, it has not yet

46. Mack, *Myth of Innocence*, 213.
47. The Greek form of the *Gospel of Thomas*, judging from the later Coptic version, did not contain miracle stories. Some would argue that this document is as old as Q. There is no positive evidence, however, that the Greek work was composed much before 125 C.E.
48. See 1 Thess 1:5-6; Gal 3:1-5; 1 Cor 12:4-11, 27-30.
49. On the relation of Jesus to Jewish charismatic leaders, see Vermes, *Jesus the Jew*, 58–82.

proved possible to formulate a consistent quantum theory of gravity. In other words, there exists a coherent description of subatomic phenomena and a coherent description of astronomical phenomena, but no coherent theory that can account for both aspects of reality. All this suggests that it behooves us to be cautious in speaking of "general laws of nature."

A second reason for admitting the possibility of miracles, at least of the healing and exorcising type, relates to a major shift of point of view among some psychologists and anthropologists who have studied religious phenomena. The older view, still held by many, is that phenomena like altered states of consciousness (including possession, visions, and journeys "out of the body") and practices like exorcism and "faith healing" are due either to lying or faking, mental pathology, the weak-minded acting out of wishes based on desperate need, or ignorant and gross superstition. Stories based on alleged experiences of this kind are judged from this point of view as lies, delusions, or worthless fantasies. An oddity related to this approach is that much of religious experience is regarded as nonsense, but the history of nonsense is regarded as scholarship.

The newer point of view takes such experiences more seriously. What the newer approaches have in common is that they allow these experiences a significant degree of reality. For I. M. Lewis, their reality is social. The experience of possession by spirits functions for persons of low social status, such as slaves or servants, as a means of gaining prestige and of exercising some control over people of higher status to whom they are responsible.[50] For Julian Jaynes these phenomena have physiological and psychological reality. Their form and function depend on the cultural setting, on the "collective cognitive imperative" accepted by the participants and their associates.[51] Felicitas Goodman has scientifically studied glossolalia and altered states of consciousness.

50. I. M. Lewis, *Ecstatic Religion: An Anthropological Study of Spirit Possession and Shamanism* (Baltimore: Penguin, 1971). Analogous interpretations of similar phenomena are given by Jeannette H. Henney ("Spirit-Possession Belief and Trance Behavior in Two Fundamentalist Groups in St. Vincent," *Trance, Healing and Hallucination: Three Field Studies in Religious Experience* [ed. Irving I. Zaretsky; New York: John Wiley & Sons, 1974; repr. Malabar, Fla.: Robert E. Krieger Publishing Company, 1982] 1–111) and Esther Pressel ("Umbanda Trance and Possession in Sao Paulo, Brazil," ibid., 113–225).

51. Jaynes, *Origin of Consciousness*, 324–25, 328–29, 340, 342, 348, 350, 360, 373–74, 381, 383–86, 402–3, 409–10, 439, 445.

In her work on glossolalia, she observed and made tape recordings of such speech and then analyzed it according to the methods of the discipline of linguistics. She also measured physiological changes in the bodies of those speaking in tongues. Such work demonstrates not only that at least some speakers in tongues are not faking, but also that it is a cross-cultural phenomenon with stable linguistic and physiological patterns.[52] In her work on exorcism, Goodman went a step further. She argued that "demonic possession" is an identifiable state distinguishable from ordinary mental illness. In addition, she argued on the basis of observation that the religious technique of exorcism works, whereas modern medical treatments in this case do not.[53]

Paul Achtemeier drew attention to the difference between the modern naturalist construction of reality and the ancient popular religious construction of reality. On the basis of the sociology of knowledge and the intentionality of perception, he urged that the ancient construction be taken seriously in interpreting texts from that time.[54] Analogously, Goodman pointed out the difference and the occasional conflict in our own time between the naturalist view of human nature (the human being as a biological-psychological system) and the "soul theory" of popular religion (spirits are real and can possess or otherwise influence human beings). Goodman's philosophical position is that the "real world" is hidden behind observable phenomena and that it is impossible to separate the observer from the observed. As an anthropologist, she argues further that what is accepted as being real in a particular situation is determined not by the individual but by the culture in which the situation is embedded. She takes her stand on the observable physical changes that accompany possession and argues that no one can prove whether the obvious changes in the brain map during "possession" are caused by physiological and psychological

52. Felicitas D. Goodman, "Glossolalia and Single-Limb Trance: Some Parallels," *Psychotherapy and Psychosomatics* 19 (1971) 92–103; idem, *Speaking in Tongues: A Cross-Cultural Study of Glossolalia* (Chicago: Univ. of Chicago Press, 1972); idem, "Glossolalia and Hallucination in Pentecostal Congregations," *Psychiatria Clinica* 6 (1973) 97–103.

53. Felicitas D. Goodman, *Anneliese Michel und ihre Dämonen: Der Fall Klingenberg in wissenschaftlicher Sicht* (Stein am Rhein: Christiana, 1980); English edition, idem, *The Exorcism of Anneliese Michel* (New York: Doubleday, 1981); idem, *How About Demons? Possession and Exorcism in the Modern World* (Bloomington, Ind.: Indiana Univ. Press, 1988).

54. Achtemeier, "Miracles and the Historical Jesus," 487–91.

processes or by an alien being invading the body. As a cultural anthropologist in a pluralistic world, she urges that all, especially authoritative and powerful naturalists, be open-minded and treat the experience and beliefs of others that differ from ours with respect.[55]

The work of social scientists on the phenomena of possession suggests that culture, or the "collective cognitive imperative," to use Julian Jaynes's phrase, has great influence on the nature and function of the phenomenon. Jaynes points out that most recorded cases of demonic possession from the Middle Ages onward in the West have involved women. In the ancient world, most of the individuals so affected seem to have been men.[56] This difference may be culturally determined or it may be a reflection of the relative stress experienced by men and women in different cultures.

One aspect of the cultural situation with regard to possession in the ancient world is that it was apparently customary for exorcists to take fees. The passage cited previously from Lucian attests to the custom. According to the tradition about Jesus, he did not take fees.[57] The relation of mighty deeds and fees was evidently an issue in the early church. The rivals of Paul in Corinth apparently worked mighty deeds and accepted some form of financial compensation. In contrast, Paul refused to accept financial support from the Corinthians (2 Cor 11:7-15, 12:11-13). It is interesting to note that the relation of "faith healing" and fees has been an issue in the twentieth century as well. Edgar Cayce became a healer reluctantly. Eventually he gave up other forms of activity to use his psychic gifts to help others. Thereafter, he accepted payment, but only what people were able to pay.[58] In Brazil there is a "spirit surgeon" at work. Edison Queiros, M.D., is a qualified medical doctor who sees paying patients in his office during regular working hours. At other times, in a ritual context and using different techniques, he heals poor people without charging a fee.[59]

55. Goodman, *How About Demons?* 123–26; idem, *Ecstasy, Ritual and Alternate Reality: Religion in a Pluralistic World* (Bloomington, Ind.: Indiana Univ. Press, 1988).
56. The affected people mentioned in the Gospels are not all male; see, e.g., Mark 7:24-30 and Luke 8:1-3.
57. The financial issue may have been of interest to the author of Mark or to those on whom he was dependent, since the woman with a flow of blood was said to have spent all she had, presumably in payments to physicians, without results (Mark 5:26).
58. See his biography by Thomas Sugrue, *There Is a River: The Story of Edgar Cayce* (rev. ed.; New York: Holt, 1945).
59. The activity of this spirit surgeon was described by David J. Hess, Visiting Professor at Colgate University, in a lecture at the Univ. of Notre Dame, April 20, 1989, entitled "Spirit Surgeons and Wounded Laws: Ideology and Spiritism in the Brazilian New Republic," sponsored by the Kellogg Institute and the Department of Anthropology.

Assuming then that the historical Jesus engaged in healing and exorcising activity, we turn now to the question of the import of that activity. This question has been debated. One position is that it authorized Jesus as a Hellenistic hero or divine man.[60] The other major position is that this activity was a sign of the dawning of the new age and that it authorized Jesus as the eschatological agent of God on the model of the prophets of Israel.[61] These two interpretations are not mutually exclusive. In the canonical Gospels, the traditions that depict Jesus as a wonder-working prophet are melded with traditions of Jesus as Messiah. Both the prophetic and messianic significance of Jesus are linked with the phrase "Son of God." The phrase "Son of God" would have recalled Psalm 2 and had primarily messianic connotations for many familiar with Jewish tradition. For those familiar with Hellenistic tradition, the phrase "son of God" (*huios theou*) would have recalled the epithet "son of Zeus" (*huios Dios*) and had connotations of a semidivine hero, such as Herakles, who became immortal by eliminating wickedness and lawlessness in obedience to God.[62]

It is difficult to say whether the historical Jesus intended this dual authorization. The Gospel of Mark portrays the miracles of Jesus both as testimony to his role as an agent of God, sharing in the divine power, and as instances in the struggle between the rule of God and the powers of Satan. The Sayings Source used by Matthew and Luke (Q) also interprets the miracles in this way. In the Q version of the controversy over the source of Jesus' exorcising power, Jesus is portrayed as saying, "But if it is by the Spirit/finger of God that I cast out demons, then the rule of God has come upon you" (Matt 12:28/Luke 11:20). Since these are the two earliest documents representing the tradition

60. This theory has been defended, e.g., by Morton Smith; see Moses Hadas and Morton Smith, *Heroes and Gods: Spiritual Biographies in Antiquity* (New York: Harper & Row, 1965); Morton Smith, "Prolegomena"; idem, *Clement of Alexandria and a Secret Gospel of Mark* (Cambridge: Harvard Univ. Press, 1973); idem, *The Secret Gospel: The Discovery and Interpretation of the Secret Gospel according to Mark* (New York: Harper & Row, 1973); idem, *Jesus the Magician*. For a history of scholarship on the "divine man" up to 1970, see David L. Tiede, *The Charismatic Figure as Miracle Worker* (Missoula, Mont.: SBL, 1972) 241–92; see also Carl R. Holladay, *Theios Anēr in Hellenistic Judaism: A Critique of the Use of This Category in New Testament Christology* (Missoula, Mont.: Scholars Press, 1977).

61. Howard Clark Kee, "Aretalogy and Gospel," *JBL* 92 (1973) 402–22; idem, *Medicine, Miracle and Magic in New Testament Times* (Cambridge: Cambridge Univ. Press, 1986) 128–29.

62. See Epictetus *Diss.* 2.16.44.

about Jesus, it is likely that they reflect the understanding of the historical Jesus.

I do not agree with Howard Kee, however, that when miracle stories symbolize the divine victory about to be achieved, the triumph of divine powers over the forces of evil, then miracle has no significance on the level of personal benefit. A comprehensive framework, like the apocalyptic framework of meaning in which the miracles are set in Mark and Q, may rightly be emphasized as their main interpretive framework and function in texts in which it appears. If Jesus healed and exorcised people, however, those people did experience personal benefit. So in the life of Jesus the value of the health and welfare of the seeking individual also played a role.[63] If the historical Jesus linked his healing activity to the rule of God, then this activity expresses an aspect of what the rule of God is about. It includes compassion for those suffering physical, emotional, mental, and spiritual distress. This understanding of the life of Jesus implies that the rule of God is not only a matter of the individual soul or spirit. By the same token, it is not strictly a matter of politics and economics. It involves the well-being of each individual and of the whole individual, as well as the manifestation of God's rule in all creation, including human society.

MIRACLES IN MARK

The first eight chapters of Mark contain fifteen miracle stories.[64] In addition to these specific accounts, five Markan summaries or editorial remarks mention Jesus' many healings or exorcisms or both.[65] Furthermore, in the narrative about the appointment of the twelve, it is said that they were to be sent out to preach and to cast out demons (3:14-15). Immediately following is an elaborated pronouncement

63. Kee distinguishes sharply between the model of the individual seeking health and welfare (his type 1) and the apocalyptic model (his type 3) (Howard Clark Kee, *Miracle in the Early Christian World: A Study in Sociohistorical Method* [New Haven: Yale Univ. Press, 1983] 293–94).

64. Mark 1:21-28; 1:29-31; 1:40-45; 2:1-12; 3:1-6; 4:35-41; 5:1-20; 5:21-24a, 35-43; 5:24b-34; 6:31-44; 6:45-52; 7:24-30; 7:31-37; 8:1-10; and 8:22-26.

65. Mark 1:32-34 (healing and exorcism); 1:39 (preaching and exorcism); 3:7-12 (healing and reference to unclean spirits); 6:5-6 (healing and teaching); and 6:53-56 (healing). On the Markan "summaries," see Charles W. Hedrick, "The Role of 'Summary Statements' in the Composition of the Gospel of Mark: A Dialog with Karl Schmidt and Norman Perrin," *NovT* 26 (1984) 289–311; idem, "What Is a Gospel? Geography, Time and Narrative Structure," *Perspectives in Religious Studies* 10 (1983) 255–68.

story whose core is a controversy over the source of Jesus' power to cast out demons (3:19b-35). Later the sending out of the twelve to preach and cast out demons is narrated (6:7-11) and their success in exorcising and healing is summarized (6:12-13). At least one-half of the narrative material in these first eight chapters is devoted to miracles.[66]

The middle section of Mark, which focuses on the predictions of the passion and teaching on discipleship, nevertheless contains two miracle stories.[67] In addition, this section includes a dialogue on the subject of exorcism.[68] The predictions of the suffering, death, and resurrection of the Son of man may have been intended to show Jesus' foreknowledge or clairvoyance, as well as to instruct the disciples within the narrative setting. At least these predictions, especially the detailed one in chapter 10, would have made and continue to make such an impression on some readers.[69]

The section narrating Jesus' messianic and prophetic activity in Jerusalem (chaps. 11–13) does not contain healings or exorcisms, but it does contain a kind of nature miracle (the cursing and withering of the fig tree) and a narrative involving clairvoyance (or prophecy and its fulfillment).[70] Like the predictions of the passion, the parable about the murder of the son of the owner of the vineyard may be seen as accurate foreknowledge from the point of view of the ending of the Gospel (12:1-11). From the point of view of readers after 70 C.E., the prophecy of the destruction of the temple in chapter 13 would also appear to be accurate foreknowledge.[71]

In the passion narrative, healings and exorcisms do not occur, but further narratives involving clairvoyance or accurate prophecy appear. According to Mark 14:9, "wherever the gospel is preached in the whole

66. So also Mack, *Myth of Innocence*, 208.
67. Mark 9:14-29 and 10:46-52; the middle section contains three miracle stories, if the healing of the blind man in Bethsaida is taken as the introduction to this section (8:22-26).
68. Mark 9:38-41; the issue is whether those who are not disciples of Jesus may use his name as a formula for exorcism.
69. The passion predictions are Mark 8:31; 9:31; and 10:32-34.
70. Jesus sends the disciples into a village and tells them what they will find and what they are to do (Mark 11:1-7); the story about the fig tree occurs in 11:12-14, 20-21.
71. On the relation of chap. 13 to social reality and history from the point of view of the author of Mark, see chap. 3, "Mark 13: An Apocalyptic Discourse."

world," what the woman who anointed Jesus had done would be told in memory of her. This remark of Jesus would be seen as prophecy fulfilled by the audience of Mark in various cities throughout the Roman Empire. As Jesus sent the disciples to fetch a donkey in the previous section, here Jesus sends them to prepare the Passover with clairvoyant instructions (14:12-16). He predicts the betrayal of Judas (14:18-21), the flight of all the (male) disciples, and the denial of Peter (14:27-31). The death of Jesus is accompanied by omens or prodigies that indicate its historic and cosmic significance.[72] The appearance of the "young man" (i.e., an angel) to the women at the tomb is another event beyond the usual order of things. This angel announces the resurrection of Jesus, which is an event of the same order as the miracles or even more extraordinary (16:1-8).

As previously noted, John Hull suggested that the miracle stories in Mark be seen in the context of the general worldview of ancient magic and folk medicine. Similarly, John Drury interprets the Gospel of Mark as a folktale in terms of its literary form and function.[73] Neil Forsyth interprets Mark in the context of the various forms and functions of the combat myth in antiquity.[74] Each of these authors has pointed out valuable analogies between Mark and other forms of literature and related religious and social contexts. These analogies are helpful in understanding the form and function of Mark. In terms of the history of religions and culture, however, the most important context for interpreting Mark is Jewish and early Christian apocalypticism.[75] In recent decades, scholars have tended to focus more on the Christology of Mark than on its apocalyptic framework and context.

Since the mid-1960s, especially in the United States, scholars have tended to read the Gospel of Mark as a critique or correction of the theology implicit in the miracle stories by subordinating them to the passion. In other words, Mark was written to discredit a "divine man" Christology.[76] That virtual consensus has not stood the test of time.

72. These omens or prodigies are the darkness from the sixth to the ninth hour (15:33) and the tearing of the curtain in the temple (15:38).

73. John Drury, "Mark," The Literary Guide to the Bible (ed. Robert Alter and Frank Kermode; Cambridge: Belknap Press of Harvard Univ. Press, 1987) 402–17.

74. Neil Forsyth, The Old Enemy: Satan and the Combat Myth (Princeton: Princeton Univ. Press, 1987) 285–97.

75. The importance of this context has been recognized, e.g., by Kee (Miracle in the Early Christian World, 146–73) and Mack (Myth of Innocence, 325–31).

76. See the history of this scholarship by Dowd, Prayer, Power, and the Problem of Suffering, 6–18.

Recent work has acknowledged the positive role the miracle stories and related material play in Mark as a whole.[77] A crucial argument in this interpretive shift is that the miracles are presented not only as activities of Jesus but as activities that the followers of Jesus can do as well. Not only are the twelve sent out to preach, heal, and exorcise, but the Gospel implies that any one who has faith may exorcise through prayer (9:23, 29). As Jesus was able to wither the fig tree by his words, the disciples (and the readers) will be able to move mountains by their faith and to obtain whatever they request in prayer. Besides having faith, the only condition is that they forgive any one who has wronged them (11:20-26). Similarly, the resurrection of Jesus is not a special privilege given to him as one like, or greater than, Elijah. On the contrary, faithful disciples will share in the resurrected life (8:34-38; cf. 9:42-48).[78]

The close association of believers with Jesus is related to typological thinking in antiquity and to the mythic mentality in general. The particular way this association is expressed in Mark, in terms of eschatological miracles and the hope for eternal life, must be seen in the context of apocalyptic tradition.

THE THEME OF SUFFERING
IN MARK

It is clear then that miraculous power and immortality constitute a major theme in the Gospel of Mark. As is well known, however, language about suffering and death constitutes an equally important theme.

The Suffering of Jesus in Mark

In the first chapter of Mark, Jesus is presented as the one announced by John the Baptist. He is authorized by a voice from heaven, by withstanding the testing of Satan, by healings and exorcisms, and by an unclean spirit whose superhuman knowledge recognizes him as the Holy One of God. His mission is presented as the proclamation of the

77. Ibid., 18–24.
78. Some of the Markan sayings of Jesus imply that not all followers of Jesus will die before the end (9:1; 13:27).

61

eschatological rule of God. In chapter 2, Jesus' activities evoke opposition; and in chapter 3, a conspiracy of the Pharisees and Herodians is formed in order to destroy him (v 6). The first narration of active opposition occurs later in chapter 3. Jesus' own family try to restrain him, because they think he is out of his mind (3:21, 31-32). Scribes from Jerusalem accuse him of being possessed by Beelzebul, the head demon. They imply that his power to exorcise is due to black magic or to a pact with the chief demon (3:22). The account of the death of John the Baptist has an ominous tone (6:14-29).

John's death is attributed to the animosity of Herodias, Herod's wife, because John had condemned their marriage as unlawful. When Herod hears of Jesus' works, he exclaims, "This man is John, whom I beheaded, raised from the dead!" (6:16). The identification of Jesus with John suggests that Jesus will meet a similar fate at the hands of the authorities. But the mention of resurrection implies, ironically, that Jesus, not John, will be raised from the dead.

In the second narrative of active opposition to Jesus, Pharisees and again scribes from Jerusalem take the initiative. They accuse Jesus and his disciples of failing to observe the tradition of the elders regarding purity and defilement (7:1-5). The next incident of this type involves the Pharisees' request for a sign from heaven (8:11-13). This request is presented as a test. The healings and exorcisms of Jesus have evoked the response among the people that he is a prophet (6:15; cf. 8:28). These mighty deeds (*dynameis*) are not enough for the Pharisees. Such could be accomplished by a common magician or deceiver. Therefore they demand a sign (*sēmeion*) from heaven to demonstrate that Jesus is a true prophet.[79] Thus even in the first major section of Mark (1:1—8:21), in which the mighty deeds predominate, there is considerable opposition and even some foreshadowing of the passion.

In the middle section of Mark (8:22—10:52), the theme of suffering and death comes to the fore. The major turning point of the plot comes in 8:27—9:1.[80] Jesus asks the disciples who they think he is. Peter

79. See *The Lives of the Prophets*, a Jewish or Jewish Christian work that speaks of the signs associated with the prophets of Israel; the text with an English translation was published by C. C. Torrey (*The Lives of the Prophets: Greek Text and Translation* [Philadelphia: SBL, 1946]); see also the introduction and translation by D. R. A. Hare in *OTP*, 2.379–99.

80. Some argue that this passage is a "recognition scene," like those that Aristotle discerned in Greek tragedies, e.g., Gilbert G. Bilezikian, *The Liberated Gospel: A Comparison of the Gospel of Mark and Greek Tragedy* (Grand Rapids, Mich.: Baker, 1977) 100–1.

declares that he is the Messiah. Rather than affirming this acclamation, Jesus instructs them to speak to no one about him. Then, using the self-designation "Son of Man," instead of Messiah, he begins to teach them that "it is necessary that the Son of Man suffer many things, and be rejected by the elders and the chief priests and the scribes, and be put to death, and after three days rise" (8:31).

It is clear that this passage does not intend to deny that Jesus is the Messiah. The evidence for this inference is that Jesus does not deny that he is and does not reject the designation as such. Further, the opening of Mark, which was its original title, designates Jesus as the Messiah (1:1).[81] Thus the audience has known from the beginning that Jesus is the Messiah. The first major section of Mark emphasizes the qualities and activities of Jesus that authorize him as the Messiah. The turning point in the action consists in several shifts: from an emphasis on mighty deeds to an emphasis on teaching; the introduction of specific announcements of and teaching about the suffering of Jesus, which was only hinted at in the first section; and from a focus on the opposition of outsiders to the misunderstanding of insiders, the disciples. The passage involving Peter's confession and Jesus' response then functions to clarify what "messiah" means. The anointed king is Son of God and doer of mighty deeds. But he is also one who must suffer and die. The paradox introduced in this passage is expressed in concrete narrative form in the passion account in which Jesus is mocked and crucified as the Messiah, the King of Israel (15:32).[82]

The passion predictions are mysterious sayings, in spite of the narrator's remark that Jesus was speaking openly.[83] No wonder the disciples did not understand them! One of the difficulties involves the use of the phrase "Son of Man." Is this use of the phrase indebted to an Aramaic idiom meaning "a man," or "someone"? Could that idiom function as a circumlocution for "I," an indirect way for the speaker

81. The Gospel opens with the words *Archē tou euangeliou Iēsou Christou*; the last two words may be translated either "Jesus Christ" or "Jesus Messiah."

82. On the passion in Mark, see Donald Senior, *The Passion of Jesus in the Gospel of Mark* (Wilmington, Del.: Michael Glazier, 1984); John R. Donahue, "Temple, Trial, and Royal Christology (Mark 14:53-65)," *The Passion in Mark* (ed. Werner Kelber; Philadelphia: Fortress, 1976) 61–79; Donald Juel, *Messiah and Temple: The Trial of Jesus in the Gospel of Mark* (Missoula, Mont.: Scholars Press, 1977).

83. The passion predictions occur in Mark 8:31; 9:31; and 10:32-34; the remark that Jesus spoke openly (i.e., not in parables or riddles, cf. 3:23; 4:2, 33-34) occurs in 8:32; the misunderstanding of the disciples is explicitly mentioned in 9:32.

to refer to himself?[84] Is it used here to allude to the heavenly figure of Daniel 7 who is described as "like a son of man" in appearance? The most likely explanation is that, by the time Mark (the evangelist, whoever he was) was writing, "Son of Man" had become a common designation of the risen Jesus in at least some Christian circles. Mark uses it to portray various phases of Jesus' life and work. He is the Son of Man with authority on earth (used of the earthly Jesus in 2:10 and 2:28). He is the Son of Man who must suffer, be put to death, and rise from the dead (8:31; 9:9, 12, 31; 10:33, 45; 14:21, 41). And he is the exalted Son of Man who will return in glory and judge humanity (8:38; 13:26; 14:62). The use of "Son of Man" as a name for Jesus in Mark thus serves to tie together his earthly activity and his exalted, heavenly status. Because of its connotations of ordinary humanity and its associations with the heavenly figure of Daniel 7, the epithet was well suited to the Markan project of reinterpreting the meaning and function of the Messiah.[85]

Another difficulty is the significance of the Greek word *dei*, an impersonal verb in the third person singular, translated "it is necessary." When Jesus says in the first passion prediction, "It is necessary that the Son of Man suffer many things" (8:31), does this remark simply mean that the opposition is so determined and powerful that Jesus' death at their hands is unavoidable? Theologically speaking, does the statement refer to the inevitable human propensity to sin, to rebellion against God, and thus to the rejection of God's eschatological agent? The answer to these questions, I think, is no. The most likely meaning is that it is God's will that Jesus suffer. Impersonal third person singular verbs, passive verbs, and sometimes indefinite third person plural verbs were often used in Jewish and Christian literature of the period to refer to the activity of God. Support for this interpretation may be found in Mark 9:12, another saying of Jesus that links the necessity of the suffering of the Son of Man to Scripture: "How is it written about the Son of Man that he suffer many things and be despised?" Scripture, read as prophecy, reveals the will of God, the divine plan for history.

---

84. This is the position of Geza Vermes; see Adela Yarbro Collins, "The Origin of the Designation of Jesus as 'Son of Man,' " *HTR* 80 (1987) 391–407.

85. The heavenly figure of Daniel 7 was interpreted messianically in a work called the *Similitudes of Enoch*. This work is preserved as chaps. 37–71 of a composite work referred to by scholars as *1 Enoch*. The *Similitudes* were probably composed in the first century C.E., or perhaps even at the end of the first century B.C.E.

The same point of view is expressed in 14:21: "For the Son of Man goes just as it is written concerning him, but woe to that man through whom the Son of Man is handed over!" The prophetic Scripture reveals that it is God's will that the Son of Man suffer. The phrase "through whom" he is handed over, rather than "by whom," may suggest that God is the ultimate agent of the action. Nevertheless, the existence of this divine plan does not release human beings from responsibility for their rebellious and murderous actions. This line of interpretation is confirmed by Jesus' prayer in Gethsemane. He asks God to "remove this cup" from him; yet he prays that God's will be done, not his own. From the point of view of the following narrative, this prayer implies that it is God's will that Jesus die.

The allusions to Scripture in 9:12 and 14:21 are puzzling. To what scriptural passages is allusion made? It is not likely that the author has Daniel 7 alone, or even primarily, in mind. The one like a son of man in that passage is a heavenly being. This being does not suffer but appears in glory after the judgment of the four beasts to receive rule and dominion. The people associated with this figure suffer, but it is hardly "written" in this passage that the one like a son of man must suffer.[86] According to 9:12, it is written that the Son of Man will be "despised" or "set at nought" (*exoudenēthē*). A similar expression occurs in the Old Greek translation of Psalm 64, a prayer for deliverance from personal enemies. The relevant part of the Greek psalm may be translated, "and their tongues have despised him" or "and their tongues have set him at nought" (LXX Ps 63:8).[87] A related expression occurs in the Greek translation of Psalm 22, a lament. The psalmist says, "But I am a worm, and no man; scorned by men, and despised by the people" (RSV).[88] Psalm 89 is a king's prayer for deliverance from his enemies.

86. C. F. D. Moule has tried to make a case for the dependence of the suffering Son of man sayings on Daniel 7 (*The Origin of Christology* [Cambridge: Cambridge Univ. Press, 1977] 13–17).

87. See Lancelot C. L. Brenton, *The Septuagint with Apocrypha: Greek and English* (London: Samuel Bagster & Sons, 1851; repr., Peabody, Mass.: Hendrickson, 1986) 734. Some manuscripts of Mark 9:12 have the verb *exoudenēthē* ("despised" or "set at nought") and that is the reading placed in the text in the Nestle-Aland (26th ed.) Greek New Testament; other manuscripts have *exoudenōthe*, one has *exouthenōthē*; a few have *exouthenēthē* (all these variants have basically the same meaning). Most of the manuscripts of the Old Greek of Ps 63:8 read *exouthenēsan* ("set at nought").

88. The Greek translation of the last phrase reads *kai exouthenēma laou* ("and an object of contempt of the people") (LXX Ps 21:6).

The Greek translation of verse 38 may be rendered, "But you have cast off and set at nought, you have rejected your anointed."[89] The reference to the Son of Man being "handed over" (*paradidotai*) in Mark 14:21 may be related to Psalm 88, another lament. The Greek version of a line in this psalm may be translated, "I have been handed over and have not gone forth" (LXX Ps 87:8).[90] Or the allusion may be to Isa 53:6 in the Greek version, "All we as sheep have gone astray; every one has gone astray in his way; and the Lord handed him over for our sins."[91] The verb "hand over" appears also in Isa 53:12 (twice). The Greek version may be translated, "Therefore he shall inherit many, and he shall divide the spoils of the mighty; because his life [or soul] was handed over [*paredothē*] to death, and he was numbered among the transgressors; and he bore the sins of many, and was handed over [*paredothē*] because of their iniquities."

It is well known that the Gospel of Mark alludes to the Psalms in the passion narrative.[92] Mark, and probably other Christians before him, interpreted the psalms of lament as prophecies of the passion of Jesus. Although the textual connections are less obvious, it seems that the fourth servant poem of Isaiah (52:13—53:12) was also interpreted as such a prophecy.

Suffering of the Followers of Jesus in Mark

Just as it is assumed that the followers of Jesus share in his power, so also will they share in his suffering. The first intimation of this fact occurs in the first major section of the Gospel, in the discourse of Jesus in parables. In the interpretation of the parable of the Sower, Jesus predicts that some who receive the word about the rule of God will be persecuted on account of the word (4:17).

In the middle section of the Gospel, each prediction of the passion of Jesus is followed by teaching on discipleship.[93] The first such teaching is a short discourse made up of a series of related sayings (8:34—

89. The Greek reads *Sy de aōpsō kai exoudenōsas.*
90. The relevant part of the Greek reads *paredothēn kai ouk exeporeuomēn.*
91. The Greek reads *kai Kyrios paredōken auton tais hamartiais hēmōn.*
92. Compare Mark 15:23 with Ps 69:21; 15:24 with Ps 22:18; 15:29 with Pss 22:7 and 109:25; 15:31 with Ps 22:8; 15:34 with Ps 22:1; and 15:36 with Ps 69:21.
93. In recent scholarship, Norman Perrin's literary analysis of this section of Mark's Gospel has been very influential; see, e.g., Perrin, *What Is Redaction Criticism?* (Philadelphia: Fortress, 1969) 40–57.

9:1). The first saying reads, "If any one wishes to follow after me, let such a one deny oneself and take up one's cross and follow me." This saying presents Jesus as a teacher who instructs by example as well as with words.[94] The second part of the instruction of this saying, "take up one's cross and follow me," picks up the theme of persecution begun in the interpretation of the parable of the Sower. The cross is a clear allusion to Jesus' death. This call to take up the cross suggests that at least some disciples will meet a violent death as well. Under the image of baptism, such a death is predicted for James and John the sons of Zebedee (10:38-39). Violent death is not valued in itself. Jesus' death is not to be imitated for the sake of being like Jesus. Rather, such a death may be necessary because of loyalty to Jesus and to the Gospel (8:35) in the face of opposition. The text alludes to a situation of persecution, actual or anticipated, in which some disciples will be interrogated and tempted to deny their faith (cf. 8:38). This allusion is made explicit in the apocalyptic discourse of chapter 13. In the context of proclaiming the Gospel to all nations, some Christians will be "handed over" to councils as Jesus was, some will be beaten in synagogues, and some will be interrogated before governors and kings (13:9).

But discipleship is not only a matter of enduring the suffering due to persecution. Returning to the first explicit teaching on discipleship, we note that the first part of the opening saying speaks about "denying oneself" (8:34). This part of the saying also recalls the interpretation of the parable of the Sower. The notion of "denying oneself" calls to mind the dangers of wealth and of desires for various things mentioned in that context (4:19). The general statement "let such a one deny oneself" is also given concrete application in the charge that the disciples should take nothing with them when they go forth to preach, heal, and exorcise (6:8-9). This theme of self-denial with regard to material goods is taken up and developed in chapter 10. The rich man is called to sell his property, give the proceeds to the poor, and join Jesus in his itinerant life of preaching and healing (10:17-23). The disciples who have left everything and followed Jesus are promised

94. On this style of teaching as typical of antiquity, see Vernon Robbins, *Jesus the Teacher: A Socio-Rhetorical Interpretation of Mark* (Philadelphia: Fortress, 1984; 1992, paperback ed. with new intro.).

compensation in this life and eternal life in the age to come (10:23-31). In these two cases, the call is not only to give up material goods but to leave one's family and to give up the ordinary ways of life as well. The story about the generosity of the poor widow (12:41-44) may suggest that almsgiving is an alternative form of self-denial for those not called to the itinerant life of voluntary poverty.

Another form of self-denial is taught in chapters 9 and 10. The followers of Jesus are also instructed to deny their desire to be first and to have authority over others. Rather, they are to be last of all and servant of all (9:33-37). The same point is made in the story about the request of the sons of Zebedee. Once again, Jesus' life is given as paradigm (10:35-45).

Self-denial is also presented as an ethical issue in traditional but intensified terms. A short discourse, made up largely of hyperbolic sayings, suggests that the disciples are not only to deny themselves the pleasures of sin but also to keep themselves strictly from occasions of sin (9:42-50). They are to deny themselves the legal privilege of divorce (10:1-12).

Discipleship is thus not entirely defined by suffering. The most comprehensive statement of discipleship in Mark is "do[ing] the will of God" (3:35). The will of God does not always involve suffering but may under certain circumstances. What are those circumstances? Let us begin with the case of Jesus.

Suffering and the Will of God in the Case of Jesus

The most explicit statement in the Gospel of Mark about the meaning of the death of Jesus is found in 10:45, at the end of the teaching on discipleship given in response to the request of the sons of Zebedee: "For the Son of Man did not come to be served, but to serve, and to give his life as a ransom for many." This is the clearest such statement in Mark, but that does not imply that it is actually clear! This saying is even more of a mystery than the predictions of the passion of the Son of Man. The first difficulty is the source of the imagery. The notion of service here continues the theme introduced in the teaching on who is the greatest (9:33-37). It may be that the background of this theme is the image of the servant of the Lord in Isaiah. But the term *ransom* does not occur there. The notion of "ransom" is introduced in Mark for the first time in 10:45. Determining its source is difficult.

The particular Greek word used, meaning "ransom, price of release" (*lytron*), appears only here and in the parallel passage in Matthew in all of the New Testament. The Greek version of the Old Testament used this noun in a variety of contexts. It occurs in descriptions of various transactions between humans: the price of freedom for a slave (Lev 25:51-52), the money paid to redeem prisoners of war (Isa 45:13), compensation for damages (Exod 21:28-32; Num 35:31-32; Prov 6:35), and buying back ancestral land (Lev 25:24-28). The word is also used in contexts of human actions directed toward God: buying back what belongs to God (Lev 27:30-33; Num 3:11-13; cf. Exod 13:1-2) and propitiating God (Exod 30:11-16).

The related verb has a rich history of metaphorical usage in the Greek version of the Old Testament. In Exod 6:6 God promises to redeem the people of Israel from the sovereignty (*dynasteia*) of the Egyptians and from slavery (*douleia*) to them. In Hos 13:14 God's power to restore the kingdom of Israel is spoken of metaphorically as the power to rescue them from the rule of Hades, to ransom them from Death. In Psalm 130 (LXX 129), God's forgiveness of sins is spoken of metaphorically as redemption or ransom, as redeeming Israel from his iniquities (vv 7-8).[95] Another usage is the notion of God redeeming (i.e., delivering) the people from their enemies (e.g., Ps 107 [LXX 106]:2).[96] Finally, in Isaiah "the redeemed" are those who are enabled to return to Zion from the exile in Babylon because God has ransomed them (Isa 35:9-10; 41:14; 43:1, 14).

Given this rich background, how should we understand the notion of Jesus' death as a ransom for many? Is it an act of compensation to God or propitiation of God on Jesus' part in behalf of others? If this

95. The verb *lytroō* is used in a similar metaphorical sense in Titus 2:14 and 1 Pet 1:18-19 of the death of Christ. Two related nouns are used in an analogous way in Heb 9:12 and 15.

96. This is the sense of the related words in Luke-Acts. "Redemption" or "deliverance" (*lytrōsis*) occurs in Luke 1:68; 2:38; "redeem" or "deliver" (*lytroō*) in Luke 24:21; and "redeemer" or "deliverer" (*lytrōtēs*) in Acts 7:35, of Moses. On this theme in Luke-Acts, see Robert Tannehill, *The Narrative Unity of Luke-Acts: A Literary Interpretation*, vol. 1, *The Gospel according to Luke* (Philadelphia: Fortress, 1986) 34–35.

is the intended meaning, then Jesus is presented as a martyr, as Eleazar is presented in 4 Maccabees:

> When he was now burned to his very bones and about to expire, he lifted up his eyes to God and said, "You know, O God, that though I might have saved myself, I am dying in burning torments for the sake of the law. Be merciful to your people, and let our punishment suffice for them. Make my blood their purification, and take my life in exchange for theirs." (4 Macc 6:26-29)[97]

Or should Jesus' death be seen as God's redeeming act, accomplished with Jesus' obedient cooperation? In this case, the model may be the suffering servant of Isaiah, whom *God* makes a tresspass offering.[98] The latter interpretation is more likely, given the divine necessity expressed in Mark 8:31 and the reference to the will of God in Jesus' prayer in Gethsemane (14:36).

Although Jesus is the agent of God and shares in the power of God, his suffering was intended by the will of God, according to Mark. His suffering and death was the chosen means of "ransoming many." This brings us to another mystery. From whom or what was Jesus' death intended to "ransom" many? Perhaps the author of Mark did not reflect on this question. Or perhaps he considered it a mystery beyond human understanding. But there are certain hints in the text of an answer. Note that John the Baptist introduces Jesus as "one who is stronger than I" (1:7). The theme of strength emerges again in the controversy over Jesus' exorcisms. In his reply to his detractors, Jesus uses a parabolic saying: "No one is able to enter the house of a strong man and to plunder his property, unless one first bind the strong man; then one will plunder his property." This saying is the conclusion to a segment of discourse that begins with a rhetorical question, "How is Satan able to cast out Satan?" and a comment, "If a kingdom is divided against itself, how is that kingdom able to stand?" (3:23-24). It is clear from the context that Jesus is the stronger one who is able to bind the "strong man," namely, Satan. Jesus as the agent of the kingdom of God is plundering the kingdom of Satan. Just as his exorcisms and healings free people from bondage to demons, so his death ransoms

---

97. Compare 1 Tim 2:6.
98. So the MT: *im tasim asham napsho* ("if/when you [God] make his soul/life a trespass offering").

many from the power of Satan. Jesus as "strong man" is the Divine Warrior incarnate. The life and death of Jesus is the eschatological combat with Satan. It is the combat myth in historic and apocalyptic mode. Perhaps the greatest irony of the Gospel of Mark is that the Divine Warrior wins his victory by dying—his defeat *is* his victory.[99]

Suffering and the Will of God in the Case of the Disciples

As already indicated, the Gospel of Mark assumes that some of the followers of Jesus will suffer persecution and die a violent death, as Jesus himself did. This actual or anticipated suffering of the disciples is placed in the same framework of meaning as the suffering of Jesus. As we have seen, Mark presents Jesus' life and death as a struggle with Satan. After Jesus' death and resurrection, that struggle is to continue and the followers of Jesus are to be God's agents in the world. As Jesus proclaimed the gospel of God (1:14), the disciples are to proclaim the gospel to all nations (13:10). The suffering that followers of Jesus are called to endure is "on account of the word" (4:17), that is, the gospel (8:35). In other words, the disciples have their part to play in preparing for "the rule of God come in power" (9:1). The images used for the suffering of the disciples, "taking up one's cross" (8:34) and "baptism" (10:38), suggest that God will redeem them through their suffering. As Jesus was vindicated, so will they be also.

CONCLUSION

Although there is much in her study that I admire, I do not agree with Sharyn Dowd that the Gospel of Mark offers "*no* solution to the problem of theodicy."[100] It is true that Mark does not offer an explicit, philosophical solution to the problem. But the Gospel does offer a solution

99. Ernest Best has argued that the death of Jesus in Mark is not primarily the result of diabolic antagonism (*The Temptation and the Passion: The Markan Soteriology* [2d ed.; Cambridge: Cambridge Univ. Press, 1990] 22, 42–44). But his own interpretation of the death as substitutionary atonement for moral evil does not make sense of the opening chapters of Mark (ibid., lvi–lxviii, 22–23). His interpretation makes the impression that Mark is incoherent. Why would Mark introduce Satan so prominently at the beginning and portray so much of Jesus' ministry as a struggle with the kingdom of Satan, if Satan and his kingdom had nothing to do with the death of Jesus and its benefits?

100. Dowd, *Prayer, Power, and the Problem of Suffering*, 160, 162.

implicit in the narrative that makes sense in an apocalyptic framework of meaning. Evil exists in the world because of the activity of malevolent spirits. These spirits have rebelled against the divine power and disrupt God's creation in many ways. Human disobedience is related to the rebellion of the spirits. But in the fullness of time, God has acted through Jesus to redeem humanity and all of creation from these forces of evil. The followers of Jesus participate in that redemption by their witness.

Thus Mark's solution to the problem of theodicy is a narrative one. All things are possible for God, but God allows evil to be part of the cosmic drama in which every creature has a role to play. The Gospel of Mark and the biblical tradition in which it stands impel us to go further and say that God not only allows what seems to us to be evil but even wills it in order to accomplish a larger purpose—the redemption of all creation. In a profound and mysterious way, the death of Jesus on the cross is at the heart of this redemption. The cross is God's answer to Job.

Chapter Three

MARK 13: AN
APOCALYPTIC
DISCOURSE

AS G. R. BEASLEY-MURRAY has so aptly pointed out, the history of scholarship on the eschatological discourse of Mark 13 is closely linked to the problem of the relationship of the historical Jesus to eschatology and apocalypticism.[1] Historically minded scholars of the nineteenth and early twentieth centuries generally emphasized two points in this regard. First, they forced other scholars and the general public to accept the idea that eschatology was central to the teaching and activity of the Synoptic Jesus. Second, they showed that this eschatology was quite different from that of the later Christian churches. Most disturbingly, they argued that Jesus was wrong in his expectation of an imminent end. The result has been a long series of attempts by exegetes and others to "save" Jesus from eschatology. For example, it has been argued that the imminent expectation of the Synoptics is due not to the teaching of Jesus himself but to that of his disciples. They took these ideas not from Jesus but from their Jewish heritage, stimulated by experiences like visions of the risen Lord or the Jewish war with Rome in 66–72 C.E.

In part because of the biting criticism of D. F. Strauss and his successors and in part because they associate imminent expectation with fanaticism, many exegetes have a strong distaste for eschatology. Some of these wish to save not only Jesus but even the author of the Gospel

---

1. G. R. Beasley-Murray, *Jesus and the Future: An Examination of the Criticism of the Eschatological Discourse, Mark 13, with Special Reference to the Little Apocalypse Theory* (London: Macmillan, 1954).

of Mark from eschatology.[2] This desire becomes evident in various ways. Some studies of Mark simply ignore chapter 13. Some exegetes even argue that the eschatological discourse is actually anti-eschatological! It has also been suggested that the discourse was added to Mark as an afterthought.[3]

It is in this context that the "Little Apocalypse Theory" must be placed. This scholarly theory, first proposed in the nineteenth century, argues that the heart of the discourse of Mark 13 was neither spoken by Jesus nor composed by Mark on the basis of early Christian tradition, but was copied from a written, coherent, apocalyptic source. In its strongest form, this theory postulated that the source was Jewish, thus emphasizing the perceived difference between its perspective and that of Jesus and Mark.[4] If the discourse appears to be a foreign body in the Gospel in the eyes of those who are biased against eschatology, if it is allegedly different from the real concerns of Jesus and the evangelist, then the theory that the narrative parts of the chapter were taken from a coherent apocalyptic source is quite attractive. I would like to address the subject of the "Little Apocalypse Theory" in the course of a survey of the exegetical problems of chapter 13. There is little evidence to support it, as we shall see.

EXEGETICAL SURVEY

Mark 13 opens with a brief anecdote (vv 1-2). The setting is given in a genitive absolute, *ekporeuomenou autou ek tou hierou* ("as he was going out of the temple," v 1). This indication of the setting links this anecdote and what follows it to the previous two chapters in which Jesus' activity is centered on the temple. Only two characters are involved, Jesus and a nameless disciple. The disciple's remark, "Teacher, look what great stones and what great buildings" (v 1), seems artificial.

2. See the criticism of such attempts by Egon Brandenburger, *Markus 13 und die Apokalyptik* (Göttingen: Vandenhoeck & Ruprecht, 1984) 9–11.

3. R. Pesch, *Naherwartungen: Tradition und Redaktion in Mark 13* (Düsseldorf: Patmos, 1968). Pesch took a different position in his later commentary (*Das Markusevangelium: II. Teil, Kommentar zu Kap. 8.27—16.20* (Freiburg: Herder & Herder, 1977).

4. The first to propose the "Little Apocalypse Theory" was Colani, who argued that it was Jewish Christian. The theory became widely influential in the form advocated by Weizsäcker, its second proponent, who concluded that it was Jewish (see Beasley-Murray, *Jesus and the Future*, 33–34).

The comment would fit better, if at all, in chapter 11 when Jesus and his disciples first arrive in Jerusalem and go to the temple for the first time. It seems to function simply to provide an occasion for Jesus' remark, "Do you see these great buildings? Not one stone will be left here upon another; all will surely be thrown down" (v 2). The references to "disciple" and "teacher" suggest that the unit is a scholastic dialogue, but the saying of Jesus is prophetic. So perhaps we should speak of a prophetic saying in a scholastic context. There are clear signs of Markan redaction in this opening dialogue, as a number of exegetes have pointed out.[5] But there is also compelling evidence that the saying of Jesus in v 2 is based on pre-Markan tradition.[6]

The most difficult question regarding Mark 13:1-2 is whether this anecdote, as formulated by Mark, presupposes the destruction of the temple that occurred in 70 C.E. The tendency of modern historical-critical scholarship has been to take allegedly prophetic texts that correspond precisely to historical events as *ex eventu* prophecy. A problem with this approach is that it rules out a priori the possibility of genuine prophecy. From the point of view of the history of religions, this procedure is dubious. Surely one of the reasons for the enduring fame and influence of people like Amos and Jeremiah, and perhaps Jesus, is that subsequent events supported their prophetic insight. They probably did make at least one unpopular but accurate prediction, respectively, whether one takes these predictions as based on divine revelation or human wisdom.

In any case, one must ask whether the prophecy placed on the lips of Jesus in v 2 corresponds so precisely to historical events that one must conclude that Mark was written after 70. For some, that Mark was written after 70 is a postulate, a heuristic starting point for interpreting the Gospel. Others point to the account in Josephus that describes Titus's activities in Jerusalem. It is said that he razed the temple and most of the wall surrounding Jerusalem (*J. W.* 7.1–4). The

5. For example, Lars Hartman, *Prophecy Interpreted: The Formation of Some Jewish Apocalyptic Texts and of the Eschatological Discourse Mark 13 Par.* (Lund: Gleerup, 1966) 219; see also the literature cited, ibid., n. 3; J. Lambrecht, *Die Redaktion der Markus-Apokalypse: Literarische Analyse und Strukturuntersuchung* (Analecta Biblica 28; Rome: Pontifical Biblical Institute, 1967) 89–90.

6. Hartman, *Prophecy Interpreted*, 220; Lambrecht, *Redaktion*, 90–91; John R. Donahue, *Are You the Christ? The Trial Narrative in the Gospel of Mark* (Missoula, Mont.: Scholars Press, 1973) 104–8.

correspondence between Mark's "no stone upon another" and Josephus's account is taken as sufficient proof that Mark wrote after 70. In fact, the correspondence is not so close. Mark's phrase may be seen as a dramatic, even hyperbolic, prediction of destruction that need not be taken as an allusion to a historical event.

The connection between vv 1-2 and v 3 is loose. There is no explicit mention of an interval of time between the first scene and the second, but the two are distinguished by a change of place and of characters. The setting of the second scene is once again given in a genitive absolute, *kathēmenou autou eis to oros tōn elaiōn* ("while he was sitting on the Mount of Olives," v 3). Besides Jesus, the characters include Peter, James, John, and Andrew (v 3). The contrast between the nameless disciple of vv 1-2 and the four named disciples of v 3 indicates that the prophetic saying of v 2 was given in the presence of a wider audience than the teaching that follows v 3. This point is made explicit by the remark that the question of the four was put to Jesus *kat' idian* ("privately," v 3). Verses 1-2 and the unit that begins with v 3 are linked by the qualification of the second scene as taking place *katenanti tou hierou* ("opposite the temple," v 3).

The relation of the anecdote in vv 1-2 and the longer scene in vv 3-37 is analogous to that between the public communication of the parable of the sower in 4:1-9 and the private interpretation of the parable and related teaching for "those who were around him along with the twelve" in 4:10-20. It is also analogous to the public teaching regarding purity in 7:1-16 and the private interpretation of that teaching for the disciples in 7:17-23. The distinction between the public exorcism in 9:14-27 and the private comments about it to his disciples in 9:28-29 should also be noted. The same compositional pattern occurs in chapter 10 in the public teaching about divorce (vv 1-9) and the further instruction of the disciples on the topic in private (vv 10-12). This contrast between public and private teaching seems to be a favorite compositional device of Mark. The two parts of this pattern do not, however, appear to correspond to tradition and redaction in any clear-cut way.

Mark 13:3-37 is a much more coherent unit than 4:10-34, the only other extended, presumably private, discourse in Mark. In the present context of Mark, vv 3-37 constitute a unified dialogue between Jesus and the four disciples; more precisely, it is a discourse occasioned by a question raised by the four. Although it is relatively coherent, it is clearly a composite literary creation, based on various elements of tradition embodied in a variety of small literary forms.[7]

Mark seems to have composed the question of the disciples in v 4 in order to link the anecdote of vv 1-2 with the discourse of vv 5-37. The question has two parts. The first asks *when* these things will be; the second what the *sign* is that will indicate when all these things are about to be accomplished. The *tauta* ("these things") in the first part of the question refers back to the prophecy of v 2 and thus to the destruction of the temple. The second part of the question antic- ipates the discourse itself. It presupposes that the destruction of the temple is part of a sequence of eschatological events (*tauta . . . panta*, "all these things"). The verb *synteleisthai* ("to be accomplished") has eschatological connotations.

Some comment should be made about the genre of vv 3-37 as a whole. Egon Brandenburger argued that it is a little apocalypse in the form of a testamentary scholastic dialogue.[8] His language reflects the fact that he believes that the author of Mark used a written source in composing this discourse and that this source was an apocalypse in form.[9] The definition of the genre "apocalypse" is, of course, disputed. If we take as an essential element of the genre the presence of a heavenly being who mediates between the human recipient of reve- lation and God, then Mark 13:3-37 is not an apocalypse. Although the Jesus of Mark is the Son of God, he is not presented as a heavenly being before his resurrection. The account of the transfiguration com- plicates the issue, but the point holds if we take that account as a proleptic revelation of the glory of the resurrected Jesus. As Bran- denburger noted, in its present form as part of Mark, the unit found in vv 3-37 fits the genre "scholastic dialogue." Some formal elements and certainly much of the content are characteristic of apocalypses. So, like the anecdote in vv 1-2, this one is a scholastic dialogue with prophetic or apocalyptic content.

ARGUMENTS FOR A WRITTEN SOURCE

The actual discourse is then given in vv 5-37. As we have already noted, many exegetes believe that Mark used a written source in

7. See the list in Brandenburger, *Markus 13*, 13.
8. Ibid., 15.
9. Ibid., 41–45.

composing this speech. This belief is the basis of the "Little Apocalypse Theory." In its simple form, this theory is that Mark adapted a preexisting but nonauthentic apocalypse by inserting and appending parenetic material. A more complex form of the theory is that the narrative portions of the discourse represent a "little apocalypse," and the parenetic portions are an authentic speech of Jesus.

A major argument for a written source has been based on the parenthetical remark in v 14b, "let the reader understand" (*ho anaginōskōn noeitō*). The assumption is that this remark was not added by the evangelist but was already in the source. For example, Brandenburger thinks that Mark could not have added this remark because his interest was oriented otherwise.[10] This conclusion is based on the postulate that vv 14-20 describe events that were already past from the point of view of the evangelist. Support for this view is found in the remark placed on the lips of Jesus in v 23, "I have told you everything beforehand" (*proeirēka hymin panta*). The latter remark does not necessarily imply that all the events narrated so far have already taken place from the point of view of the author (perceived as the final editor). It is equally likely that the prophecy has been fulfilled in part and the author is confident of the fulfillment of the remainder. The remark in v 23 then would function as a claim for the validity of the as yet unfulfilled portion of the prophecy. We will return to this issue in discussing the meaning of vv 14-23 from the point of view of the evangelist.

Another important argument for a written source is the claim that the word *tauta* ("these things") has different referents in vv 29 and 30. This claim is related to the hypothesis that two discourses were combined in the composition of Mark 13: an authentic, parenetic speech, and a Jewish or Jewish Christian apocalypse. The different referents of "these things" in vv 29 and 30 allegedly show that the coherence of each discourse has been destroyed by their combination.[11] Verse 29 is taken to be part of the authentic parenetic discourse. Here "these things" refers to the temptations narrated in vv 5-6, 21-23, and 9b-13. Verse 30, with its imminent expectation ("this generation will not pass away until all these things have taken place") is

10. Ibid., 25.
11. See the discussion of Wendt by Beasley-Murray, *Jesus and the Future*, 44–49.

assigned to the written source, the little apocalypse. Here "these things" refers either to the description of the arrival of the Son of Man in vv 24-27 or to the whole account of vv 7-9a, 14-20, and 24-27. According to Beasley-Murray, this point has been the main argument for the existence of a Christian discourse prior to the composition of Mark 13.[12] He also pointed out that the argument is circular. The phrase "these things" in v 29 can be taken to refer to the temptations of vv 5-6, 21-23, and 9b-13 alone only if one has decided a priori that it cannot refer to the remarks that immediately precede it or to any of the remarks that are assigned to the alleged source.

The determination of the antecedent of *tauta* ("these things") in v 29 depends on the translation of *engys estin* in the same verse. If the latter clause is to be translated "he is near," then *tauta* refers to the events leading up to the appearance of the Son of Man (i.e., the account ranging from v 6 to v 23). If it is to be translated "it is near," and "it" represents the "end" (*to telos*, v 7), then *tauta* refers to the series of events from v 8 through v 27. It is more likely that *engys estin* means "he is near," because it would be odd to say that "the end" is at the gates (v 29). The image of the Son of Man at the gates, however, fits well with the parable about the master and the doorkeeper in vv 34-36.

So if *tauta* ("these things") in v 29 refers to the series of events from v 6 to v 23, then the phrase *tauta panta* ("all these things") in v 30 refers to the entire series from v 6 to v 27. There is a parallel between the *tauta* and *tauta . . . panta* of v 4 and the *tauta* and *tauta panta* of vv 29 and 30.[13] This parallel suggests that vv 29 and 30 belong together, since together they reprise the opening question of the disciples. It is clear that there is no contradiction between v 29 and v 30 that could support the hypothesis that a written source was used in the composition of Mark 13.

A further influential argument for the use of a source is an alleged contradiction between v 30 and v 32.[14] In v 30 Jesus claims to know that the end will come within the current generation. In v 32 he

12. Ibid.

13. Joachim Gnilka, *Das Evangelium nach Markus* (2 vols.; Zurich: Benziger, 1978–1979) 2.184.

14. Weizsäcker emphasized the "contradiction" of v 32 with its context (Beasley-Murray, *Jesus and the Future*, 36).

professes ignorance about the timing of the end. A related issue is the alleged contradiction between the picture of the end as preceded by signs, implied by the narrative portions of the discourse, and the view of the end coming suddenly, implied by vv 32-37. With regard to the tension between vv 30 and 32, Paul Schwartzkopff's comments are apt. There is no ground for viewing the two verses as inconsistent. Verse 32 does not imply an *absolute* ignorance on the part of Jesus as to the time of the end, only a *relative* one. Thus the confession of ignorance is consistent with the conviction that the end would come within a generation.[15]

In his last book, Johannes Weiss addressed the broader issue of the alleged contradiction between the two views of the end. He argued that the apparent contradiction is characteristic of much of the New Testament. It unites two fundamental attitudes of the primitive Christian life.[16] Beasley-Murray argued that in the teaching of the Synoptic Jesus, signs have a dual function: they unveil the divine kingdom and call for a moral response. It is in the moral or existential sphere that the two views can be reconciled. Since the end will come with unexpected suddenness, it will take the ungodly unawares, for they do not know the issue of their distress. The believers also do not know when the end will come, but the understanding of the nature of the times will encourage them to endure steadfastly.[17] Thus the alleged contradiction between v 30 and v 32 or between two perspectives discerned within the chapter does not compel the conclusion that one or two coherent pre-Markan sources were used in the composition of the eschatological discourse.

As briefly noted earlier, the alternation between eschatological or apocalyptic narrative units and parenetic units has often been assumed to imply the use of one or two coherent sources.[18] The conclusion that the two basic types of literary form in the discourse derive from two coherent speeches goes far beyond the evidence. Even the notion that the discourse can be divided neatly into narrative and parenesis is questionable. Most adherents of the "Little Apocalypse Theory" have concluded that v 7 belongs to the apocalyptic source. But this verse

15. Cited by Beasley-Murray, *Jesus and the Future*, 135–37.
16. Summarized by Beasley-Murray, ibid., 124.
17. Herein Beasley-Murray follows Schwartzkopff (ibid., 180).
18. For example, F. Hauck (cited by Beasley-Murray, ibid., 70).

has a parenetic as well as a narrative element. The audience is told that there will be "wars and rumors of wars," but is also exhorted not to be alarmed. Similarly, most who hold the theory include vv 14-20 in the little apocalypse. Here also prophecy and parenesis are combined. The setting up of the desolating sacrilege is announced, but those in Judea are also urged to flee to the mountains (v 14). Further instructions follow in vv 15-16, 18.

Thus the arguments in favor of the use of a written, coherent source in Mark 13 are not compelling. The question remains whether it is possible to interpret the speech as a composition of Mark in a way that relates it intelligibly to a plausible social setting for the Gospel. Let us look at the speech unit by unit.

MARK 13 IN SOCIAL CONTEXT

Verses 5b-8 form a unit in that they contain parenesis related to a series of events that are designated "the beginning of the birth pangs" (v 8).[19] Much of the material in these verses is widespread eschatological tradition, deriving ultimately from the Old Testament.[20] It is likely, nevertheless, that this material relates to the social setting of Mark. The introductory exhortation, "Beware that no one leads you astray" (v 5b), suggests that the possibility of members of the audience following false teaching or leadership is the major issue in this unit. The source of this false leadership is indicated in general terms in v 6, "Many will come in my name." Some have argued that "in my name" characterizes the "many" as Christians and that these false leaders claimed to be Jesus returned. In spite of its popularity, this hypothesis is implausible. There is little evidence apart from this passage and its parallels that any Christians made such a claim. Further, *epi tō onomati mou* should be translated "requisitioning or claiming my name [i.e., Jesus]" or "with my name," rather than "in my name."[21] This translation implies that the false leaders are not Christians. It is said further that these leaders will say *egō eimi*. Some have argued that this clause

19. Vaganay described this unit as "signs that are forerunners" and related it to the destruction of Jerusalem (cited by Lambrecht, *Redaktion*, 12). Lambrecht himself labeled the unit "Pseudochrists and wars" (ibid., 111).
20. Hartman, *Prophecy Interpreted*, 147–50, 176, 203–4.
21. Heitmüller, *Im Nahmen Jesu*, cited by Beasley-Murray, *Jesus and the Future*, 107–8.

should be translated "I Am" and that it refers to a claim to divinity.[22] Such a translation is possible grammatically, but again it is difficult to find relevant evidence outside Mark that would illuminate this remark in its context. It is more likely that *egō eimi* should be translated "I am he." Since we do not have external evidence of Jesus pretenders, the "name" in question is probably not "Jesus," but "Christ" or "Messiah." The most likely historical allusion here is to the Jewish messianic pretenders who came forward during the Jewish war with Rome, beginning with Menahem in 66 C.E. According to Josephus, he returned from Masada to Jerusalem in that year like a king.[23] From the point of view of Mark, these pretenders were competing with Jesus for the title and role of God's anointed.

Even if this exhortation is derived from older tradition, the context suggests that it was of real concern to Mark and his audience. If Mark was written after 70, there would have been little reason to warn the audience against these men. Political eschatology did not die out, since there were two more revolts in the first half of the second century. The last revolt was associated with another messianic pretender, Simon, called Bar Cochba ("Son of the Star") by some and Bar Cosiba ("Son of the Lie") by others. Since virtually no one argues that Mark was written during the time of Simon, and before him the issue was most pressing between 66 and 69, this unit then suggests a date during that period for Mark.

The "wars and rumors of wars" of v 7 and the rising up of nation against nation and kingdom against kingdom in v 8 also fit a situation early in the first Jewish war against Rome. The warning that "the end is still to come" (v 7) and the statement that "This is but the beginning of the birthpangs" either express the insight that the war will be long and hard rather than resolved immediately by divine intervention or indicate that the war has been in progress already for some time. If the war were already over, it would hardly have been necessary to point out that the end had not yet come. It would have been clear to all that the war did not issue immediately in the end time. The admonition that this is but the beginning suggests that some thought

22. Werner Kelber, *The Kingdom in Mark: A New Place and a New Time* (Philadelphia: Fortress, 1974) 115.
23. Josephus, *J. W.* 2.433–48; see the discussion in Richard A. Horsley and John S. Hanson, *Bandits, Prophets, and Messiahs: Popular Movements in the Time of Jesus* (Minneapolis: Winston, 1985) 118–27.

that divine intervention would occur immediately, at the onset of hostilities.

Verses 9-13 are differentiated as a unit by the repetition of the warning "Beware" (*blepete*) at the beginning of v 9 (cf. v 5b). The end of the unit is marked by the general hortatory statement "But the one who endures to the end will be saved" (v 13b; cf. v 8d).[24] Scholars have generally concluded that these verses reflect the experience of early Christians.[25] There is little in the passage, however, that indicates a specific social setting. The sorts of experiences described could have taken place in any city of the eastern Mediterranean from the time of the death of Jesus onward.[26]

After the summary statement of v 13b, v 14 begins a new unit: "But when you see the desolating sacrilege. . . ." Most of those who hold to the "Little Apocalypse Theory" define this unit as vv 14-20. Weizsäcker differentiated the unit in this way because he considered the sayings about false prophets in vv 6 and 21-23 to be authentic sayings of Jesus; thus he needed to separate them from the allegedly inauthentic apocalypse.[27] It seems more appropriate to define this unit as vv 14-23. The *tote* ("at that time") of v 21 does not refer to a new time and thus introduce a new unit. Rather, it raises a new issue with regard to the same time period described in vv 14-20.[28] Verse 23, like 13b, is a summary statement that concludes its unit.

This unit clearly alludes to the book of Daniel in several verses. The "desolating sacrilege" in v 14 is an allusion to one or more verses in Daniel: 9:27; 11:31; 12:11. Mark 13:14 is linguistically closer to Dan 11:31 and especially to 12:11 than to 9:27. But it is noteworthy that

24. Like many others, Vaganay considered vv 9-13 as a unit and designated it "preliminary signs" related to the destruction of Jerusalem (cited by Lambrecht, *Redaktion*, 12). Lambrecht himself labeled the unit "Persecutions" (ibid., 142–43).

25. For example, Hartman, *Prophecy Interpreted*, 219.

26. See the discussion in Gerd Theissen, *Lokalkolorit und Zeitgeschichte in den Evangelien: Ein Beitrag zur Geschichte der synoptischen Tradition* (Novum Testamentum et Orbis Antiquus 8; Freiburg, Schweiz: Universitätsverlag; Göttingen: Vandenhoeck & Ruprecht, 1989) 133–34.

27. Cited by Beasley-Murray, *Jesus and the Future*, 33–34; Pfleiderer's analysis was similar (ibid., 36–37); so also that of Weiffenbach (ibid., 39–41) and Wendt (ibid., 44–49). Holtzmann and Loisy no longer considered vv 14-20 as a unit, because they believed that vv 15-16 came from Q (ibid., 50–51).

28. Wellhausen apparently concluded that vv 14-22 came from the "little apocalypse" (cited by Beasley-Murray, *Jesus and the Future*, 55); so also F. Hauck (ibid., 70) and Bultmann (ibid., 70–72). Vincent Taylor took vv 14-23 as a unit (ibid., 106–7) as did Joachim Gnilka (*Markus*, 2.180).

the destruction of Jerusalem and the temple are mentioned in the context of Dan 9:27 (Mark 13:26). Such mention is not made in association with the other two passages.[29] The remark in Mark 13:19 about a tribulation such as has not been from the beginning of the creation until now is an allusion to Dan 12:1.[30]

Many of those who have argued for the use of a written source have maintained that the sacrilege implies desecration of the temple, not destruction. They dated the source prior to 70, since desecration implies the possibility of rededication and thus continuation of the temple.[31] Those who think that Mark was written after 70 argue that the earlier meaning of the sacrilege in the source was reinterpreted by Mark as a prophecy of destruction.[32] For example, in his early work, Otto Pfleiderer argued that vv 14-20 came from a Jewish Christian source written in the 60s prior to the destruction of Jerusalem and that the abomination of desolation in this source referred to the murderous acts of the Zealots in the temple mentioned by Josephus (*J.W.* 4.196; 6.93–110).[33] In his later work Pfleiderer argued that the source was Jewish and that the allusion to Daniel expressed the expectation that an idol would be set up in the temple. This expectation was awakened by the events under Caligula and kept alive by the Jewish revolt. Since nothing like this actually happened in 70, he dated the source to the 60s.[34]

B. H. Streeter, influenced by Wilhelm Bousset, argued that the "abomination of desolation" refers to a personal Antichrist who would rule Jerusalem until destroyed by Christ at the parousia.[35] A. E. J. Rawlinson and E. Lohmeyer took similar positions.[36]

A. Piganiol argued that the apocalyptic source reflected in vv 14-20 was written in 40 C.E. in response to the crisis under Caligula. This

29. Desmond Ford, *The Abomination of Desolation in Biblical Eschatology* (Washington, D.C.: Univ. Press of America, 1982) 151–54.
30. On the relation of Mark 13:14-20 to Daniel and other Old Testament passages, see Hartman, *Prophecy Interpreted*, 151–54.
31. For example, Weizsäcker (cited by Beasley-Murray, *Jesus and the Future*, 34) and Wellhausen (ibid., 53–54). See now Theissen, *Lokalkolorit*, 133–76.
32. For example, B. W. Bacon (cited by Beasley-Murray, *Jesus and the Future*, 88–92).
33. Ibid., 36–37.
34. Ibid., 38–39.
35. Ibid., 57–59.
36. Ibid., 67–68, 108–10.

position, with modifications, has been taken up by many exegetes from his time until the present.[37]

Maurice Goguel argued that the "abomination of desolation" in v 14 has nothing to do with the events of 40 C.E., for that crisis was temporary. In Mark it is simply a traditional apocalyptic idea with no definite referent. Mark's version was produced in a time when it was realized that the fall of Jerusalem was not the sign that preceded the parousia.[38]

Robert Eisler revived a patristic interpretation according to which the desolating sacrilege is Pilate's setting up the imperial standards in Jerusalem in 19 C.E. He argued that this event led Jesus to come forward, since he saw it as a sign of the end.[39] Desmond Ford argued that the author of Luke understood the sacrilege of Mark 13:14 to refer to the standards of the Roman army as it surrounded Jerusalem in 70.[40] Vincent Taylor suggested that the "abomination," like the name "Babylon" in 1 Peter and the book of Revelation, is a reference to Rome as the embodiment of satanic power, the Antichrist.[41]

In *Das älteste Evangelium*, Johannes Weiss argued that the "abomination of desolation" cannot refer to the past activity of the Romans, because this would go against the removal of the end until after the Gospel had been preached to all nations. Thus "Let the reader understand" cannot mean "Let the church realize that the old prophecy is in the process of fulfillment or has just been fulfilled." The verb *noein* ("to understand") here implies that the Danielic prophecy is intended in the words of Jesus, but the fulfillment is not envisaged. What Mark does is pass on a still unfulfilled prophecy of Jesus.[42]

The variety of opinions expressed indicates the difficulty of the problem. If we take the admonition to the reader in v 14 as an aside

37. For example, Hölscher (discussed by Beasley-Murray, "The Rise and Fall of the Little Apocalypse Theory," *ExpTim* 64 [1953] 346–49); B. W. Bacon (idem, *Jesus and the Future*, 88–92); C. H. Dodd (ibid., 98–101); C. C. Torrey (ibid., 153–56); H. H. Rowley (ibid., 157–59); L. Gaston, *No Stone on Another: Studies in the Significance of the Fall of Jerusalem in the Synoptic Gospels* (NovTSup 23; Leiden: Brill, 1970); Theissen, *Lokalkolorit*, 145–76.
38. Cited by Beasley-Murray, *Jesus and the Future*, 72–73.
39. Ibid., 92.
40. Ford, *The Abomination of Desolation*, 144.
41. Cited by Beasley-Murray, *Jesus and the Future*, 106–7.
42. Ibid., 120–22.

written by the evangelist, the implication is that the "desolating sacrilege" of Daniel is an element of high importance at the final stage of the composition of the Gospel. Its importance is also indicated by the fact that it is the primary answer to the disciples' question about a sign (v 4). The desolating sacrilege is a "sign" (*sēmeion*) in two senses. It is a signal for those in Judea to act and it is an instructional sign for all of the audience that the end is near.[43] According to vv 21-22, false messiahs and false prophets would appear during the tribulation associated with the desolating sacrilege. Like v 6, these verses suggest a context after the outbreak of the Jewish war.

Given the climactic role of the sacrilege, however, and its close temporal association with the appearance of the Son of Man (v 24a), it seems unlikely that the Gospel was written after the destruction of the temple and the city of Jerusalem. Cosmic upheaval and the arrival of the Son of Man are to take place *in those days*. From the point of view of the evangelist, it is most likely that the prophecy of v 14 is as yet unfulfilled. The call to flee and the realistic description of the hardships involved suggest that the sacrilege was to be followed immediately by a divine intervention. This intervention was to be a judgment on Jerusalem analogous to that upon Sodom and Gomorrah. The analogy is suggested by the command to flee to the mountains and not to turn back (cf. Mark 13:14c-16 with Gen 19:17).[44] Taken together, these factors suggest that Mark was written after the outbreak of the war, after the appearance of at least a few "false messiahs" and "false prophets," but before the destruction of the temple.

The next unit is universally defined as vv 24-27, the narrative account of the arrival of the Son of Man. In Daniel 7 the judgment of the four beasts (vv 9-12) is followed by the appearance of the one like a son of man (vv 13-14). Similarly in Mark 13 the divine judgment on Jerusalem implied by vv 14-23 is followed by the arrival of the Son of Man (vv 24-27). According to the latter passage, the activity of the

43. On the meaning of "sign" (*sēmeion*) in Mark 13, see Lambrecht, *Redaktion*, 295.

44. On the similarities between Mark 13:14-16 and Gen 19:17, see Hartman, *Prophecy Interpreted*, 151–54. He also discusses the eschatological use of the story of the destruction of Sodom and Gomorrah elsewhere in the New Testament.

Son of Man involves gathering the elect and establishing the eschatological community under his leadership.[45] The absence of any indication that the Son of Man functions as judge in this pericope has puzzled some, and others have suggested that it is implied. But if the judgment is already implied in vv 14-23, it is not necessary here.

The final unit of the chapter consists of the instruction and admonition of vv 28-37.[46] The parable of the Fig Tree (vv 28-29) takes up again the disciples' question about the sign (v 4). The newly emerging leaves of the fig tree relate to summer as "these things" relate to the appearance of the Son of Man. "These things" refer to all the events narrated in vv 6-23, especially to "the desolating sacrilege" of v 14. The sacrilege is the sign that indicates "when these things will be" (v 4a), that is, the destruction of the temple. It also signifies that "all these things are about to be accomplished" (4b), that the appearance of the Son of Man will occur soon thereafter.

Verse 30 is a saying that asserts that the end will come before the passing away of the current generation. Verse 31 is a confirmation formula that strengthens the force of the previous saying. Verse 32 is the saying affirming that only the Father knows the day and the hour of the end. As indicated earlier, there is no contradiction between this statement and v 30. The references to a "day" and an "hour," rather than to a month and a year, even if rhetorical, indicate imminent expectation.

The parable about the absent master and the doorkeeper follows in vv 33-36. Here we see the moral dimension discussed by Beasley-Murray. The notion of the sudden arrival of the end has the function of admonishing the audience to vigilance. This vigilance is not the sort that involves standing on a mountaintop waiting to be rescued by heavenly powers. The master leaves each of the slaves with his or her own work to do (v 34). The discourse implies that an important part of the work of at least some of the members of the audience is to preach the gospel (v 10) and to bear testimony before governors and kings (v 9). Others presumably have various tasks to which they must attend. The discourse thus provides a framework of meaning

45. See the discussion by Ernst Lohmeyer summarized by Beasley-Murray, *Jesus and the Future*, 108–10.
46. Lambrecht, *Redaktion*, 286.

within which the audience can understand their work and their suffering. Verse 37 then concludes the discourse with a general admonition to "Watch." Like v 14b ("Let the reader understand"), this last verse breaks out of the narrative context to address the audience as well as the four disciples questioning Jesus ("what I say to you [the four] I say to all").

JESUS AND MARK 13

Some exegetes deny all or part of the discourse to the historical Jesus because of the role played in it by the notion of a sign (*sēmeion*, v 4). They argue that Jesus refused to give signs and denied them a role in eschatology. In support of this conclusion they refer to Mark 8:11-13 and to Luke 17:20-21. Mark 8:11-13 does not warrant the conclusion. In that anecdote, Pharisees ask Jesus for a sign to test him and he refuses them: "Truly I tell you, no sign will be given to this generation" (8:12). The underlying argument seems to be that in this verse Mark transmits the teaching of the historical Jesus, whereas in chapter 13 he reproduces a Jewish or Jewish Christian source. As we have noted, some would argue that Mark reproduces the source only to refute it. In any case, there is no contradiction between 8:12 and chapter 13. In the anecdote about the Pharisees, a sign is refused to outsiders. The phrase "this generation" in 8:12 should not be taken absolutely but as a reference to negatively disposed or faithless outsiders (cf. 8:12 with 8:38 and 9:19). In chapter 13, a small group of insiders is informed about an eschatological sign. Just as Jesus' messianic identity is at first withheld from outsiders and revealed only to insiders, so also eschatological secrets are at first kept hidden and later revealed. Both types of secret are revealed by Jesus at the trial before the Sanhedrin (14:62).

In Luke 17:20-21, the Pharisees ask Jesus when the kingdom of God is coming. His response is "The kingdom of God is not coming with things that can be observed; nor will they say, 'Look, here it is!' or 'There it is!' For, in fact, the kingdom of God is among you." This anecdote, at least from the point of view of the author of Luke, does not reject the notion of public, cosmic, eschatological events, as some exegetes have argued. The attached speech of Jesus (17:22-37) makes abundantly clear that Luke expected the arrival of the Son of Man to be a public event. The point of the opening anecdote is that the kingdom of God is effective in and through Jesus. But his public activity was the beginning, not the end, of the fulfillment of the eschatological events. The rejection of observation or signs in v 20 is not absolute but relative to the search for signs of a coming reality that in fact was already present. In the following speech, the warning about those who say "Look there" or "Look here" is primarily an admonition against pretenders. Nevertheless, the overall impression made by the speech of 17:22-37 is that the Son of Man will arrive suddenly, without being preceded by signs.

From the perspective of the author of Luke, the lack of signs preceding the arrival of the Son of Man is not due to a theological rejection of signs in principle, but to the need to revise the eschatological scenario of Mark. Like Mark, Luke includes references to outsiders seeking signs for the wrong reasons (11:16, 29; 23:8). But Luke also uses the notion of signs positively. The angels give the shepherds a sign by which they can recognize the Savior (2:11); Simeon declares that Jesus himself will be a sign (2:34). The refusal of a sign to those who test Jesus is not absolute, as in Mark, but they are given "the sign of Jonah." As Jonah was a sign to the people of Nineveh, so will the Son of Man be to "this generation" (11:29-30).

It is striking that Luke preserves the disciples' request for a sign in the eschatological discourse later in the Gospel (cf. Mark 13:4 with Luke 21:7). If the author of Luke rejected signs in principle, he would have eliminated the word from the question or portrayed Jesus as correcting the disciples on this point. The notion of signs is not rejected, but its use here differs from that in Mark. The link between the destruction of the temple and the whole sequence of eschatological events visible in Mark 13:4 is not reproduced in Luke 21:7. In Luke the disciples' question focuses on the destruction of the temple only. The *panta* ("all") modifying *tauta* ("these things") in the second part of the question in Mark is missing in Luke, and the verb *synteleisthai* ("to be accomplished") is replaced with the neutral *ginesthai* ("to take place"). The Danielic "desolating sacrilege" is missing from Luke. But the notion of a sign is still present in v 20: "When you see Jerusalem surrounded by armies, then know that its desolation has come near."

In Mark there is a close temporal link between the crisis in Jerusalem and the arrival of the Son of Man. The latter event, preceded by cosmic disturbances, is connected with the previous one by the words "But in those days after that tribulation" (*alla en ekeinais tais hēmerais meta tēn thlipsin ekeinēn*, 13:24). In Luke this connection is loosened in two ways. First, the destruction of Jerusalem is to be followed by the "times of the Gentiles" (*kairoi ethnōn*, 21:24). There is no indication that this period is a long one, but it does remove the arrival of the Son of Man from the period of the tribulation itself. The other way in which Luke breaks this connection is by the lack of any indication of time in the introduction to the appearance of the Son of Man in v 25. Mark's "in those days after that tribulation" is removed and nothing is put in its place. The reason for these changes is that the destruction of the temple had already occurred when Luke was written; sufficient time had passed so that the latter event could not be taken as immediately preceding the arrival of the Son of Man. But the notion of signs is preserved not only for the crisis in Jerusalem but also for the coming of the Son of Man. The sign for the latter event is no longer the crisis in Jerusalem itself, but "signs in the sun, the moon, and the stars, and on the earth distress among nations confused by the roaring of the sea and the waves" (v 25).

It is beyond the scope of this essay to discuss in detail the history of the notion of signs in the Synoptic tradition. It should be noted, however, that the Sayings Source combined the teaching about the sudden arrival of the Son of Man with at least a limited notion of the importance of signs, since the sayings about the sign of Jonah were probably in Q in a form close to that of Luke's version of them.

Likewise, my intention here is not to make a case for the authenticity of Mark 13 as a speech of Jesus. I have pointed out that the arguments for the use of a written source in this chapter are not persuasive. But the hypothesis that the author of Mark was dependent on oral tradition in composing the discourse is a likely one. The proposal that the context for the handing on of this tradition was the catechesis of the early church is attractive.[47] The possibility that much of the tradition

47. Vincent Taylor argued that vv 28-37 represent the catechetical teaching of the church in Rome (Beasley-Murray, *Jesus and the Future*, 106–7), but there are no compelling reasons to link such tradition with Rome. Building on the work of C. H. Dodd, Beasley-Murray has argued that the eschatological tradition of Mark 13 was part of the primitive Christian catechesis developed as a medium of conveying traditions of the instruction of Jesus ("Second Thoughts on the Composition of Mark 13," *NTS* 29 [1983] 414).

in Mark 13 goes back to the historical Jesus, including a version of vv 14-23, and that he himself alluded to Daniel should not be ruled out unless good reasons can be articulated for doing so.

CONCLUSION

Far from being fanatical, the eschatological discourse of Mark 13 provided a framework of meaning in a difficult situation. It interpreted the original audience's situation for them so that they could renew their faith and carry on their work. In the light of the high-handed way many exegetes have treated this text, I must agree with the following remarks of F. Busch, although I do not follow him in his overall interpretation. "The first presupposition for the grounding of that hypothesis [the 'Little Apocalypse Theory'] is the construction of a Christ who in every respect was adapted to the colourless features of a century whose representative must needs perpetually call the artless, magnificent view of Mark 13 'bizarre.' If this presupposition, this prejudice is renounced, then all the reasons for the hypothesis tumble down."[48]

48. Translation by Beasley-Murray, *Jesus and the Future*, 150–52.

Chapter Four

THE PASSION
NARRATIVE
OF MARK

THE "PASSION NARRATIVE" in Mark refers to the account of the suffering and death of Jesus in chapters 14 and 15 of that Gospel. Some scholars consider the passion narrative to have a broader scope, but all would include at least some of the material now found in these two chapters. There is disagreement not only on the extent of the passion narrative but also on the question whether the author of Mark was the first to compose such an account or whether he used a previously existing narrative as the foundation for his own. This essay is an exploration of these disputed issues.

REVIEW OF SCHOLARSHIP

In the traditional reading of the passion narrative, the question of historical fact is not raised. The readers and hearers take the account as a representation of the end of Jesus' life and enter into it, focusing on the significance of the story for the individual and the community. When critical tools were applied to the Gospel of Mark, however, the historical question and many related questions were raised. Scholars began to ask about the relation between the author of Mark and the events that took place in the last days of Jesus' life. Was the author an eyewitness? If not, did he have access to the memories of eyewitnesses? They also raised questions about the relation between history and tradition. When the account alludes to passages from the Old Testament, can the events in question still be taken as historical, or were they pious fictions inspired by the Scriptures?

An early form critic of the New Testament, Karl Ludwig Schmidt, observed that the passion narrative had a distinctive place in the history of the Gospel tradition. The account of Jesus' suffering and death contrasts strongly with the story of his deeds and words. The latter was composed on the basis of individual stories and small collections of stories that do not appear in a reliable relationship to historical events. Rather, they appear in a secondary and artificial framework. It is only by chance, if at all, that correct chronological or topographical information is preserved in the introductions or conclusions to such stories or collections. This body of tradition preserves only a modest remnant of the actual itinerary of the activity of Jesus. The passion narrative, however, is the only section of the Gospels in which exact temporal and topographical information is given, even the day and the hour. Literarily speaking, it is clear that a larger, continuous narrative was intended from the beginning.

The difference between the two types of tradition is explained by the hypothesis that individual stories were useful to the Christian storytellers, leaders of liturgy, and apologists when the topic was a particular deed or saying of Jesus. Such stories were not adequate when the subject was the death of Jesus. The larger extended narrative was necessary to put individual features in context, such as the betrayal of Judas, the preparation of the Passover meal, and the trial before Pilate. Although stories like the founding of the Lord's Supper and the crucifixion were probably used independently, it was only the larger narrative that could serve liturgical and missionary needs effectively by answering the question how it could be that the people who received Jesus' mighty deeds brought him to the cross. Schmidt suggested that the whole narrative was read in the liturgy. In terms of literary genre, he identified it as the first of a series of Christian acts of the martyrs. Just as such acts are more reliable historically than legends about the martyrs, so also is the passion narrative more accurate historically than the other forms of the tradition about Jesus. The early fixing of the content and perspective of the passion narrative explains also the greater agreement among the four Gospels in this section than in the rest. The relative silence of Jesus in this narrative is also taken as a sign of its early date and primitive character.[1]

1. Karl Ludwig Schmidt, "Die literarische Eigenart der Leidensgeschichte Jesu," *Die Christliche Welt* 32 (1918) 114–16; repr. in *Redaktion und Theologie des Passionsberichtes nach den Synoptikern* (ed. Meinrad Limbeck; Darmstadt: Wissenschaftliche Buchgesellschaft, 1981) 17–20.

Martin Dibelius agreed with Schmidt that the passion narrative is a special case. He argued that the speeches in Acts and the Pauline summaries of early Christian preaching are evidence that the primary interest of the most primitive theology was the passion and the Easter story. Their significance lay in the fact that they were perceived as the first act of the end of the world. In them salvation was visible in a succession of events. The passion narrative was composed early because it was necessary to set these events in context in order to explain the paradox of the cross and settle the issue of responsibility. We must presuppose the early existence of a self-contained passion narrative because preaching, whether for mission or for worship, required some such text. Further arguments in favor of a pre-Markan passion narrative included the observations that the passion narrative is relatively fixed in the Synoptics, the Gospel of John is parallel to the synoptics only in the passion narrative, and the passion narrative is relatively self-sufficient. Only one narrative can immediately be separated out (14:3-9). Otherwise the passion of Jesus runs in a closed sequence from the death of Jesus to the empty grave.[2]

Dibelius thought that he had found further support for a pre-Markan passion narrative in the tension between the chronology of the earlier account and that of Mark. He contended that the introduction to the passion (14:1-2, 10-11) must be earlier than Mark's Gospel because it contradicts his chronology. The motive for the secret arrest of Jesus is the nearness of the feast. Thus it assumes that Jesus was arrested before the Passover evening. But Mark assumes that Jesus and the disciples celebrated Passover together before the arrest.[3] Although Dibelius concluded that it was impossible to determine the exact range of the earliest passion story, he thought that it ended with an appearance of the risen Jesus to the disciples, since such an appearance is predicted in 14:28, and not with the empty tomb story.[4]

Unlike Schmidt and Dibelius, Rudolf Bultmann concluded that the passion story as we have it in the Synoptic Gospels is not an organic unity. Even here the story is made up of separate pieces. Most of the

2. Martin Dibelius, *From Tradition to Gospel* (New York: Scribner's, 1935) 22–23, 178–80; the first edition of this work appeared under the title *Die Formgeschichte des Evangeliums* (Tübingen: Mohr/Siebeck, 1919).
3. Ibid., 180–81.
4. Ibid., 181.

units are not bound to their context in the passion narrative. But once the particular stories were bound together into a whole, it was essentially the nature of the facts that determined their particular order. *Like* Schmidt and Dibelius, Bultmann nevertheless concluded that the author of Mark had already before him a passion story that was a continuous narrative. This passion story was a short narrative of historical reminiscence about the arrest, condemnation, and execution of Jesus. It was the kerygma, as we know it from the prophecies of the passion and resurrection in Mark 8:31; 9:31; 10:33-34; and in the speeches of Acts, that led to a coherent narrative.[5]

This brief narrative was expanded first of all with stories that elaborated individual moments of the narrative: the preparation of the Passover (14:12-16), the hearing before the Sanhedrin (14:55-64), and the trial before Pilate (15:3-5). Then the narrative was elaborated with secondary expansions that are less closely tied to the overall context: the anointing (14:3-9), the prophecy of the betrayal (14:17-21), the last supper, which replaced an older account of a meal (14:22-25), the Gethsemane story (14:32-42), Peter's following and denial (14:53-54, 66-72), the Barabbas episode (15:6-15a), and the mocking of Jesus (15:16-20a).[6]

Bultmann did not accept Dibelius's thesis that 14:1-2, 10-11 constituted the introduction to the older passion narrative, since these verses have no organic continuation in Mark. Rather, these verses must be taken as a secondary introduction to a collection of stories that Mark had before him and into which he inserted 14:3-9.[7]

The primitive historical narrative reconstructed by Bultmann began with a brief account of the arrest, which had a sequel, subsequently replaced, about how Jesus was taken away and sentenced. Bits of the original account may be preserved in 14:53a, 65; 15:1-5. The account then continued with the story of the leading away to the crucifixion and the execution itself (15:15b, 20b-24a, perhaps 27, and 37). The individual items are not stories as such, but short statements making up a historical narrative.[8]

5. Rudolf Bultmann, *The History of the Synoptic Tradition* (trans. John Marsh; rev. ed.; New York: Harper & Row, 1968) 275.
6. Ibid., 275–77.
7. Ibid., 277.
8. Ibid., 279.

Vincent Taylor made a case for regarding the passion narrative as a composite section in which primary and secondary elements can be distinguished. He built his case on literary and stylistic features. He argued that the primary element of the passion narrative consists of short summary passages, written in relatively good Greek, which have a certain continuity and give an outline to the story, although broken and incomplete. These passages include 14:1-2, 10-11, 26, 43b-46, 53a; 15:1, 15, 22-24, 37, 39. He defined the secondary element as inter-calated narratives and shorter appended or inserted passages, many of which were written in a vivid style characterized by Semitisms. The intercalated passages include the anointing (14:3-9), the story of Geth-semane (14:32-42), the trial before the priests (14:55-64), the denial of Peter (14:54, 66-72), and the mockery by the soldiers (15:16-20). The appended or inserted passages are 14:28, 47, 48-50, 51-52, 65; 15:25, 33, 38, 40-41, 47. He identified the primary element as a simple straightforward narrative that was probably composed for the com-munity at Rome. He suggested that Mark discovered the simple nar-rative in Rome and then expanded it with reminiscences of Peter.[9]

In 1970 Eta Linnemann argued that there was no pre-Markan passion narrative. She viewed the Markan passion narrative as a collection of short, independent reports rather than a reworking of a connected account. Her work pushed some of Bultmann's observations to their logical conclusion. Like Bultmann, she concluded that the Gethsemane pericope was originally independent. She translated *apechei* (14:41) as "the account is closed" and took this as an expression of Jesus' acceptance of God's will. On this basis she was able to conclude that the story does not report a phase of Jesus' passion; it interprets the entire event of the passion.[10]

She argued further that Mark composed the pericope concerning the arrest of Jesus (14:43-52) by combining three originally indepen-dent traditions. The first was a biographical apophthegm, partially preserved in vv 43, 48-49. In this unit Jesus reproached the members

9. Vincent Taylor, *The Gospel According to St. Mark* (2d ed.; Grand Rapids, Mich.: Baker, 1966) 653–64. A similar theory was proposed by E. R. Buckley ("The Sources of the Passion Narrative in St. Mark's Gospel," *JTS* 34 [1932/33] 138–44); see the brief discussion of Buckley's work by Marion L. Soards, "The Question of a Pre-Markan Passion Narrative," *Biblebhashyam* 11 (1985) 146.

10. Eta Linnemann, *Studien zur Passionsgeschichte* (Göttingen: Vandenhoeck & Ruprecht, 1970) 24–28.

of the arresting party for their guile. Its primary focus, however, was on the arrest of Jesus as being in accordance with the Scriptures. She thus maintained that the unit interprets the passion as a whole, not just a phase of it.[11] The second tradition was a narrative about the arrest of Jesus through the betrayal of Judas. This unit originally began with 14:1-2, 10-11 and continued with vv 44-46. She contended that this narrative was not a simple report. Its message is that the betrayer was a disciple and it thus raises a question for the hearers.[12] The third tradition is manifest in fragments of a story concerning the arrest of Jesus involving resistance on the part of the disciples and their flight. These fragments are preserved in vv 47 and 50. The flight of the naked young man in vv 51-52 is taken as an appended example of the general flight narrated in v 50.[13]

Linnemann argued that the greater part of the pericope concerning the crucifixion consisted of isolated details.[14] She held that it would be difficult to find a motive for inserting the schema of hours into an older narrative, whereas it is easy to imagine a storyteller using such a schema to make possible the narration of the crucifixion when little was known about it. So she included the verses that express this schema in her reconstruction of the original form of the pericope: vv 22a (introduction), 24a, 25a, 33, 34a, 37, 38 (conclusion).[15] Christian scribal or exegetical activity produced a number of individual motifs relating to Jesus' death. Before the pericope came to Mark, one of these scribes or exegetes inserted many of these motifs into the old crucifixion account.[16] When the narrative came to Mark, it already included the mention of the wine mixed with myrrh (v 23), the casting of lots for Jesus' clothes (v 24b), the mention of the criminals crucified with Jesus (v 27), the mocking of Jesus by gesture (v 29a) and perhaps also by speech (vv 30a and 31b), the citation of the prayer from Psalm 22 in v 34b, and the episode in vv 35-36. Verse 25b is editorial and belongs to this pre-Markan stage. She also concluded that the translation of Jesus' prayer (v 34b) and the translation of Golgotha (v 22b) are pre-Markan. Thus the crucifixion pericope that Mark had in front

11. Ibid., 44–47.
12. Ibid., 47–50.
13. Ibid., 50–52.
14. Ibid., 146–54.
15. Ibid., 155–57.
16. Ibid., 157.

of him consisted of vv 15, 22-25, 27, 29a, 30a, 31b, 33-38.[17] In the pre-Markan form of the crucifixion account, the opening of the curtain in the temple (v 38) signified that in the death of Jesus on the cross the majesty of God was revealed.[18]

According to Linnemann, the Markan contributions to the crucifixion account are: the linking of the isolated episode in vv 20b-21 (Simon of Cyrene with introduction) to the crucifixion narrative; the composition of v 26, which corresponds to the insertion of 15:2; the composition of vv 29b and 30b in the light of 14:58; the composition of vv 31a and 32ab in the light of 14:61-62; and the composition of v 32c, which creates a link with v 27. The evangelist is also responsible for 15:39. The link between 15:40-41 and the crucifixion narrative is due to Mark; he may have composed vv 40-41, but they could have been independent tradition like the mention of Simon of Cyrene.[19]

Linnemann's conclusion then is that Mark composed the passion narrative in the same way that he composed the rest of the Gospel, out of individual pericopes. His method, however, was different. In the rest of the Gospel, he could simply reproduce the individual units one after another. But when he had several stories that related to the same phase of the passion of Jesus, he had to fuse them into a single story. This procedure explains the literary difference between the passion narrative and the rest of the Gospel, along with the coherence of the natural course of events that Mark used as an organizing principle in composing the passion narrative.[20]

In 1971 Ludger Schenke published a book attempting a careful distinction between tradition and redaction in Mark 14:1-42 (the plot against Jesus, the anointing, the traditions related to the last supper, and the prayer of Jesus in Gethsemane). He concluded that Mark composed this portion of the passion narrative out of individual units.[21] In a later, shorter book he analyzed Mark 14:53—15:47 into three distinct layers: the oldest account, a pre-Markan redaction, and the Markan redaction. He concluded that the oldest tradition presented Jesus' passion on the model of the suffering just one, a motif common

17. Ibid., 157–58, 169.
18. Ibid., 162–63.
19. Ibid., 169–70.
20. Ibid., 173–74.
21. Ludger Schenke, *Studien zur Passionsgeschichte des Markus: Tradition und Redaktion in Markus 14, 1–42* (Würzburg: Echter, 1971).

in the book of Psalms.[22] Some of his detailed arguments will be examined below.

In 1976 a group of scholars working in the United States, Werner Kelber, John Donahue, Vernon Robbins, Norman Perrin, Kim Dewey, Theodore Weeden, and John Dominic Crossan, published a collection of essays on the passion narrative in which they emphasized the creativity of Mark as an author. Kelber served as the editor of the volume. They reached the following conclusions. Since virtually all major Markan themes converge in Mark 14–16, from the perspective of the history of tradition, Mark 14–16 does not differ appreciably from what is known about the literary genesis and composition of Mark 1–13. Since Mark 14–16 constitutes a theologically inseparable and homogeneous part of the Gospel, the classic form-critical thesis concerning an independent and coherent passion narrative prior to Mark is called into question.[23]

In the following year, Rudolph Pesch published volume 2 of his commentary on Mark. He took a position diametrically opposed to that of the Kelber volume. He presented Mark primarily as a collector and faithful reproducer of the tradition. He argued that Mark used a historically reliable passion narrative that consisted of what is now found in Mark 8:27—16:8. Mark allegedly made only minor changes in this preexisting passion narrative.[24] In 1979 Pesch published a study in which he argued that the pre-Markan passion narrative was composed in and for the oldest Christian community in Jerusalem.[25]

In spite of the challenge expressed in the volume edited by Kelber and in his later work on the subject,[26] the studies published on the passion narrative in the 1980s conclude that there was a pre-Markan passion narrative of some kind, although there is little agreement on

22. Idem, *Der gekreuzigte Christus: Versuch einer literarkritischen und traditionsgeschichtlichen Bestimmung der vormarkinischen Passionsgeschichte* (Stuttgart: Katholisches Bibelwerk, 1974).

23. *The Passion in Mark: Studies on Mark 14–16* (ed. Werner H. Kelber; Philadelphia: Fortress, 1976) 156–57.

24. Rudolf Pesch, *Das Markusevangelium* (HTKNT 2; 2 vols.; Freiburg/Basel/Vienna: Herder, 1976–77).

25. Idem, *Das Evangelium der Urgemeinde: Wiederhergestellt und erläutert* (Freiburg/Basel/Vienna: Herder, 1979).

26. Werner H. Kelber, *The Oral and the Written Gospel* (Philadelphia: Fortress, 1983) 184–99; see the critical comments by Joel B. Green, *The Death of Jesus: Tradition and Interpretation in the Passion Narrative* (Tübingen: Mohr/Siebeck, 1988) 158–69.

its specific form. T. A. Mohr, whose book was published in 1982, and Etienne Trocmé, whose most recent book on the subject appeared in 1983, agree with Pesch in concluding that this narrative may go back to the oldest Christian community.[27] In 1987 Maria Ruhland published a study in which she argued that a primitive apocalyptic admonitory narrative, including the denial of Peter and related material, was the generative core of the pre-Markan passion narrative.[28] In the following year, John Dominic Crossan published a book arguing that the oldest passion narrative is the source used by the *Gospel of Peter*.[29] The most recent comprehensive study of the issue is the book by Joel Green, also published in 1988, which concluded that there was a pre-Markan passion narrative whose birthplace and social setting was the Lord's Supper.[30]

ASSESSMENT OF THE EVIDENCE

The Form-Critical Arguments

Karl Ludwig Schmidt was surely right in noting a significant literary difference between Mark 1–13 and 14–15.[31] The Gospel begins with minimal orientation in time and space: "John was baptizing in the wilderness" (1:4). Those readers familiar with the activity of John the Baptist would be aware of the approximate time in which he was active. The context suggests an area within Judea. It is said that Jesus went to John to be baptized "in those days." The following account of Jesus' deeds and teachings has some specific indications of place (Capernaum in 1:21; 2:1; 9:33; Bethsaida in 8:22; Caesarea Philippi in 8:27; Jerusalem in 10:32; 11:11, 15, 27; Jericho in 10:46; Bethphage and Bethany in 11:1; the temple in 11:11, 15, 27; 12:35; 13:1, 3; Bethany

27. Till Arend Mohr, *Markus- und Johannespassion: Redaktions- und traditions- geschichtliche Untersuchung der Markinischen und Johanneischen Passionstradition* (Zurich: Theologischer Verlag Zürich, 1982); Etienne Trocmé, *The Passion as Liturgy: A Study in the Origin of the Passion Narratives in the Four Gospels* (London: SCM, 1983).

28. Maria Ruhland, *Die Markuspassion aus der Sicht der Verleugnung* (Eilsbrunn: Ko'amar, 1987); see the review by W. R. Telford in *JTS* 40 (1989) 182–85.

29. John Dominic Crossan, *The Cross That Spoke: The Origins of the Passion Narrative* (San Francisco: Harper & Row, 1988).

30. Joel B. Green, *The Death of Jesus: Tradition and Interpretation in the Passion Narrative* (Tübingen: Mohr/Siebeck, 1988).

31. So also Charles W. Hedrick, "What Is a Gospel? Geography, Time and Narrative Structure," *Perspectives in Religious Studies* 10 (1983) 256, 260–61.

in 11:11-12; opposite the treasury in 12:41; the Mount of Olives in 13:3). For the most part, however, topographical references are general and vague (Galilee in 1:14; 9:30; along or beside the Sea of Galilee in 1:16; 2:13; 3:7; 4:1; in a synagogue in 3:1; 6:2; on a mountain in 3:13; 9:2; the country of the Gerasenes in 5:1; in a house in 7:17, 24; 10:10; the region of Tyre in 7:24; the region of the Decapolis in 7:31, the region of Judea and beyond the Jordan in 10:1; on a journey in 10:17). In 6:45 Jesus instructs the disciples to go in the boat to Bethsaida. After he walks to them on the sea, however, they arrive at Gennesaret (6:53). It is noteworthy that the indications of place become more specific in chapters 8–10, still more specific in chapters 11 and 13, and then very specific in chapters 14:1—15:39. After the specificity of 14:1—15:39, the vagueness about the location of the tomb in 15:42—16:8 is striking.

The account of Jesus' deeds and teachings has some specific indications of time (forty days of testing in 1:13; a sequence of events on a particular Sabbath and the following day in 1:21-35; "on that day, when evening had come" in 4:35; "six days later" in 9:2). A sequence of three days is indicated in 11:11-12, 19-20. But on the whole the indications of time in chapters 1–13 are even more vague than the topographical references ("after some days" in 2:1, "on the sabbath" in 2:23, "when it was evening" in 6:47, "in those days" in 8:1). The most common temporal connectives in Mark are "and" (*kai*, often translated "then" in the NRSV) and "immediately" (*euthys*, 1:10 and frequently).

The situation changes in chapters 14–15. Although no indication of the year is given, the passion narrative proper begins with a specific indication of time, "two days before the Passover and the Feast of Unleavened Bread" (14:1). On this day, it is implied, both the plot of the chief priests and scribes and the anointing in Bethany took place (14:1-11). The next section is introduced with a reference to "the first day of Unleavened Bread, when the Passover lamb is sacrificed" (14:12). This temporal reference seems to confuse the Day of Preparation and the first day of the feast. As Schenke has suggested, the confusion probably occurred because Mark did not reckon days from sunset to sunset, as most Jews of his time did. According to the Jewish reckoning, the Passover lamb is sacrificed on Nisan 14; the Feast of Passover and Unleavened Bread begins on Nisan 15. But from the point of view of those who reckon days from sunrise to sunrise, the sacrifice of the lamb and the Passover meal take place on the same day. He argued that the reference to the time when the Passover lamb is sacrificed is pre-Markan, whereas the reference to "the first day of Unleavened Bread" is Markan.[32] All the incidents recounted in the rest of chapter 14 take place on this day. Indications of place are relatively specific: in a house in Jerusalem discovered through a sign (14:12-16), the Mount of Olives (14:26), Gethsemane (14:32), the house and courtyard of the high priest (14:53-54, 66).

The reference "as soon as it was morning" (*kai euthys prōi*, 15:1) indicates a new day. All the events described in chapter 15 occur on this day. Indications of place are specific in the section including 15:1-39 (the official residence of Pilate in 15:16 and Golgotha in 15:22). As already mentioned, it is noteworthy that the location of the tomb in the burial story is quite vague.

The literary coherence and specificity of chapters 14–15 certainly give them a greater historylike character than chapters 1–13. But critics today are acutely aware that historylike does not necessarily mean historically reliable. It is not immediately apparent that a larger, continuous narrative was intended from the beginning. One must nevertheless struggle with the question why chapters 14–15 are more successful as continuous narrative than chapters 1–13. Schmidt's explanation is that the style of Mark varies according to the nature of his sources. Linnemann suggested that the actual events of the passion lent themselves more easily to the construction of a continuous narrative. Kelber argued that textuality is more suited to describing death than orality is; it was only when Mark set out to compose a written gospel that the death of Jesus could be treated. Kelber's explanation seems to be the weakest. As Green has pointed out, much early Christian preaching focused on the death of Jesus. There were literary patterns in Judaism that could be drawn upon for making sense of the passion. There are no historical or aesthetic-literary reasons why a written passion narrative could not have been composed prior to Mark.[33] It is more difficult to choose between Schmidt's and Linnemann's explanations. More specific evidence is needed; such evidence will be discussed later.

32. Schenke, *Studien zur Passionsgeschichte*, 22–23.
33. Green, *Death of Jesus*, 158–69.

The form-critical approach taken by Schmidt and Dibelius has certain strengths. The argument that there was both a need (preaching and catechesis) and a setting in life (the liturgy) for an extended narrative that would make sense of Jesus' death is persuasive. Schmidt was also on the right track in attempting to define the genre of the passion narrative as a whole. The reader's attention goes to the whole rather than to the individual units. Some of the units are difficult to label in terms of the traditional form-critical categories. Schmidt's definition of the genre as "acts of a martyr" is supported by the book of Revelation. There both Jesus and those who die for their Christian faith are called *martyres* ("witnesses" or "martyrs," Rev 1:5; 2:13). But this evidence is not pre-Markan. Further, Jesus does not seem to have been presented in the pre-Markan passion narrative as a "martyr" in the primary sense of the term, as one who bears witness in verbal testimony. It is this sense that dominates the terminology of the book of Revelation and that seems to have been the earliest Christian usage. Schmidt himself points out that the emphasis in the passion narrative is on Jesus' silence. But he was certainly right to attempt to grasp the passion narrative as a generic whole. Finally, Schmidt had a valid insight in his remarks about the primitive character of the passion narrative. The relative silence of Jesus is maintained during the passion in all four Gospels. This probably early and primitive motif is circumvented primarily by speeches before Jesus' arrest and after his resurrection. It is also modified by the addition of sayings to the older passion narrative (e.g., 14:48-49, 62; see below). One could extend this insight by remarking that the relatively undeveloped theological interpretation of the death of Jesus in the passion narrative is also a sign of its early and primitive character.

The Prelude (Mark 14:1-31)

Dibelius's argument about the tension between the chronology of the alleged introduction to the passion source (14:1-2, 10-11) and that of Mark is not persuasive. The remark "for they said, 'Not during the festival, or there may be a riot among the people'" (14:2) does not necessarily imply that the source narrated Jesus' arrest as occurring before the feast. To conclude that it does is to force an alien logic upon the narrative. The remark may be taken simply and loosely as an explanation why it was necessary to arrest Jesus "by stealth" (14:1). In any case, Bultmann argued persuasively that these verses could not have been the introduction to a pre-Markan passion narrative, since they have no organic continuation in what follows. In 14:43, the next occasion on which Judas appears as a character in the narrative, he is introduced as "one of the twelve." This introduction would not be necessary if he had already been introduced (as "Judas Iscariot, who was one of the twelve") in the same document in what is now preserved as 14:10. Linnemann argued that the account of the betrayal with a kiss (14:44-46) may be seen as the original continuation of the conspiracy described in 14:1-2, 10-11. But she did so in the context of an argument that the resulting reconstructed unit circulated independently. If one is attempting to reconstruct a continuous narrative beginning with 14:1, v 43, with its superfluous introduction of Judas, would need to be included, since it provides the link between the story of the prayer in Gethsemane and the arrest.

The plot to arrest Jesus in 14:1-2, 10-11 could not have been an independent unit, since it requires a continuation. As noted, Bultmann thought that it was the introduction to a collection of stories that Mark used in composing chapter 14. Schenke argued that all four of these verses were composed by Mark.[34] In any case, it is unlikely that these verses constituted the introduction to a pre-Markan passion narrative.

There are indications that 14:1-31 is a section composed by Mark from individual units. The placement of the story of the anointing (14:3-9) between the two parts of the story about the plot is a sign of Markan editing. This is the familiar technique of intercalation used elsewhere in Mark (3:19b-35; 5:21-43; 6:6b-30; and 11:12-26). The narrative about the preparations for the Passover (14:12-16) could have circulated independently. It fits the form-critical category "biographical apophthegm" and could have been told to show what Jesus was like. Its point lies in the miraculous foreknowledge of Jesus. Only this story and the notice in 14:26 that they sang a hymn suggest that the meal was a Passover meal. The story containing the prediction of the betrayal (14:17-21) does not follow smoothly on the story about the preparation of the meal. The major instance of discontinuity is the lack of Passover motifs in vv 17-21. Further instances are the use of

34. Schenke, *Studien zur Passionsgeschichte*, 139.

different terms for the followers of Jesus in the two stories ("disciples," *matēhtai*, in vv 12-16; and "the twelve," *hoi dōdeka*, in vv 17-21) and the unclarity about whether only the twelve or a wider group shared the meal with Jesus. Verses 12-16 imply a larger group, but vv 17-21 imply that only the twelve were present. The unit containing the words over the loaf and the cup (14:22-25) does not follow smoothly on either the story about preparation (vv 12-16) or on the prediction of the betrayal (vv 17-21). It does not follow coherently on vv 12-16 because there is no indication that the loaf and cup were part of a Passover meal. It does not follow smoothly on vv 17-21 because its introduction (v 22a) competes with the introduction to vv 17-21, especially with v 18. The prediction of the betrayal (vv 17-21) and the words over the bread and cup (vv 22-25) appear to be independent stories placed one after the other, rather than two parts of a single narrative description of the same meal.

The following unit (14:26-31) has important ties with subsequent incidents in the passion narrative. Jesus' prediction that all the disciples would take offense and be scattered (v 27) is fulfilled in the account of the arrest (14:50). The promise that Jesus, after he was raised up, would go before them to Galilee (v 28) is repeated in 16:7. Peter's denial, predicted in v 30, is narrated in 14:54, 66-72. These connections would seem to support the idea that the unit in vv 26-31 was part of a coherent, pre-Markan passion narrative, if such a narrative existed. The main problem with drawing this conclusion is that the unit does not fit smoothly and coherently in its immediate context. It is not historically certain that "Gethsemane" originally designated a place on the Mount of Olives. It has often been suspected that the association of the place-name with the Mount of Olives is a result, rather than a cause, of the association of the two place-names in Mark 14. The presence of the two place-names, without any explicit comment on the relation between them, suggests that the two units have been secondarily joined. Furthermore, the Gethsemane story does not follow smoothly on the preceding unit. The transition is rough and the failure of the disciples to stay awake is not an illustration or a fulfillment of the prophecy that they would take offense. The tensions between these two pericopes could be resolved either by taking the unit containing the prediction of desertion and denial (vv 26-31) as a Markan composition to prepare for later elements in the narrative (whether these elements are pre-Markan or redactional) or by taking the Gethsemane story (vv 32-42) as an intercalation into an earlier sequence in which the arrest followed immediately on the predictions of vv 26-31.[35]

The Gethsemane Story (Mark 14:32-42)

The evidence seems to support Schenke's conclusion that 14:26-31 was composed by Mark, whereas the Gethsemane story was the first unit of the pre-Markan passion narrative.[36] The reasons for this conclusion will become apparent when the earliest recoverable form of the Gethsemane story is reconstructed. The saying "the Son of Man is handed over into the hands of sinners" (the last part of v 41) is a Markan addition to emphasize the fact that the first part of the passion predictions is about to be fulfilled (cf. 9:31; 10:33). The remark that "He took with him Peter, James, and John" (14:33a) is also a Markan addition. The special role of these three disciples is a Markan theme. The other passages that mention these three disciples as singled out are probably Markan compositions (cf. 5:37; 9:2; 13:3).[37] The command to all the disciples to "Sit here while I pray" (14:32b) was probably added by Mark in the process of distinguishing the three special disciples from the rest. The threefold return of Jesus in vv 39-41 is not original because the use of the aorist tense in the reproof of Simon in v 37 implies that the disciples will not have a further chance to stay awake. The present tense and parenetic character of v 38 ("Keep awake and pray") suggest that it was added at the same time as the threefold return.

The addition of the threefold return of Jesus shifted the focus of the story significantly. The narrative structure involving a single prayer and a single discovery of the sleeping disciples places the emphasis on Jesus as the suffering just one who is alone and unsupported by friends, yet willing to accept the suffering ordained by God.[38] The triple return places the emphasis on the disciples and their inability to stay awake and watch. The new emphasis fits well with the Markan theme of the failure of the disciples. This resonance suggests that Mark

35. Schenke argues that 14:26-31 was composed by Mark (ibid., 353, 423); Taylor considered the Gethsemane story to be an intercalated narrative (*Mark*, 653).
36. Schenke, *Studien zur Passionsgeschichte*, 353, 360–62, 423, 561.
37. Ibid., 483–85.
38. On the echoes of the motif of the suffering just one, see ibid., 545–47.

added the threefold elaboration and the command to keep awake and pray.

The original ending of the story was probably v 42 ("Get up, let us be going. See, my betrayer is at hand"), which follows well upon the reproof of Peter in v 37. If v 35 ("And going a little farther, he threw himself on the ground and prayed that, if it were possible, the hour might pass from him") is a secondary summary of the prayer of v 36 ("Abba, Father, for you all things are possible; remove this cup from me . . ."), then the references to the "hour" in both vv 35 and 41 are probably redactional. If v 42 ("Get up, let us be going. See, my betrayer is at hand") is the original ending of the story, then the Gethsemane story and the story of the arrest were already linked prior to Mark. The exclamation *apechei* in v 41 goes logically with the third reproof of Jesus, whether it is translated "The account is closed" or "It is enough!" If the triple return is secondary, so is this exclamation.

Linnemann argued that the original ending was "The account is closed. The hour has come." She argued further, as previously noted, that the narrative interprets the whole passion and therefore could have circulated independently. But it is hard to imagine such a story circulating independently. The ending as she has reconstructed it leaves the audience hanging. Thus it seems more likely that the narrative was always attached to the subsequent story of the passion (though not necessarily to the latter in its present form). It thus interprets the whole passion of Jesus as an introduction to the passion narrative proper.[39] Mark expanded this "prelude" by composing (using individual units of tradition) and prefixing the account in 14:1-31.[40]

The Arrest (Mark 14:43-52)

The story of the arrest contains a number of secondary expansions. The two analogous episodes in v 47 (someone draws a sword and cuts off the ear of the slave of the high priest) and vv 51-52 (the young man fleeing naked) seem especially to be secondary insertions. Both give reactions of disciples to the arrest, but neither is prepared for or followed up. The strike with the sword in v 47 depicts the failure of

39. Ibid., 547.
40. Ibid., 552.

a disciple analogous to that of Peter when he rebukes Jesus in 8:32-33. This similarity suggests that it is a Markan insertion. Likewise, the flight of the naked young man (vv 51-52) is an image for the flight of all the disciples (v 50). The question must be left open whether these two insertions are Markan compositions or his use of particular traditions. The response of Jesus in vv 48-49 (reproaching the crowd for treating him like a bandit and referring to the fulfillment of Scripture) also seems to be secondary. These two verses disturb the context. They do not relate satisfactorily to the arrest, since it has already taken place. With their presence, the immediately following flight of the disciples is unmotivated. The reference to the fulfillment of Scripture, without mentioning any particular text, points to Markan redaction. The phrase *en tō hierō didaskōn* ("teaching in the temple," v 49) is also redactional. The strong correspondence between vv 43 and 48 could have been introduced by the redactor as he imitated v 43 in composing v 48. These observations are supported by the fact that v 50 follows well upon v 46. Verse 50 could well have been the conclusion of the original arrest story.[41]

The Sequel to the Arrest
(Mark 14:53-72)

An interrogation of Jesus by chief priests is mentioned twice (14:53, 55-64 and 15:1). Mistreatment of Jesus by his captors is also mentioned twice (14:65 and 15:16-20a). The intercalation of the denial of Peter into the trial before the Sanhedrin is a typically Markan technique. These observations suggest that Mark added the denial of Peter and the trial before the Sanhedrin to the earlier passion narrative.[42] This conclusion implies that 15:1 was part of the pre-Markan passion narrative.[43] It would have followed the statement in 14:53a that they took Jesus to the high priest. The remark that "all the chief priests, the

41. Ibid., 356–58.

42. On the secondary character of the trial before the Sanhedrin and its composition (using older traditions) and insertion by Mark, see John R. Donahue, *Are You the Christ? The Trial Narrative in the Gospel of Mark* (Missoula, Mont.: Scholars Press, 1973) 5–102.

43. Schenke argued that 15:1 originally read "the high priest and the whole Sanhedrin" instead of "the chief priests with the elders and scribes and the whole Sanhedrin" (*Der gekreuzigte Christus*, 31).

elders, and the scribes were assembled" in v 53b is probably redactional, composed by Mark as an introduction to the trial before the Sanhedrin (14:55-65).[44]

The episode concerning Barabbas (15:6-15a) is intercalated into the story of the trial before Pilate (15:2-5, 15b). The literary technique again suggests Markan redaction.[45] This hypothesis is supported by the connection between Jesus' remarks at the time of his arrest and the story about Barabbas. Jesus' remarks (14:48-49) distance him from the category "bandit" (*lēstēs*). It is clear from the writings of Josephus that this term was used in the first century as a designation of a kind of insurrectionist.[46] In 15:7 Barabbas is associated with rebels (*stasiastai*), and Jesus is contrasted with him in the unit as a whole. Instead of seeking mercy for the "King of the Jews," the crowd demands the release of a revolutionary murderer. Since it was apparently Mark who added 14:48-49, it is likely that he inserted 15:6-15a as well.[47]

The Trial Before Pilate
(Mark 15:1-15)

Like others before him, Bultmann argued that the question of Pilate to Jesus ("Are you the King of the Jews?") and Jesus' answer ("You say so") in 15:2 are secondary additions to the original story of the trial before Pilate. The reason for the addition was that the description had to be presented from the standpoint that Jesus was executed for his messianic claims.[48] But this standpoint need not be judged secondary. Given the interests and needs of the early Christian communities, it is unlikely that the earliest form of the passion narrative was a simple historical report. Bultmann himself concluded that it was impossible to distinguish the historical from the legendary in this

---

44. Ibid., 32.

45. Schenke thinks that the Barabbas episode was added by a redactor prior to Mark (ibid., 50). Detlev Dormeyer argued that an earlier form of the Barabbas story was part of the oldest passion narrative, namely, vv 6, 11, 7, 15 (*Die Passion Jesu als Verhaltensmodell: Literarische und theologische Analyse der Traditions- und Redaktionsgeschichte der Markuspassion* [Münster: Aschendorff, 1974] 185).

46. Richard A. Horsley and John S. Hanson, *Bandits, Prophets, and Messiahs: Popular Movements in the Time of Jesus* (Minneapolis: Winston, 1985) 48–87.

47. Schenke argued against the hypothesis that Mark added the Barabbas episode, but noted some of its Markan characteristics (*Der gekreuzigte Christus*, 50 n. 7).

48. Bultmann, *History*, 272.

material.[49] Thus the point of this part of the pre-Markan passion narrative could well have been to show that Jesus was crucified as a royal or messianic pretender. Although Pilate's question in 15:2 is shaped by a Christian perspective, it is also possible—even likely—that the general point of the narrative reflects historical fact.

Bultmann also concluded that the original basis of the trial before Pilate (15:1-5) contained a statement regarding Jesus' being sentenced by Pilate. The end of the trial was displaced by the Barabbas story, and v 15b ("and after flogging Jesus, he handed him over to be crucified") is a remnant of the original conclusion.[50] This hypothesis is not necessary. The interest of the author of the passion narrative and the tradents of the tradition beforehand may have been primarily in the ideas that Jesus was on trial as King of the Jews (15:2; from a Roman point of view, as a pretender to kingship) and that Pilate "handed him over" to be crucified (v 15b). The transition from v 5 to v 15b is rough, but it may be deliberately so. Pilate's response to Jesus' ambiguous answer (v 2b) and his silence (vv 4-5) was to hand him over to be flogged and then crucified.

The Mockery by Roman Soldiers
(Mark 15:16-20a)

Bultmann concluded that the story about the mocking of Jesus by the Roman soldiers (15:16-20a) is a secondary explanation of the remark regarding flogging (*phragellōsas*) in v 15b.[51] Since v 15b implies that the flogging took place before Jesus was handed over to the soldiers who were charged with the order to crucify him, the story about the mocking is presented as a separate and subsequent incident. There is some repetition involved in the transitions (cf. v 15b with v 20b), but this could be an original narrative device just as easily as a sign of secondary expansion. More persuasive is Schenke's conclusion that only *ho estin praitōrion* ("that is, the governor's official residence") in v 16 is secondary. The rest of the scene follows well on the trial

---

49. Ibid., 245.
50. Ibid., 279; Schenke followed Bultmann in the conclusion that the original ending of the story has been displaced, but he held that v 2 is part of the original narrative, having been moved from its original position after v 5 (*Der gekreuzigte Christus*, 53–54).
51. Bultmann, *History*, 272.

before Pilate without the Barabbas story. It picks up the important theme "King of the Jews" in v 18 (cf. v 2) and then leads logically into the account of the crucifixion. All this speaks for the originality of this scene in the narrative context.[52]

The Crucifixion (Mark 15:20b-32)

Bultmann considered the journey to the cross and the crucifixion (15:20b-24a) to be part of the primitive passion narrative, which he took to be an ancient historical account.[53] Schenke considered the statement about Simon of Cyrene (v 21) and the translation of the Aramaic place-name Golgotha into Greek (v 22b) to be secondary additions to the older narrative. He argued that the statement regarding Simon is secondary because it reflects the interest of Hellenistic Jewish Christians in Jerusalem.[54] This judgment is related to his thesis that Aramaic-speaking members of the oldest Christian community composed the earliest passion narrative in Aramaic in Jerusalem. This conclusion is based on what he considers to be secondary translations of Aramaic words, such as the translation of Golgotha in v 22b. But the presence of such translations does not necessarily imply that the earliest form of the narrative was composed in Aramaic. It could just as well have been composed by bilingual Christians who translated Aramaic expressions for members of the audience who did not know Aramaic. Since the arguments for judging vv 21 and 22b as secondary are not compelling, it is better to consider them as part of the earliest recoverable account of the journey to the cross and the crucifixion (15:20b-24). The brief reference to Simon is best understood as historical reminiscence.

Bultmann contended that the time reference in 15:25, "It was the third hour when they crucified him," is due to the editing of Mark. He based this conclusion on the repetition in the immediate context; *kai estaurōsan auton* ("and they crucified him") in v 25 is a doublet of *staurousin auton* ("they crucified him") in v 24.[55] As already noted,

---

52. Schenke, *Der gekreuzigte Christus*, 55.
53. Bultmann, *History*, 273, 279.
54. Schenke, *Der gekreuzigte Christus*, 83–84, 90–92; Linnemann also concluded that v 21 is secondary, for some of the same reasons (*Studien zur Passionsgeschichte*, 146).
55. Bultmann, *History*, 273.

Linnemann argued that the references to the hours of the day in the crucifixion account are original.[56] Schenke concluded that v 25 is secondary, but he attributed it to a pre-Markan redaction.[57] Using the methods of statistical study of vocabulary and stylistic analysis, Detlev Dormeyer concluded that 15:25 was composed by Mark, because the word *hōra* ("hour") is a preferred word in the Markan redactional vocabulary and because *ēn de* ("and it was") introduces a parenthesis; such parentheses are characteristic of Markan redaction.[58]

Dormeyer's arguments are circular, since it is not certain that all or even most of the passages he adduces as Markan redaction in Mark 1–13 were actually composed by Mark.[59] The repetition pointed out by Bultmann and Schenke is worthy of note, as is the fact that the verb in v 24 is in the historical present tense, whereas that of v 25 is in the aorist.[60] But these features do not compel the conclusion that v 25 is secondary. The historical present is used in v 24 in the course of narrating a sequence of events ("And they crucified him, and divided his clothes among them . . ."). Verse 25 ("It was the third hour when they crucified him") may be seen as an aside or parenthesis, but authors are as capable of making these as editors. The aorist tense is used because the verse is retrospective; it comments on an event already narrated. Linnemann's argument that the schema of hours was used in the oldest account as a narrative device is the most persuasive suggestion.

Bultmann considered 15:26, the comment about the inscription of the charge against Jesus, to be editorial, like 15:2. As previously noted, this judgment is dependent on the conviction that the standpoint that Jesus was executed for his messianic claims is necessarily secondary. But such is not the case. There is no apparent reason why such

56. Linnemann, *Studien zur Passionsgeschichte*, 146, 155–57.
57. Schenke, *Der gekreuzigte Christus*, 84, 92, 95.
58. Dormeyer, *Die Passion Jesu*, 194; cf. 67.
59. On the unreliability of vocabulary statistics and style criticism when used in isolation, see Soards, "The Question of a Pre-Markan Passion Narrative," 163–64, with reference to Robin Scroggs, "Section VIII: The Crucifixion," in W. Kelber, A. Kolenkow, and R. Scroggs, "Reflections on the Question: Was There a Pre-Markan Passion Narrative?" *SBL Seminar Papers 1971*, 505–85.
60. The difference in tense is apparently one criterion used by J. Schreiber to distinguish two pre-Markan traditions in the crucifixion account (Schreiber's work was summarized by John Donahue, "Introduction: From Passion Traditions to Passion Narrative," *The Passion in Mark*, 12).

a perspective could not have characterized the earliest passion narrative.[61]

Bultmann thought that 15:27, the statement about Jesus being crucified between two bandits, perhaps belonged to the earliest account.[62] Linnemann concluded that v 27 was secondary, but that it was already part of the passion narrative that Mark had before him.[63] Schenke included v 27 in his reconstruction of the original account.[64] Verse 27 is one of the many rather isolated details whose presence in the crucifixion narrative was pointed out by Linnemann. Whether their presence is due to the manner of composition of the author of the earliest account or to a pre-Markan redaction is a question that must remain open for the present.

The comment in 15:28 that Jesus' crucifixion between two bandits, the circumstance mentioned in v 27, was a fulfillment of Scripture was probably not an original part of the Gospel of Mark, but was added during the course of the transmission of the Gospel to harmonize this text with that of Luke 22:37.[65]

The remark that those who passed by the crucified Jesus derided him, shaking their heads (15:29a), is probably original. It alludes to LXX Ps 21:8, a psalm alluded to elsewhere in the passion narrative (15:24 to LXX Ps 21:19 and 15:34 to LXX Ps 21:2). As Schenke has argued on literary grounds, the original mocking scene consisted of 15:29a, 31b, 32: "Those who passed by derided him, shaking their heads and saying, 'He saved others; he cannot save himself. Let the Messiah, the King of Israel, come down from the cross now, so that we may see and believe.' Those who were crucified with him also taunted him."[66] This conclusion is supported by the fact that v 32 ("Let the Messiah, the King of Israel, come down") alludes to 15:2 (Jesus was condemned as King of the Jews), a passage that was probably part

---

61. Schenke included 15:26 in his reconstruction of the original form of the crucifixion account (*Der gekreuzigte Christus*, 85, 102); so also Dormeyer, *Die Passion Jesu*, 195. Linnemann states arguments for the secondary character of v 26, but they are not compelling (*Studien zur Passionsgeschichte*, 147).

62. Bultmann, *History*, 279.

63. Linnemann, *Studien zur Passionsgeschichte*, 157–58, 169.

64. Schenke, *Der gekreuzigte Christus*, 102; Dormeyer also included v 27 in his reconstruction of the earliest account (*Die Passion Jesu*, 196).

65. Bruce M. Metzger, *A Textual Commentary on the Greek New Testament* (New York: United Bible Societies, 1971) 119.

66. Schenke, *Der gekreuzigte Christus*, 92–94.

of the earliest passion narrative; whereas v 29b ("You who would destroy the temple and build it in three days") alludes to 14:58 ("We heard him say, 'I will destroy this temple that is made with hands, and in three days I will build another, not made with hands'"), a passage that was secondarily added to the passion narrative.[67] Since Mark added the narrative about the trial before the Sanhedrin, as already argued, 15:29b-31a was probably added by him as well.[68]

The Death of Jesus (Mark 15:33-39)

The death of Jesus is recounted in 15:33-39. Bultmann concluded that the temporal references in v 33 ("and when it was the sixth hour") and v 34 ("at the ninth hour") were due to the editorial work of Mark, like v 25. As previously noted, the case for the secondary character of v 25 is not strong. If the temporal reference in v 25 is original, then those in vv 33 and 34 are probably original also. Schenke argued in a fashion similar to Bultmann's, but he brought forward additional arguments. He called this schema of units of three hours artificial and thought that it was imposed on the narrative. He also contended that v 33 constitutes a break in the temporal and geographical unity of the story: darkness covered the *whole land*, and during a unit of three hours, nothing happens. He also noted that no reaction to the darkness is recorded. The centurion's remark is too far removed to be such a reaction.[69] Bultmann had argued that the reaction of the centurion was to the signs and wonders recorded in v 33 (the darkness) and possibly v 38 (the splitting of the temple curtain).[70] Since the darkness occurs *before* the death of Jesus and no reaction is recorded, Schenke concluded that v 33 was a secondary insertion. He argued that the source of the motif was the Old Testament notion of the day of the Lord (day of judgment) as a day of darkness and mourning (e.g., Amos 8:9). He suggested that the point of this verse is that the cross of Jesus is the eschatological judgment. This theme connects the verse with 15:29b-30. Therefore v 33 was added by Hellenistic Jewish Christians in Jerusalem, as vv 29b-30 were.[71]

---

67. Ibid., 85.
68. Schenke argued that 14:58 and 15:29b–31a were added in a redaction of the passion narrative prior to Mark in Hellenistic Jewish circles in Jerusalem (ibid., 94–95).
69. Ibid., 85.
70. Bultmann, *History*, 274.
71. Schenke, *Der gekreuzigte Christus*, 95.

Schenke's judgment that the schema of hours is artificial may be relevant for the issue of historicity, but not for the history of tradition. As Linnemann pointed out, the schema may be taken as a narrative device. The argument that v 33 breaks the geographical and temporal unity of the story is equally uncompelling. The aesthetic canons of the author may not have required geographical unity. The presence of darkness for a period of three hours is a vivid narrative detail. To say that the darkness defines Jesus' death as the eschatological judgment goes beyond the evidence. The omen suggests that the death is a cosmic event, but it is difficult and probably unnecessary to be any more specific. The omen makes an impression on the reader even without a narrated reaction by a character. In short, there seems to be no good reason for regarding v 33 as secondary. The same holds for the temporal reference at the beginning of v 34.

Schenke maintained that the cry of Jesus in v 34 ("Eloi, Eloi, lema sabachthani?"), consisting of an Aramaic version of Ps 22:1a, must be original because it derives from the oldest stage of the passion narrative, which was composed in Aramaic. He inferred that the Greek version of the cry (which translated is "My God, my God, why have you forsaken me?") was added very early when the account was first translated into Greek. But he also argued that vv 35, 36b (the bystanders' comment that he was calling Elijah and the suggestion of one of them that they wait to see whether Elijah comes) are secondary because the misunderstanding of the cry of Jesus is meant to be deliberate in the context of mockery. These verses have a polemical point against the chief priests and scribes. The evangelist must have added these verses, since he added the reference to scribes in v 31a—these are the typical enemies of Jesus whom he introduced into the passion narrative at various points (cf. 14:43, 53; 15:1)—and since *tines* ("some") in v 35 refers back to v 31a.[72] Further support for the redactional character of vv 35-36 lies in the fact that these verses develop the Gospel's Elijah theme (cf. 9:9-12).[73] If vv 35-36 are redactional, the cry of Jesus in v 34 may have been added to prepare for the

---

72. Ibid., 99.

73. It seems arbritary to separate out v 35a as original, just because it alludes to a psalm (LXX Ps 68:22). Such allusions are found in the earliest recoverable parts of the passion narrative, but it is not necessarily the case that all such allusions belong to the earliest stage.

mockery involving the deliberate misunderstanding of *Eloi* ("My God") as "Elijah." The cry must be given in Aramaic, as well as in Greek, so that the wordplay may be manifest. Thus the earlier account may simply have read *kai tē enatē hōra eboēsen ho Iēsous phōnē megalē* ("and at the ninth hour, Jesus cried out with a loud voice," v 34a) [*kai*] *exepneusen* ("and expired," v 37).

According to Bultmann, the prodigy related to the temple in 15:38 is a novelistic motif that goes with the darkness of v 33.[74] From this point of view, there is no reason to regard v 38 as secondary, unless one presupposes that the original account was a historical report free of legendary embellishment. On the other hand, Schenke argued that v 38 is secondary, like v 29b, because it signifies that the judgment on the old temple has begun. This judgment involves not so much the beginning of the destruction of the building as the loss of its function as the place of prayer and service of God. This loss is due to the death of Jesus, which means the end of the temple cult and of Judaism itself. Since God has left the temple, the place of the temple has been taken by the new community of salvation.[75] One could make a case that this interpretation expresses what 15:38 meant for the evangelist on the basis of a comparison with 11:12-24, although Schenke's expression of it is overstated.[76] It is questionable that the evangelist held that Judaism itself had come to an end. But Schenke attributed both the verse and the interpretation to the hypothetical Hellenistic Jewish Christian redaction prior to Mark.[77] It makes more sense to conclude, as did Eta Linnemann, that this verse was the original ending of the account of the death of Jesus.[78] The term *eschisthē* should be translated "was divided," "separated," or "opened." The curtain before the Holy of Holies was opened, as the heavens were at the baptism of Jesus (*schizomenous tous ouranous*, 1:10).[79] Both passages are taken from

74. Bultmann, *History*, 273–74, 282.
75. Schenke, *Der gekreuzigte Christus*, 100.
76. The argument seems even more overstated in light of the argument of Heikki Räisänen that the cursing of the fig tree does not involve antitemple symbolism (*The 'Messianic Secret' in Mark* [Studies of the New Testament and Its World; Edinburgh: T. & T. Clark, 1990] 24–25).
77. Schenke, *Der gekreuzigte Christus*, 101.
78. Linnemann, *Studien zur Passionsgeschichte*, 162–63.
79. David Ulansey, among others, has argued that the veil in question was the outer veil, which hung in front of the doors at the entrance to the temple ("The Heavenly Veil Torn: Mark's Cosmic *Inclusio*," *JBL* 110 [1991] 123–25).

tradition. In both cases, the verb *schizō* signifies the opening of that which normally hides the godhead. Both verses imply a theophany. In its original context, 15:38 implies that the death of Jesus was God's will and that Jesus was vindicated.

Bultmann regarded the statement of the centurion in 15:39 as a dogmatic motif, although he did not speculate as to the stage at which it became part of the passion narrative.[80] Schenke contended that, although v 39 plays an important role in Markan theology, the verse was part of the original form of the passion narrative.[81] It is more likely, as Linnemann argued, that Mark composed v 39.[82] The centurion's acclamation is not a response to the darkness, to the opening of the temple curtain, or to the cry of Jesus. Its function is to make the point that it is precisely the crucified Jesus who is God's Son. This point expresses the heart of Mark's Christology.

It is likely that the pre-Markan passion narrative ended with the death of Jesus and the theophany expressed in 15:38. The purpose of this document was to interpret the death of Jesus. It is unlikely that the events of burial and resurrection were included.[83] The vagueness concerning the location of the tomb suggests that the story about the burial was not part of the older passion narrative. The burial story is more like chapters 1–13 of Mark than the passion narrative proper with its topographical specificity. The focus on the death would fit the most likely social setting of the text: either an annual commemoration of the death of Jesus held in conjunction with Passover or the more frequent ritual of the Lord's Supper. The theophany of 15:38 would make a fittingly dramatic conclusion and an appropriate theological point, namely, the vindication of Jesus. The resurrection of Jesus was assumed but not narrated in this particular document.

---

80. Bultmann, *History*, 283–84.
81. Schenke, *Der gekreuzigte Christus*, 102–3.
82. Linnemann, *Studien zur Passionsgeschichte*, 170.
83. Schenke concluded that the earliest form of the passion narrative ended with the story of the burial and that the empty tomb story was placed in its present context by Mark (*Der gekreuzigte Christus*, 74, 77). Dormeyer also concluded that the earliest form of the passion narrative ended with the burial (15:46) but that a pre-Markan redactor added 16:1, 2b, 4a, 5, 6, 7, 8a (*Die Passion Jesu*, 221–29). Joel Green argued that the primitive passion account included the statement about the women at the crucifixion site but not the burial or resurrection stories (*Death of Jesus*, 310–13).

CONCLUSION

Several factors suggest that the hypothesis of a pre-Markan passion narrative is a sound one. Within the current form of Mark 14:32—15:39, a series of incidents can be discerned that have an apparently pre-Markan connection. These incidents have a greater narrative coherence than other portions of the Gospel of Mark. In part, this coherence is due to the inner logic of the events narrated, but probably also to the nature of the source used by Mark in this case. This source interpreted the death of Jesus by narrating it in terms of the traditional type of the suffering just person. Like the typical just one, Jesus placed his trust in God (the Gethsemane story), suffered without protest, and was vindicated (the opening of the veil before the Holy of Holies). This early document knew nothing of an atoning or sacrificial interpretation of Jesus' death. Such notions were familiar to the evangelist from other strands of tradition, and he made use of them at earlier points in the Gospel to interpret the death of Jesus. The notion of atonement appears in the saying that the Son of Man came to give his life as a ransom for many (10:45), and the sacrificial interpretation is suggested by the saying over the cup, that his blood was poured out for many (14:24). Such notions had already been combined with the motif of innocent suffering in 2 Macc 7:38. What is distinctive about the pre-Markan passion narrative, as reconstructed, is the combination of the role of the suffering just one with that of the Messiah. The occasion for the composition of the pre-Markan passion narrative was probably the need for a meaningful account of the death of Jesus to be read at the annual commemoration of his death in conjunction with Passover or at the celebration of the Lord's Supper. Such a liturgical document would have had missionary and catechetical significance as well.

Chapter Five

THE EMPTY TOMB
AND RESURRECTION
ACCORDING TO MARK

THE NARRATIVE CONCERNING the empty tomb in the Gospel of Mark is related to the phenomenon we call "the resurrection of Jesus." A number of interpretations of the resurrection of Jesus have been articulated, each based on a different set of fundamental presuppositions.

PERSPECTIVES ON THE RESURRECTION
OF JESUS

Some Christians argue, "Since the resurrection of Jesus is the heart of Christian faith, if he was not raised, Christian faith is a delusion." This argument is a restatement of 1 Cor 15:12-19. Others assert, "What is impossible with humankind is possible with God." This is a reformulation of a widespread ancient idea that appears in the prayer of Jesus in Gethsemane according to Mark (14:36).[1] This approach to the resurrection of Jesus is based on the authority of individual passages of Scripture that function as principles. For some, such a principle solves everything as far as the resurrection is concerned. With regard to the first example, one could dispute that the restatement accurately reflects Paul's argument. Or one could dispute that the resurrection

---

1. On the widespread character of this notion in the ancient world, especially in Greco-Roman culture, see Sharyn Echols Dowd, *Prayer, Power, and the Problem of Suffering: Mark 11:22-25 in the Context of Markan Theology* (Atlanta: Scholars Press, 1988).

of Jesus is the heart of Christian faith. On the latter point, one could show that entire books of the New Testament do not use resurrection language. The problem with the second example—that all things are possible for God—is that it does not help us much in most of the rest of life (keeping a house clean, getting a meal on the table, solving family problems).

Another approach is what we might call the canonical perspective. The underlying argument is basically: "The New Testament says that Jesus was raised, therefore he was." At present, this perspective has a growing number of adherents. A sophisticated version of it implies that we cannot know for certain whether Jesus was raised, or prove that we was, but the New Testament provides the language or the symbol system of Christian belief. To be Christian means to experience oneself and one's world in its terms.[2] The problem with this approach becomes apparent as soon as one recalls that the New Testament also says that slavery is to be accepted as part of Christian life. One could object that the resurrection of Jesus is foundational to Christianity, whereas acceptance of slavery is not. Such an objection, however, changes the rules of the game. The canonical perspective should take the entire canon into account. If one is to pick and choose, then criteria must be articulated for determining what is foundational and what is not.

A kind of pastoral perspective is often expressed: "People need assurance about life after death; therefore, I will tell them that the resurrection of Jesus gives them such assurance." It may well be that human beings need to believe in life beyond the grave. But most of us, except perhaps in foxholes and their equivalents, want to know that our beliefs are reliable. Some, even among the terminally ill, when presented with this argument will respond, "If that is all you can say, turn on the TV."

Many of the more reflective approaches, which we may call philosophical, share as a starting point the profound idea that death is not

2. This general perspective is that of the postliberal, cultural-linguistic school of theology, which characterizes the work of George Lindbeck, Stanley Hauerwas, and others. See the discussion of this point of view (in general, not in relation to the resurrection in particular) by Frederic B. Burnham, "The Bible and Contemporary Science," *The Bible and the Intellectual Life, Religion and Intellectual Life* 6 (1989) 60–61.

the end. Various formulations have been proposed. One posits individual, conscious afterlife in some form. Another affirms immortality through one's children, their children, and so on. A third envisions the extension of the individual into later time by the effects of one's deeds, writings, or other accomplishments. Along these lines, process theology speaks of a kind of objective immortality through one's chemical remains and the effects of one's deeds on society.

Another type of approach reflects the apparent importance of the natural sciences for thinking about the resurrection of Jesus. One point of view says that resurrection is physically impossible. No corpse could be resuscitated. Those who take this point of view reason from an alleged general law of nature to a specific historical situation. The position taken by Rudolf Bultmann is an example of this point of view, one that has been enormously influential in New Testament studies and theology in the twentieth century.[3] This position is not based on the actual results of research in any one of the special sciences. It is rather the product of a general worldview in which the natural scientific focus on the empirical has been made absolute and functions as a secular myth.

Another perspective of this general type interprets the resurrection as the transformation of matter from one form into another. Jesus' physical body was transformed into a spiritual state as water becomes steam.[4]

Whereas Bultmann assumed that historical inquiry must work within the limits set by the natural sciences, another position is that the point of view of the historian need not be determined by the natural sciences. A historical event is always particular; all the elements of one event will never be repeated exactly. For example, Richard R. Niebuhr asks whether it is not within the realm of historical probability that the elements of the resurrection of Jesus were present only once.[5]

3. Rudolf Bultmann, "Neues Testament und Mythologie: Das Problem der Entmythologisierung der neutestamentlichen Verkündigung," *Offenbarung und Heilsgeschehen* (BEvT 7; Munich: A. Lempp, 1941); repr. in *Kerygma und Mythos*, vol. 1 (ed. H. W. Bartsch; Hamburg-Volksdorf: Hebert Reich, 1948); ET: "New Testament and Mythology: The Mythological Element in the Message of the New Testament and the Problem of Its Reinterpretation," *Kerygma and Myth: A Theological Debate* (ed. H. W. Bartsch; rev. ed. Reginald Fuller; New York: Harper & Row, 1961).

4. C. F. D. Moule, "Introduction," *The Significance of the Message of the Resurrection for Faith in Jesus Christ* (ed. C. F. D. Moule; SBT 2/8; Naperville, Ill.: Allenson, 1968) 9–10.

5. Richard R. Niebuhr, *Resurrection and Historical Reason* (New York: Scribner's, 1957).

Recently there has been more interest in the implications of the social sciences for understanding the resurrection of Jesus than the natural sciences. A sociological perspective begins with the function of the resurrection of Jesus for the group of his disciples. An old and negative form of this approach is the theory that the disciples consciously and deliberately fabricated the story of the resurrection to cope with the death of Jesus and to continue his work. A more psychological approach has been taken by those who argue that the appearances of the risen Jesus were individual and, in some cases, collective visionary or hallucinatory experiences.

A socio-psychological theory of cognitive dissonance is very persuasive for some today. Cognitive dissonance may be defined as conflict between one's view of reality or one's expectations of the future and what seems on the surface to be the case. In more technical terms, it consists of dissonant or inconsistent relations among cognitive elements.[6] Dissonance or tension among perceptions or beliefs creates pressure to resolve or reduce that tension. The means of reducing the tension include changes in behavior, changes in cognition, and the seeking out of new information. This theory was applied first to apocalyptic expectations in the United States in the mid-twentieth century.[7] Before long, it was used to explain phenomena in the ancient world, including the resurrection of Jesus.[8] This theory could provide a psychological explanation for the appearances of the risen Jesus: they were visions produced unconsciously in order to resolve the tension created by the death of Jesus. The arrest and crucifixion of Jesus seemed to be disconfirming events of his disciples' belief that he was the definitive agent of God. Most applications of the theory to biblical literature, however, have focused on changes in behavior, such as increased missionary activity, and changes in beliefs attested by hermeneutical activity.[9]

6. Leon Festinger, *A Theory of Cognitive Dissonance* (Stanford, Calif.: Stanford Univ. Press, 1957).

7. Leon Festinger et al., *When Prophecy Fails: A Social and Psychological Study of a Modern Group that Predicted the Destruction of the World* (Minneapolis: Univ. of Minnesota Press, 1956).

8. Hugh Jackson, "The Resurrection Belief of the Earliest Church: A Response to the Failure of Prophecy?" *JR* 55 (1975) 415–25.

9. John G. Gager, *Kingdom and Community: The Social World of Early Christianity* (Englewood Cliffs, N.J.: Prentice-Hall, 1975) 37–43; Robert P. Carroll, *When Prophecy Failed: Cognitive Dissonance in the Prophetic Traditions of the Old Testament* (New York: Seabury, 1979) 124–28.

Two final perspectives should be mentioned: the historical and the literary. The historical approach is the attempt to determine what *probably*—not possibly—took place. Anything conceivable is possible; for example, that Jesus rode out of the tomb on a giant turtle. The historian asks the question, What can we construct from the evidence? The best discussion of the resurrection of Jesus from this point of view is that by Van Harvey in *The Historian and the Believer*.[10] The literary perspective has come into its own most recently.[11] The literary approach raises the question of the form and the nature of the claims being made in the sources. Are they scientific, mythological, historical, metaphorical, psychological, or what?

New Testament scholarship begins with the historical and literary approaches for several reasons:

1. The resurrection of Jesus is said to have taken place in the first century. Only those who debate this claim can avoid the historical approach.

2. The evidence about the resurrection is found in literary texts.

3. Christianity has always claimed to be a historical religion. It is not founded on timeless insight or deep experience in the Jungian sense. It is founded on events among people. Therefore the literary and historical approaches are essential.

4. All the other approaches depend on these two.

THE OLDEST TEXT: 1 CORINTHIANS 15

In taking a historical and literary approach to the resurrection of Jesus, it is most appropriate to begin with the oldest text that refers to it in some detail, namely, Paul's first letter to the Corinthians. This letter was written in the early 50s of the first century. Very few New Testament scholars today would date the earliest Gospel before 66 C.E. In chapter 15, beginning in verse 3, Paul cites pre-gospel tradition about the resurrection of Jesus. The terms *received* and *handed over* in vv 1 and 3 are technical terms that show he is reporting tradition.[12]

10. Van A. Harvey, *The Historian and the Believer* (New York: Macmillan, 1966).
11. See, for example, Norman Perrin, *The Resurrection according to Matthew, Mark, and Luke* (Philadelphia: Fortress, 1977).
12. Compare 1 Cor 11:23 in which the same verbs are used in citing the words of Jesus over the bread and wine at the last supper. That these terms were technical in the Hellenistic and Roman periods is shown by Hans Conzelmann, *1 Corinthians* (Hermeneia; Philadelphia: Fortress, 1975) 195.

The use of non-Pauline words and phrases in vv 3-5 supports the conclusion that we have tradition here.[13] Paul has clearly elaborated this tradition at least by adding comments about his own experience in vv 8-11. Whether he added comments to the tradition preserved in vv 3-7 is debated.[14]

First Corinthians 15 is an important historical source not only because it is early but also because it is written by a participant in the phenomenon under discussion. Paul's language shows clearly that he considered his experience of the risen Lord to be of the same nature as those of Peter and the rest of the twelve: "He appeared to [or was seen by] Cephas . . . he appeared also to [or was seen also by] me" (vv 5, 8).[15] Further, in this passage Paul does not simply repeat the tradition and state his experience. He goes to considerable lengths to explain how the notion of resurrection is to be understood (vv 35-50).

Paul's understanding of the resurrection of Jesus does not involve the revival of his corpse. The resurrected person has a "spiritual body" (v 44) that is not a slightly modified form of the physical body. The spiritual body is as different from the physical body as the plant is from the seed (vv 36-37). The physical body is terrestrial whereas the spiritual body is celestial (vv 40-41). Figurative use of language about seeds and plants was very common in the ancient world. To understand Paul's intention in using this figurative language, we must look very closely at his argument. The most important thing to notice is that Paul emphasizes the discontinuity between the seed and the plant: "What you show is not the body which is to be. . . . But God gives it a body as he has chosen, and to each kind of seed its own body" (1 Cor 15:37-38). In other words, for Paul the seed "dies" and God creates a plant in its place. Paul seems to have in mind here the phenomenon

13. See John Kloppenborg, "An Analysis of the Pre-Pauline Formula in 1 Cor 15:3b-5 in Light of Some Recent Literature," *CBQ* 40 (1978) 351–52, and the literature cited there.
14. See the discussion by Pheme Perkins, *Resurrection: New Testament Witness and Contemporary Reflection* (Garden City, N.Y.: Doubleday, 1984) 88–91.
15. The remark that Jesus appeared to Paul "last of all" (1 Cor 15:8) is not evidence that he distinguished the type of appearance he was granted from those of Peter and the twelve. On the contrary, it marks his experience as the last in a series of the same type of experiences. The remark that Jesus appeared to him "as to one prematurely born" (v 8) does not imply that the nature of the *appearance* was any different. It was Paul who was different—he was not even a disciple yet. This interpretation is supported by the remark in the following verse that he was persecuting the church of God (i.e., even at the time that Jesus appeared to him).

whereby the sprout of a new plant springs forth from that which is planted, such as a bean or a potato, and the "seed" itself shrivels and eventually decomposes. Of course, for Paul there is continuity between the dead person buried and the person who is raised. This is not, however, primarily *material* continuity in the sense of a relatively slight transformation of the body. It is rather the continuity of the person.

According to this interpretation, the phrase "that which you sow" in v 36 refers figuratively to the whole (dead) person who is buried. It is the whole person who "is not made alive unless one dies." In v 37 the referent of "that which you sow" has shifted a bit. Such a shift is not uncommon elsewhere in Paul's letters. In v 37 "that which you sow" refers figuratively to the physical, earthly body. It is not the same as "the body that will come into being," the spiritual, resurrected body.

In vv 42-44 there is a series of verbs, all of which are in the third person singular. The implied subject of these verbs needs to be expressed in an English translation. The possibilities include "he," "she," "one," and "it." The Greek is somewhat ambiguous. The antecedent of the implied subject could be the "seed" (*kokkon*) mentioned in v 37 or "that which you sow" (*ho speireis*) mentioned in vv 36 and 37. Both of these are rather distant from the series of verbs that begins in v 42. Since v 42 begins with the statement "So also [is] the resurrection of the dead [plural]," the most appropriate subject to supply is "[one of] the dead." Thus the following statements should be translated, "One is sown in corruption, one is raised in incorruption; one is sown in dishonor, one is raised in glory; one is sown in weakness, one is raised in power; one is sown as a body characterized by the principle of earthly life [*sōma psychikon*], one is raised as a body characterized by spirit [*sōma pneumatikon*]." The translation "one is sown as a body" seems odd only if one is unaware that Paul sometimes used the word *body* (*sōma*) to characterize the whole human person, albeit from a specific point of view (Phil 1:20; 1 Cor 6:15 [cf. 1 Cor 12:27]; 7:4; 9:27; 13:3; 2 Cor. 10:10; Rom 6:12; 12:1).[16]

Paul's understanding of resurrection is like that of Daniel 12. Most English translations of Dan 12:2 are misleading. For example, the RSV

16. See the classic study of the range of meaning of *sōma* in Paul's letters by Bultmann, *Theology of the New Testament* (2 vols.; New York: Scribner's, 1951–55) 1.192–203.

refers to "those who sleep in the dust of the earth." This translation is supported by the versions, but not by the MT. The Hebrew phrase is best translated "those who sleep in the land of dust."[17] This expression is not an allusion to bodies in graves. "The land of dust" is a description of Sheol or Hades, where the shades of the dead are confined.[18] Those who "awake" are not reunited with their physical bodies, but "shine like the brightness of the firmament," "like stars" (v 3). In other words, they are given celestial bodies, like those of the heavenly beings. That Paul's understanding of resurrection was similar to that expressed in Daniel 12 is supported by Paul's comparison of resurrected bodies to the sun, moon, and stars in 1 Cor 15:40-41. Both Daniel 12 and 1 Corinthians 15 express the notion of resurrection in terms of astral immortality.[19] Neither the book of Daniel nor Paul shows any interest in what happens to the physical body. Presumably it decays and has no importance for the resurrected person. This interpretation of Daniel 12 is supported by the description of personal afterlife for the righteous in the book of *Jubilees*: "And their bones shall rest in the earth, and their spirits shall have much joy" (*Jub.* 23:22). It is important to note that both Daniel 12 and the book of *Jubilees* are of Palestinian provenance.[20]

In Paul's understanding Jesus was transformed into a completely different kind of existence. The remark in v 50, "flesh and blood cannot inherit the kingdom of God, nor does the perishable inherit the imperishable," implies that the resurrection "body" is not material in the same way that the earthly body is. This interpretation is confirmed by the contrast in 2 Corinthians 5 between the earthly body as a "tent"

17. The NRSV gives this translation in a note to Dan 12:2.
18. R. H. Charles, *A Critical and Exegetical Commentary on the Book of Daniel* (ICC; Oxford: Clarendon, 1929) 327–28; see also George W. E. Nickelsburg, Jr., *Resurrection, Immortality, and Eternal Life in Intertestamental Judaism* (Cambridge: Harvard Univ. Press, 1972) 17.
19. On the notion of astral immortality in the ancient world, see Franz Cumont, *Lux Perpetua* (Paris: P. Geuthner, 1949).
20. On the variety of conceptions of resurrection and other forms of personal afterlife in Palestinian Judaism, see Friedrich Schwally, *Das Leben nach dem Tode: Nach den Vorstellungen des alten Israel und das Judentums einschliesslich das Volksglaubens im Zeitalter Christi* (Giessen: J. Ricker, 1892); K. Schubert, "Die Entwicklung der Auferstehungslehre von der nachexilischen bis zur frührabbinischen Zeit," *Biblische Zeitschrift*, n.f. 6 (1962) 177–214; H. C. C. Cavallin, *Life after Death: Paul's Argument for the Resurrection of the Dead in I Cor. 15*, Part 1, *An Enquiry into the Jewish Background* (Lund: Gleerup, 1974) 33–101.

that is to be folded up or destroyed and the heavenly "body" as an eternal "building" waiting for us in the heavens.[21] Thus for Paul, and presumably for many other early Christians, the resurrection of Jesus did not imply that his tomb was empty.

APPEARANCES AND EMPTY TOMB

Thus it is not surprising, although it is noteworthy, that the tradition Paul cited does not mention the empty tomb. In his own elaboration and discussion of the theme, Paul also does not mention the empty tomb. The summaries of the gospel in the book of Acts, which some scholars believe are older than the book of Acts itself, also fail to mention the empty tomb.[22] The fact that Paul, especially, does not mention it has led some scholars to argue that the tradition about the empty tomb was an apologetic invention intended to support the early Christian proclamation about the resurrection.[23] This theory has several problems. If such were the origin of the tradition, it is odd that it is not used apologetically in the book of Acts. Further, if the empty tomb story was invented to "prove" the resurrection of Jesus, it is odd that the only witnesses to the emptiness of the tomb, at least in Matthew and Mark, are women.[24] The status of women in the ancient world was such that a story fabricated as proof or apology would probably not be based on the testimony of women.

The empty tomb story is difficult for everyone, regardless of perspective. There is a major textual problem regarding the original ending of Mark. Text-critical principles and linguistic studies indicate that the

21. Paul's language about being "further clothed" rather than "naked" does not imply material continuity from earthly body to heavenly "body" (2 Cor 5:2-4). Rather it expresses his opposition to the notion that the soul is completely immaterial.

22. Acts 2:22-24; 3:13-15; 4:10-12; 5:30-32. The book of Acts is, of course, considerably later than the Gospel of Mark. Whether one can reconstruct sources used by the author of Acts is disputed. It is generally agreed that no continuous source was used in chaps. 1–5 (Ernst Haenchen, *The Acts of the Apostles: A Commentary* [Philadelphia: Westminster, 1971] 81–90). The empty tomb is presupposed in Acts 2:25-31 and 13:34-37. These passages may be dependent on older tradition, but it is not clear that such tradition is as old as the Gospel of Mark (ibid., 3–4, 409, 411). The passages in question may represent a strand of tradition unknown to Mark and Paul.

23. Rudolf Bultmann, *The History of the Synoptic Tradition* (trans. John Marsh; rev. ed.; New York: Harper & Row, 1963) 290.

24. In Matthew, of course, the guards see the angel and know that the tomb is emtpy. It is generally agreed, however, that the story of the guards at the tomb and the lie that they spread about the disciples stealing the body is later than the empty tomb story and is definitely apologetic. One of the problems that this story addresses indirectly is the reliability of women as witnesses.

original ending was 16:8.[25] Another difficulty is that the list of women varies among the Gospels; some argue that it varies even within Mark. The status of the stone varies among the Gospels. Within Mark, why do the women go without having a plan for moving the stone? Whether Jesus was anointed before burial varies among the Gospels. Within Mark, why do the women intend to anoint Jesus on the second day after his death? Assuming that Mark ended with 16:8, the women are told to tell but they do not. Why not? Was the empty tomb tradition new with Mark? Is their silence meant to explain why the tradition about the empty tomb was not known before Mark was written?

Another problem is who really buried Jesus. According to Acts 13:29 it was his enemies. According to the Synoptics it was Joseph of Arimathea. It is quite credible that Acts 13:29 is as precise a historical report of the burial of Jesus as can be reconstructed. The Joseph story may be an apologetic legend; at least it seems to grow into one, as is evident from a comparison of the four canonical Gospels.

Some argue that the very fact that the empty tomb tradition is only loosely related to the tradition of appearances of the risen Jesus is evidence that the empty tomb tradition is equally old.[26] Most New Testament scholars at present accept the argument that the Gospel of Mark is the oldest Gospel. In the opinion of this majority, Mark 16:1-8 is therefore the oldest attestation of the tradition that the tomb was empty.[27] One's judgment about the age of the empty tomb tradition will depend on the literary question regarding the origin of this passage.[28] The options are: (1) it is based on a pre-Markan passion narrative; (2) it is based on another source, oral or written, adapted by the author of Mark; and (3) it was composed by the author of Mark.

25. At least these studies indicate that the material that follows Mark 16:8 in many manuscripts is not original. Some scholars argue that the original ending of Mark has been lost or suppressed. See, for example, Bultmann, *History*, 285 n. 2. In this essay, the assumption is made that the Gospel ended with 16:8, since that is the earliest recoverable ending. Any attempt to reconstruct an earlier ending would be unduly speculative.
26. So, for example, Perkins, *Resurrection*, 90.
27. P. Benoit has argued that John 20 contains an older form of the empty tomb tradition (cited by Joachim Jeremias, "Die älteste Schicht der Osterüberlieferungen," *Resurrexit: Actes du symposium international sur la résurrection de Jésus* [ed. E. Dhanis; Rome: Libreria Editrice Vaticana, 1974] 189–90; ET: J. Jeremias, *New Testament Theology: The Proclamation of Jesus* [New York: Scribner's, 1971] 304–5); but this hypothesis is unlikely; see John Dominic Crossan, "Empty Tomb and Absent Lord (Mark 16:1-8)," *The Passion in Mark: Studies in Mark 14–16* (ed. Werner H. Kelber; Philadelphia: Fortress, 1976) 138–45.
28. As Crossan puts it, there may have been a presumption that the tomb was empty

THE LITERARY HISTORY OF
MARK 16:1-8

Those who assume a pre-Markan passion narrative that included some form of the empty tomb story explain the agreements and continuities between chapters 15 and 16 as evidence for the use of the same source for the two chapters. Those who dispute the existence of such a source, or who think it ended with the death or burial of Jesus, explain the elements of continuity as the result of composition or editing by the author of Mark. I have concluded that there was a pre-Markan passion narrative that ended with the account of the death of Jesus.[29] The statement about the women in 15:40-41 was placed there by Mark to prepare for the narrative about the discovery of the empty tomb. The story about the burial (15:42-46) may be based on tradition, but at least its placement is due to Mark. It lacks the topographical specificity of the pre-Markan passion narrative; the vagueness about the location of the tomb is not in keeping with the character of the older narrative. The second statement about the women in 15:47 is also due to Mark. It too prepares for the empty tomb story.

Several types of arguments are brought forward as evidence that the author of Mark made use of a brief, self-contained source in composing 16:1-8. The burial scene at the end of chapter 15 and the empty tomb story are said not to "match."[30] The names of the women are said to differ in the two chapters.[31] The burial described in 15:46 is said not to be incomplete. Thus there is tension between the account of the burial and the motivation for the women's visit to the tomb. It is also claimed that, from the point of view of the author of Mark, Jesus was already anointed for burial by the anonymous woman in the anecdote recounted in 14:3-9. Early form critics saw the passage about the woman anointing Jesus as an insertion by the author of Mark into the pre-Markan passion narrative.

---

prior to the formulation of Mark 16:1-8 (or its source), but a presumption is not a tradition ("Empty Tomb," 136).

29. See chap. 4, "The Passion Narrative of Mark."

30. See, for example, Perkins, *Resurrection*, 115.

31. Bultmann argued that Mark 16:1-8 was independent of the sections of Mark that went before. If the narrative about the empty tomb had followed upon the narratives of the crucifixion and burial, he argued, the names of the women would not have needed to be given again in 16:1 (*History*, 284–85). Given the importance of the events being narrated, however, it is understandable that the names would have been given each time. The repetition is softened by variation in the form of the name of the second woman (see above). But this repetition does not necessarily imply the use of a source.

The names of the women are given for the first time in 15:40 as Mary Magdalene, Mary the mother of James the younger and Joses, and Salome. Here they are presented as witnesses to the crucifixion. Two of these women are mentioned again in 15:47 as Mary Magdalene and Mary the mother of Joses. In this context they are presented as witnesses to the burial of Jesus by Joseph of Arimathea. In the beginning of the empty tomb story, three women are introduced as Mary Magdalene, Mary the mother of James, and Salome. There is no compelling reason to think that the three women referred to in 16:1 are not the same three mentioned in 15:40. It is true that the references to them are not verbally identical. But the differences may be explained perfectly well as stylistic variations that avoid monotonous repetition. It is the wording of the reference to the second woman that varies. In the second two instances the reference is shortened, first in one way, then in another. Such shortening is understandable given the lengthiness of the full reference in the first instance (15:40). Thus these differences are not evidence for the use of a source in 16:1-8.[32]

The account of the burial of Jesus by Joseph of Arimathea in chapter 15 does not mention anointing of the body with aromatic spices. Raymond Brown has made a credible case that, from the point of view of the author of Mark, this burial is a dishonorable burial, the type afforded a criminal.[33] He argues that Joseph performs it not out of reverence for Jesus but in order to observe the commandment of Deut 21:22-23: "When someone is convicted of a crime punishable by death and is executed, and you hang him on a tree, his corpse must not remain all night upon the tree; you shall bury him that same day, for anyone hung on a tree is under God's curse. You must not defile the land that the LORD your God is giving you for possession." The relevance of this commandment, or one like it, is implied in Mark 15:42-43: "And when evening had come, since it was the day of Preparation, that is, the day before the sabbath, Joseph of Arimathea, a respected member of the council . . . went to Pilate." The implied reference to sunset (*opsias genomenēs*, v 42) supplies the motivation for Joseph's

32. The fact that the third woman, Salome, is not mentioned as a witness to the burial is not significant for the question of sources. It does not seem to be sufficient evidence to warrant the conclusion that the pericope about the burial was once a separate anecdote.
3. Raymond E. Brown, "The Burial of Jesus (Mark 15:42-47)," *CBQ* 50 (1988) 233–45.

request that Pilate allow him to bury the body. In the case of a dishonorable burial, anointing was not necessarily customary and should not be supplied by the modern reader. If this is an accurate reading of the burial story in its historical and literary context, this burial would have seemed incomplete to the disciples of Jesus. Thus within the narrative of Mark the coming of the women to the tomb to anoint the body would be motivated and would fit with the previous narrative.

The argument that Mark would not have composed a narrative involving women going to the tomb to anoint Jesus, because he had already been anointed by the anonymous woman, is not strong. The relationship between the two passages may be understood in terms of Markan compositional technique. In the first place, the intention of the women is ironic: there will be no body to anoint, since Jesus has not remained in the grave.[34] Second, the appearance of the motif of anointing in chapter 16 reminds the reader of the earlier passage and encourages reflection on its significance.

Another argument brought to bear is that certain verses in this passage are "overloaded" with particular kinds of markers. The point is that the source had its markers and the author of Mark added his own. For example, 16:2 is said to "pile up" temporal indicators.[35] The first such indicator is *lian prōi* ("very early"). Since a similar Greek phrase appears also in 1:35 (*prōi ... lian*), its use here is attributed to the author of Mark.[36] The second is *tē mia tōn sabbatōn* ("on the first day of the week" or "on the first day after the Sabbath"). It has been argued that this temporal expression is a Semitic phrase that Mark has retained from his source.[37] If this is a Semitic expression obscure enough to warrant the conclusion of the use of a source here, it is odd that the author of Luke preserves it without correction in the parallel to this passage (Luke 24:1) and also uses it in Acts 20:7, when, presumably, composing freely.[38] The third indicator is *anateilantos tou hēliou* ("after the sun had risen"). A "double step" compositional technique has been recognized elsewhere in Mark, in which

---

34. See the discussion of irony in David Rhoads and Donald Michie, *Mark as Story: An Introduction to the Narrative of a Gospel* (Philadelphia: Fortress, 1982) 59–62.

35. Perkins, *Resurrection*, 117.

36. For example, R. Pesch, cited by Perkins, ibid. See also Crossan, "Empty Tomb," 146–47.

37. J. Kremer, cited by Perkins, *Resurrection*, 117. Crossan argues that this phrase fits the Markan chronological framework ("Empty Tomb," 147).

38. See Haenchen, *Acts*, 586.

a second phrase qualifies the first. [39] If one rejects the theory that the phrase "on the first day of the week" comes from a source, then the first two indicators may be seen as one: "very early on the first day of the week." Then the phrase "after the sun had risen" may be seen as a second phrase, qualifying the first in typical Markan fashion. More significantly, the temporal markers in 16:1-2 may be seen as the author's attempt to explain why the women did not try to anoint Jesus sooner. They had to wait until the Sabbath was over to purchase the spices (v 1); then they went to the tomb at the earliest feasible time—as soon as it was light (v 2).

Another kind of "overloading" has been perceived in 16:8. This verse has several references to fear. The second clause states that *tromos* ("trembling") and *ekstasis* ("astonishment") seized the women. The word *tromos* does not appear elsewhere in Mark. It appears four other times in the New Testament in the combination *phobos kai tromos* ("fear and trembling"). The word *ekstasis* is used in Mark 5:42 to express the astonishment of the onlookers when Jesus raises the daughter of Jairus from the dead. Some argue that these two words expressing fear are rare, whereas the verb used in the last clause ("and they said nothing to anyone, for they were afraid [*ephobounto*]") and the related noun (*phobos*) occur often in Mark in connection with the disciples.[40] Against this argument it must be pointed out that *tromos* is hardly a rare word. In addition, the word *ekstasis* appears twice in Mark, in both cases in the same sense, and both times the context is related to resurrection. Linguistic arguments alone do not compel the conclusion that the "overloading" of this verse with references to fear is evidence for the use of a source.

Both cases of alleged "overloading" may be understood as features of composition rather than of editing. The several indications of time in v 2 may be understood in various ways, for example, as an attempt at verisimilitude or at accurate reporting. The several expressions of fear in v 8 may have been used for dramatic effect. It may well be that the last two clauses link this incident with an aspect of the theme of discipleship in the Gospel. But such a link does not necessarily imply that the preceding clause comes from a source.

39. Perkins, *Resurrection*, 117 and 140 n. 13, citing Rhoads and Michie, *Mark as Story*, 47–49.
40. Perkins (*Resurrection*, 121–22) and those cited by her (ibid., 143 n. 44).

These linguistic arguments, weak in themselves, are meant to bolster a form-critical argument against the unity of this passage.[41] Legendary elements in the passage have been pointed out, such as the motif of the large stone and the implicit quest for a helper to remove the stone.[42] Similarly, apocalyptic elements relating to narratives about the appearance of an angel, the genre "angelophany" or "angelic epiphany," have been noted. The discernment of both legendary and apocalyptic elements in Mark 16:1-8, however, does not warrant the conclusion that they could not occur together in a single, unified narrative.[43]

Some see the command of the angel to the women to go and tell the disciples and Peter that "he goes before you to Galilee" in v 7 as secondary and thus as evidence of a source. For example, Bultmann argued that the speech of the angel originally functioned simply to point out the empty tomb as evidence for the resurrection (v 6). In his view the author of Mark added the command in v 7 to link the empty tomb tradition connected with Jerusalem to the tradition of appearances in Galilee.[44] This argument, however, is bound up with Bultmann's opinion that the Gospel of Mark could not have ended with 16:8. His reconstruction of how the Gospel "must have ended" is overly speculative. Nevertheless, many scholars have agreed with him that v 7 was added to an existing story.[45] The most obvious reason for seeing this verse as Markan composition is its connection with 14:28. Soon after Jesus and the disciples arrive on the Mount of Olives, Jesus tells them that after he is raised he will go before them to Galilee. In chapter 16 the angel asks the women to remind the disciples of this promise.

The link between 16:7 and 14:28 is obviously insufficient evidence by itself to require the conclusion that a source was used in 16:1-8.

41. E. Bickermann attempted to define a literary form that could be called "translation story" or "removal story" and then to argue that the source used by the author of Mark in 16:1-8 was such a story ("Das leere Grab," ZNW 23 [1924] 281–92). Bultmann rightly disagreed and concluded that there is insufficient evidence that such a story lies behind Mark 16:1-8 (History, 290 n. 3). The conclusion that the literary form "translation story" does not define Mark 16:1-8 or its alleged source does not mean that such stories or the notions they express had no influence on the passage.

42. Perkins, Resurrection, 118.

43. F. Neirynck has written an extensive survey of attempts to reconstruct the source used in Mark 16:1-8 (cited by Perkins, ibid., 138 n. 2 and 139 nn. 9 and 10).

44. Bultmann, History, 285, 287. So also J. Delorme (cited by Perkins, Resurrection, 121, 143 n. 41). But see the reservations of Fuller and Pesch (ibid., 143 n. 41).

45. For example, J. Kremer, J. Delorme, R. H. Fuller, and A. Lindemann (cited by Perkins) and Perkins herself (Resurrection, 116, 120, and 140 nn. 16 and 17).

A deeper reason for seeing 16:7 as redactional, rather than as part of a unified composition by the author of Mark, is the perceived tension between the command of the angel and the response of the women. Wilhelm Bousset argued long ago that the statement in v 8, "and they said nothing to anyone," referred originally to the discovery of the empty tomb (v 6), not to the command that they give the disciples the message about Galilee (v 7). According to Bousset, the point of their silence was to explain why the story of the empty tomb had remained unknown for so long.[46] A number of scholars have contended that the reminder that Jesus goes before the disciples to Galilee implies the restoration of Peter after his denial and of all the disciples after their flight.[47] Pheme Perkins concluded that the implication of restoration may be the import of 16:7 as pre-Markan tradition, but not of the passage as a whole in the intention of the author. She seems to imply that the tension between v 7 and the context supports the hypothesis that a source was used.[48] At the same time, however, she admits that the element of restoration may be seen as a feature of Markan redaction. Her own interpretation of the passage as a whole makes sense of the tension as a paradoxical affirmation that the disciples will be Jesus' witnesses, in spite of their incomprehension and fear, combined with an implicit warning to the readers not to repeat the pattern of both the male and the female disciples.[49] Another possibility is that the silence of the women is not to be taken literally but is a conventional expression of the human reaction to the numinous. In any case, it should be apparent that the hypothesis of a source is unnecessary to explain or resolve the tensions in the passage.

MARK 16:1-8 AS A
UNIFIED COMPOSITION

Mark 16:1-8 may be seen then as a unified and effective composition. It continues chapter 15 logically and appropriately. Joseph buried the body of Jesus just before or just as the Sabbath was beginning. It is

46. Wilhelm Bousset, cited by Bultmann, *History*, 285.
47. Fuller, E. L. Bode, Rhoads and Michie (cited by Perkins, *Resurrection*, 121, 143 n. 42).
48. Perkins, *Resurrection*, 121.
49. Ibid., 121 and 122–23.

implied, however, that the women do not accept that burial as adequate. As soon as the Sabbath ends, presumably at sunset or shortly thereafter, the women purchase the aromatic spices needed to anoint Jesus (v 1). Then they wait, presumably for the sake of safety or propriety, until sunrise to go to the tomb (v 2). Their question to one another on the way to the tomb, "Who will roll away the stone for us from the door of the tomb," creates dramatic tension and leads the reader to expect something extraordinary to occur (v 3). The arrival of the women at the tomb is narrated very strikingly. They see that the stone has already been rolled away from the entrance to the tomb. The extraordinary character of this situation is brought out by the remark that the stone was very large (v 4). Some scholars have argued that the removal of the stone is significant for how the reader of Mark is intended to conceive of the resurrection of Jesus. We shall return to this point later. The next verse builds dramatically on the previous one. The extraordinary situation of the stone is followed by an even more uncanny incident. When the women enter the tomb, a young man is there dressed in a white robe (v 5). It is clear that this young man, in spite of the parallel with the young man in 14:51-52, is not presented as a human being.[50] It is a well-known apocalyptic convention to speak of angelic beings as "men."[51] The white robe is also a conventional attribute of heavenly beings.[52] The reaction of the women is described in very strong terms: *exethambēthēsan* ("they were amazed").[53]

The description of the appearance of the angel is so restrained that it does not seem appropriate to characterize the passage as an angelic epiphany. More importantly, the focus of the passage is on the empty tomb, not on the angel; his role is to point out its significance. Thus the young man plays the role of the *angelus interpres*, a narrative role

50. If the author of Mark had intended to imply that the "young man" of 16:5 was identical with "a certain young man" mentioned in 14:51, he would have used the definite article in 16:5.

51. See, for example, Dan 8:15-16; 9:21; 10:5. The term translated "young man" in Mark 16:5 is *neaniskos*. A related word, *neanias*, is used of angels in 2 Macc 3:26 and 33 and in Josephus *Ant.* 5.277.

52. See Dan 7:9; 2 Macc 11:8-10; Acts 1:10.

53. The author of Mark is the only New Testament writer to use this word. It may express simple surprise (9:15) or the deepest kind of emotion (14:33); see Vincent Taylor, *The Gospel According to St. Mark* (2d ed.; Grand Rapids, Mich.: Baker, 1966) 396, 552, 606.

common in apocalyptic literature and other texts influenced by it.[54] His exhortation to the women that they not be amazed (v 6) is a typical angelic reassurance relating to the consternation and fear of the human recipient of revelation.[55] The rest of the speech of the angel, including v 7, has the narrative function of interpreting the empty tomb. The remarks following the reassurance, from "You seek Jesus, the Nazarene, who was crucified" to "see the place where they laid him" (v 6), have at least the implicit function of making the point that the women have come to the right place. They have not confused the grave of Jesus with another, empty grave. In the center of this first pronouncement is the key interpretation of the empty tomb, "he has been raised" (ēgerthē). In the narrative context of Mark 16, the announcement of the resurrection of Jesus serves to interpret the empty tomb. As I shall argue, in the history of the tradition their relationship is the opposite: the author of Mark has interpreted the early Christian proclamation of the resurrection of Jesus by composing a narrative about the empty tomb.[56]

The second pronouncement of the angel, "But go, tell his disciples and Peter, 'He goes before you into Galilee; there you will see him, just as he said to you' " (v 7), indicates the significance of the empty tomb for the disciples. It is the first stage in the fulfillment of the prophecy Jesus gave them on the Mount of Olives. At the moment in which the angel is speaking to the women within the narrative, the first part of Jesus' prophecy, "after I am raised up" (14:28), has been fulfilled. Some scholars have argued that the renewed promise, "there you will see him" (16:7), refers to the parousia, that is, to the return of Jesus on the clouds as Son of Man.[57] This interpretation is unlikely because language of "power" and "glory" associated with the parousia

54. So Bultmann, *History*, 287, 290. The *angelus interpres* sometimes interprets a vision (Dan 7:15-18; 8:15-26) and sometimes explains a situation (Dan 9:21-23; 10:2-14). Note that this same device is used to comment on the significance of the ascension in Acts 1:10-11.

55. Compare, for example, Dan 8:17-18; 10:8-12.

56. See the discussion by Perkins (*Resurrection*, 119) of the kerygmatic elements in Mark 16:6.

57. Theodore J. Weeden, *Mark: Traditions in Conflict* (Philadelphia: Fortress, 1971) 111–16; and N. Q. Hamilton, "Resurrection Tradition and the Composition of Mark," *JBL* 84 (1965) 415–21. Werner Kelber and John Dominic Crossan hold this view, but understand the parousia in Mark in terms of the realization of the kingdom of God in the activity of the followers of Jesus in Galilee (Kelber, *The Kingdom in Mark* [Philadelphia: Fortress, 1974] 105, 107, 140, 146; Crossan, "Empty Tomb," 146, 148–49).

elsewhere in Mark (9:1; 13:26; cf. 14:62) does not occur here. The parousia and Galilee are not associated anywhere else in the Gospel. It is more likely that the promise alludes to the same tradition of appearances that Paul recounts in 1 Cor 15:5.[58]

It was standard literary practice in the ancient world to allude to well-known events that occurred after those being narrated in a text without actually narrating those later events.[59] The *Iliad* is perhaps the best-known example of this technique.[60] Thus the fact that the appearances are not narrated in Mark does not necessarily mean that the author believed that they did not occur or wanted to suppress them. The main problem is how to interpret the relationship between the angel's announcement and the conclusion of the narrative in v 8.

The first part of v 8, "And they went out and fled from the tomb, for trembling and amazement had seized them," is understandable as an example of the typical human reaction of terror in the presence of the numinous. The second part of the verse, "and they said nothing to any one, for they were afraid," is a stupifyingly abrupt ending to the Gospel. Werner Kelber has historicized this ending, claiming that it means that the twelve and the members of Jesus' family rejected his intention that the kingdom of God on earth, the Christian community, be established in Galilee. The twelve never got the message. In any case, they and the family of Jesus preferred to stay in Jerusalem, closer to the center of power as they understood it and the place with which their own eschatological expectations were associated.[61] It is surprising that a scholar with so much literary sensitivity, who has argued that the Gospel of Mark is "parabolic,"[62] should insist on defining the meaning of v 8 so absolutely. It seems more appropriate to see this ending as deliberately provocative and open-ended, as numerous scholars in this century have taught us to read the parables of Jesus. It lures the reader to reflect on the events narrated and on one's own relation to those events. The disciples function in a complex way as both positive and negative examples or role models.

58. Perkins, *Resurrection*, 120.
59. See J. Lee Magness, *Sense and Absence: Structure and Suspension in the Ending of Mark's Gospel* (Atlanta: Scholars Press, 1986).
60. Ibid., 30–31.
61. Werner H. Kelber, *Mark's Story of Jesus* (Philadelphia: Fortress, 1979) 83–87.
62. Idem, *The Oral and the Written Gospel* (Philadelphia: Fortress, 1983) 117–29.

With regard to the eschatological events, the lack of narration of the appearances makes the impression on the reader that the chain of eschatological events is not yet completed. The narratives of the appearances of the risen Jesus in Matthew, Luke, and John round off the story. Matthew and Luke still express eschatological expectation, but it is balanced by the sense of the presence of the risen Lord with the community. Mark lacks such a satisfying denouement. One result is that the readers are asked to complete the story not only by imagining the fulfillment of the promise of appearances, as 14:28 and 16:7 should probably be interpreted, but also by imagining the fulfillment of the dramatic and vivid promises that the Son of Man would return (13:24-27; 14:62).

THE ANCIENT NOTION OF TRANSLATION

The idea that a human being could be removed from the sphere of ordinary humanity and made immortal is very ancient. The oldest narrative known to me of such an event is found on a tablet excavated in Nippur that contains part of the Sumerian flood story.[63] The hero of this story is the king Ziusudra. A deity informs him that there will be a flood and instructs him to build a huge boat. After the flood Ziusudra offers sacrifice. Near the end of the passage that is preserved, it is said that the gods Anu and Enlil cherished Ziusudra. They give him life like a god. They give him breath eternal like (that of) a god. They cause him to dwell at the place where the sun rises. These honors are granted him apparently because he is the preserver of vegetation and the seed of humankind.

In the Akkadian *Gilgamesh Epic*, Gilgamesh journeys through a great mountain range and over the Waters of Death to reach the flood hero, who in this epic is named Utnapishtim.[64] The purpose of the quest is to obtain the secret of immortality. In tablet XI of the epic, Utnapishtim recounts the story of the flood for Gilgamesh. At the end of the story he tells how the god Enlil announced: "Henceforth Utnapishtim and his wife shall be like unto us gods. Utnapishtim shall reside far away, at the mouth of the rivers."[65] Earlier in the epic it was

63. See S. N. Kramer's translation in *ANET*, 43–44.
64. See E. A. Speiser's translation in *ANET*, 73–97.
65. Ibid., 95.

said that Utnapishtim had "joined the Assembly (of the gods)."[66] In the *Atrahasis Epic*, which includes a Babylonian version of the flood on tablet III, a similar story is told about the flood hero Atrahasis and his wife.[67]

In the Hebrew Bible it is not the flood hero Noah who was translated but the antediluvian patriarch Enoch. His destiny is tersely related in Genesis 5. It is said that "Enoch walked with God" (vv 22 and 24) and that "he was not, for God took him" (v 24). It is not said that Moses was translated. The book of Deuteronomy states that he died in the land of Moab (34:5). But it also states that God buried him and that no one knows the place of his burial (v 6). These latter remarks suggested to later readers that Moses had in fact been translated. The translation of Elijah is described in vivid detail in 2 Kings 2. This transition, unlike that of Enoch, is explicitly said to have been witnessed (by Elisha).

The oldest Greek texts that speak of translations of human beings are the *Iliad* and the *Odyssey*. According to the *Iliad*, Tros, the lord of the Trojans, had three sons. One of these, Ganymedes, because of his unsurpassed beauty, was caught up by the gods to themselves, made immortal, and made the cupbearer of Zeus (20.230–35). The mortal Tithonos is mentioned in this context as the descendant of one of Ganymedes' brothers (20.237). Earlier the epic mentioned his translation by the goddess Dawn (11.1). This allusion presupposes a tradition that Dawn had made Tithonos immortal to be her spouse and to dwell by the River Okeanos where Dawn rises (cf. 19.1–2).[68]

In book 4 of the *Odyssey*, Menelaos, the husband of Helen, tells Telemachos how he tricked the god Proteus into advising him how to make his way home and giving him news of his companions. Proteus's revelations include a prophecy that Menelaos will not die; rather the gods will cause him to dwell on the Elysian Plain at the (spatial) end of the world, where life is as pleasant as on Mount Olympos. The reason given for this great blessing is that he is, as husband of Helen,

66. Ibid., 88.
67. Ibid., 104–6.
68. The story of Kleitos, the mortal son of Manios, has similarities with both the story of Ganymedes and of Tithonos. Kleitos was carried off by Dawn to live among the gods because of his beauty (*Od.* 15.248–52).

139

a son of Zeus (4.560–70).[69] Menelaos is to join Rhadamanthys, who apparently was transported to the Elysian Plain earlier, according to tradition. The details of his story are lost, but it is interesting to note that he was also said to be a son of Zeus (*Il.* 14.321–22). The similarity between "son of Zeus" and "son of God" should be noted.

All these traditions imply that the human beings translated became gods, that is, immortal. They seem to assume that in these cases the soul (*psychē*) was never separated from the body.[70] In some cases, however, the human being in question dies first and then is made immortal. The *Aithiopis*, a continuation of the *Iliad* that survives only in references to it in other authors, tells how Memnon, the Ethiopian prince, brought help to the Trojans. He is slain by Achilles, whereupon Memnon's mother, Dawn, obtains permission from Zeus to carry his body to the end of the earth in the East and there to grant immortality to her son.[71] According to the same epic poem, when Achilles was slain and placed on his funeral pyre, his mother, the divine Thetis, carried his body from the pyre to White Island. The extract does not say so, but the story probably continued with an account of how she restored him to life there and made him immortal.[72]

All the traditions discussed so far involve immortal life in regions on the surface of the earth, most of which are normally not accessible to humanity. Another type of translation story involves removal beneath the earth and subterranean immortality, often in a cave.[73] This type of immortality is analogous to that of the "heroes," who died, were buried, and from their graves gave proof of a higher existence and powerful influence.[74] It is noteworthy that the later belief in heroes required a grave at which the continued existence and potency of the hero was localized.[75] Erwin Rohde's reconstruction of one of the

69. Women, as well as men, were said to have been translated. There is a tradition that Helen herself was made immortal and made to dwell on the White Island or in the Islands of the Blest (Erwin Rohde, *Psyche: The Cult of Souls and Belief in Immortality among the Greeks* [New York: Harcourt Brace Jovanovich, 1925] 83 n. 21). The nereid Leukothea was once the mortal Ino (*Od.* 5.333–35). There was also a tradition that Iphigeneia, the daughter of Agamemnon, was not sacrificed but was translated by Artemis and made immortal in the land of the Taurians (Rohde, *Psyche*, 64).
70. Rohde, *Psyche*, 57.
71. Ibid., 64.
72. Ibid., 64–65.
73. Ibid., 89–92.
74. Ibid., 97.
75. Ibid., 98.

traditions associated with the hero Hyakinthos is instructive. Originally a chthonic deity, he was later transformed into a hero, who died, was buried, and then was translated to heaven.[76]

The case of Asklepios as hero is also instructive. According to this tradition, he was a mortal who was transformed into an immortal by a flash of Zeus's lightning.[77] Part of this tradition is that Asklepios was buried.[78] Thus his story also is that of a hero who died, was buried, and then was translated.

The focus on the tomb in Mark may have been inspired by the importance of the graves of the heroes in the Greco-Roman world. Even if the location of the tomb of Jesus was unknown to the author of Mark, and even if there were no cultic observances at the site of the tomb, it would still be important as a *literary* motif in characterizing Jesus as herolike.[79]

An example that does not involve the death of the hero but is instructive for the role of the angel in Mark 16 is the case of Kleomedes of Astypalaia, related by Pausanias and several other writers. Kleomedes killed his opponent in the boxing match at the seventy-first Olympic festival (486 B.C.E.) and was therefore disqualified. In his anger at this turn of events, he behaved destructively upon his return home and caused the death of some boys. He fled to the temple of Athena and hid in a chest. When his pursuers forced open the chest, Kleomedes was not inside. Envoys were sent to inquire of the oracle. They were told that he had become a hero and must be honored with sacrifice. The oracle is able to explain a supernatural occurrence to human inquirers because the oracle sees such events as one spirit sees another.[80] This perspective is instructive both for the role of the angel at the empty tomb and for the role of the demons or unclean spirits in Mark who know that Jesus is the Son of God.

Finally, the case of Herakles should be mentioned. In agony because of the poison on his garment, he made his own funeral pyre and mounted it. Apollodorus says, "While the pyre was burning, it is said

---

76. Ibid., 99–100.
77. Ibid., 100, 582.
78. Ibid., 101.
79. On the hypothesis that there were cultic observances performed at the tomb of Jesus from an early date, see Perkins, *Resurrection*, 93–94, 119.
80. Rohde, *Psyche*, 129–30. See also the story of Aristeas, related by Herodotus and discussed by Arthur S. Pease, "Some Aspects of Invisibility," *HSCP* 53 (1942) 29.

that a cloud passed under [Herakles] and with a peal of thunder wafted him up to heaven. Thereafter he obtained immortality, and being reconciled to Hera he married her daughter Hebe, by whom he had sons."[81] The traditional mythic view is obviously that immortal life is much like mortal life and that Herakles was embodied in his afterlife. Another interpretation is that the pyre burned away the mortal part of his nature (inherited from his mortal mother), so that the immortal part (inherited from his father Zeus) could ascend to the gods.[82] The Pythian priestess had promised Herakles immortality upon completion of the ten labors or tasks (Apollodorus *Library* 2.4.12). Later writers interpreted this as an honor granted because of his great benefactions to humankind.

In the Hellenistic and early Roman periods these traditions of translation and deification were widespread. The Hellenistic Babylonian historian Berossus, writing in Greek, retold the ancient flood story. In his version the flood hero is named Xisouthros. In recounting his translation, Berossus says that he "disappeared" (*aphanē*), a term that had become almost technical in describing such occurrences.[83] A new element in the account is Berossus's explanation of the event: he was translated because of his piety. Josephus describes Enoch's translation with the words "he returned to the divinity" (*Ant.* 1.85). He uses an expression similar to Berossus's in describing the translation of Elijah: "Elijah disappeared from among human beings." A little further on, he says of both Enoch and Elijah that "they became invisible and no one knows of their death" (*Ant.* 9.28). The expression "become invisible" is synonymous with "disappear" and is also typical of Hellenistic accounts of translation.[84]

The terminology used by Josephus makes clear that he was presenting Enoch, Moses, and Elijah as Jewish forefathers who had not

81. Apollodorus *The Library* 2.7.7 (trans. James G. Frazer; LCL; Cambridge: Harvard Univ. Press, 1921) 1.271–72.
82. So Lucian *Hermotimus* 7, cited by Frazer, ibid., 271.
83. For the text of Berossus, see Felix Jacoby, *Die Fragmente der griechischen Historiker, part 3: Geschichte von Staedten und Voelkern, C: Autoren ueber einzelne Laender* (Leiden: Brill, 1958) 380; for other examples of the use of this term, see G. Lohfink, *Die Himmelfahrt Jesu* (SANT 26; Munich: Kösel, 1971) 41 n. 58.
84. On these passages, see Christopher Begg, " 'Josephus's Portrayal of the Disappearances of Enoch, Elijah, and Moses': Some Observations," *JBL* 109 (1990) 691–93. Begg's note is a response to an article by James D. Tabor, " 'Returning to the Divinity'; Josephus's Portrayal of the Disappearances of Enoch, Elijah, and Moses," *JBL* 108 (1989) 225–38.

died but had been translated alive and made immortal, like the fore-fathers of the Greeks and Romans.[85] Another Jewish writer who wrote in Greek shows that the idea of resurrection could be associated with the Greco-Roman ideas of translation and deification. Phocylides was a Greek poet from Miletus who lived in the sixth century B.C.E. Around the turn of the era, a Jewish poet wrote a work under the name and in the style of Phocylides (hence he is known as Pseudo-Phocylides), possibly in Alexandria.[86] A section of this poem is devoted to death and afterlife. The author advocates moderation in grief (lines 97–98) and the duty of burying the dead (99). He then advises against opening the graves of the deceased (100–102). The rejected practice may be secondary burial[87] or the removal of bodies from their graves in order to dissect the corpses.[88] The following statement is given as the reason: "For in fact we hope that the remains of the departed will soon come to the light again out of the earth. And afterwards they become gods" (103–104).[89] The coming to light of the remains of the departed out of the earth is a clear expression of hope in the bodily type of res-urrection, which will be discussed later. The statement that the dead become gods after being raised is an expression of the idea of res-urrection in Greco-Roman terms. The word *god* in Greek is synony-mous with the word *immortal*. So Pseudo-Phocylides is using typical Greek language of the blessed dead to express the idea that the res-urrected faithful are exalted to the angelic state. We should recall at this point that the community at Qumran referred to angelic beings as "gods" (*elim*).

THE RESURRECTION OF JESUS IN MARK

At the time the Gospel of Mark was written, two basic notions of resurrection were current: one that emphasized its heavenly character

85. In spite of the statement in Deuteronomy that Moses died, Josephus did not believe that he did (see Begg, "Some Observations," 692).

86. P. W. van der Horst, *The Sentences of Pseudo-Phocylides* (Leiden: Brill, 1978) 81–83. Van der Horst dates the work between 30 B.C.E. and 40 C.E.

87. The placement of bones in an ossuary was a common form of secondary burial in the ancient world (Jack Finegan, *The Archaeology of the New Testament* [Princeton: Princeton Univ. Press, 1969] 216–18).

88. Van der Horst, *Pseudo-Phocylides*, 82, 183–84.

89. Translation by van der Horst, ibid., 95; the Greek text is given on p. 94; see also the discussion on pp. 186–88.

and one that emphasized its bodily character. The heavenly type was expressed in Daniel 12, as was pointed out earlier.[90] The bodily or physical type is attested by 2 Maccabees. This work contains the story of seven brothers and their mother who were tortured and killed during the persecution of Antiochus IV Epiphanes. Among the tortures were the cutting out of the tongue and the cutting off of hands and feet. Regarding the torture of the third son, the text reads: "When it was demanded, he quickly put out his tongue and courageously stretched forth his hands, and said nobly, 'I got these from Heaven, and because of his laws I disdain them, and from him I hope to get them back again'" (2 Macc 7:10-11).[91] There is no sign in the book of Daniel of a belief in bodily resurrection of the type present in 2 Maccabees. In the later period, however, the two types could be combined, as the example of Pseudo-Phocylides shows.[92]

Two elements are constant, however, in Jewish literature of the time, namely, that resurrection is a collective event and that it is an event of the future.[93] The notion of resurrection did not necessarily imply its universality.[94] The picture of Daniel 12 is collective but not universal: "Many . . . shall awake" (v 2). In 2 Maccabees the emphasis is on the restoration of individuals, because of the narrative context. Nevertheless, the implicit context of the resurrection is the apocalyptic notion of the renewal of all creation.[95] Thus one of the innovations of the Christian movement was the claim that God had raised a single

90. The heavenly notion of resurrection is also expressed in the Epistle of Enoch (chaps. 91–104 of *1 Enoch*). The righteous "will shine like the lights of heaven" and the gate of heaven will be opened to them. They will "have great joy like the angels of heaven" and will "be associates of the host of heaven" (*1 Enoch* 104:2, 4, 6; the translation cited is by M. A. Knibb in *The Apocryphal Old Testament* [ed. H. F. D. Sparks; Oxford: Clarendon, 1984] 312). See also the Similitudes of Enoch, in which it is said that the resurrected righteous "will become angels in heaven" (*1 Enoch* 51:4; *Apocryphal Old Testament*, 231).

91. See also 2 Macc 14:37-46.

92. Pseudo-Phocylides incorporates several different understandings of afterlife with little concern for systematic coherence (see van der Horst, *Pseudo-Phocylides*, 188–89).

93. The idea that individual humans who had been translated would return to the earth at the end was widespread in Jewish literature of the second temple period, but these were men who had not died and thus did not need to be resurrected (e.g., Mal 4:5 [MT 3:23]; *1 Enoch* 90:31).

94. Many texts speaks only of a resurrection of the just, e.g., *Pss. Sol.* 3:10-12 [3:13-16].

95. On the apocalyptic background of the resurrection in 2 Maccabees and the reasons for its muted character, see Nickelsburg, *Resurrection*, 93–109.

individual, Jesus. Paul explained the resurrection of Jesus as the beginning of the renewal that would soon be followed by the resurrection of those who belong to him (1 Cor 15:20-23, 51-52).

The author of Mark was heir to the shocking but simple Christian proclamation that God had raised Jesus from the dead and to the tradition that the risen Jesus had appeared at least to Peter and to the twelve. In writing an extended narrative that expressed the good news (*euangelion*; 1:1) of God's activity through Jesus, this author was faced with the challenge of narrating the resurrection. I have argued elsewhere that the genre of Mark is history in the apocalyptic mode.[96] My working hypothesis in this essay is that Mark 16:1-8 is fiction. In composing the story of the empty tomb, the author of Mark interpreted the proclamation that Jesus had been raised.

I am aware that objections have been raised to the notion that evangelists made up episodes and speeches.[97] With regard to speeches, it is widely known that Thucydides, the ancient historian with the most rigorous standards of evidence, stated explicitly that he constructed the speeches in his history of the Peloponnesian War by giving "whatever seemed most appropriate to me for each speaker to say in the particular circumstances, keeping as closely as possible to the general sense of what was actually said" (1.22).[98] I submit that the author of Mark did something analogous. He was convinced that what actually had happened was that Jesus had been raised from the dead. In composing 16:1-8, he described that event in what seemed to him the most appropriate way. So I am not arguing that the author of Mark made up this episode out of whole cloth. He regarded the resurrection of Jesus as an event attested by those to whom the risen Jesus had appeared. Since he did not have evidence for the details regarding how Jesus was raised, he supplied those details in accordance with his sense of what must have happened. Because the male disciples had fled from the scene of the arrest, presumably to avoid being arrested

96. Adela Yarbro Collins, "Narrative, History, and Gospel: A General Response," *Genre, Narrativity, and Theology* (ed. Mary Gerhart and James G. Williams; *Semeia* 43; Atlanta: Scholars Press, 1988) 145–53; see also chap. 1 above, "Is Mark's Gospel a Life of Jesus? The Question of Genre."

97. Eleonore Stump, "Visits to the Sepulcher and Biblical Exegesis," *Faith and Philosophy* 6 (1989) 367–68.

98. Cited by Oswyn Murray, "Greek Historians," *The Oxford History of the Classical World* (ed. John Boardman et al.; New York: Oxford Univ. Press, 1986) 193–94.

themselves, and since the author apparently assumed that they were in hiding at the time of the crucifixion and burial, it seemed most appropriate to have female disciples discover the empty tomb.

The creation of the empty tomb story shows that the author of Mark had a notion of resurrection closer to that of 2 Maccabees than to that of Daniel 12. Resurrection for Mark is not the giving of a new, spiritual body to the inner person in a way that the former body does not matter. For Mark it is either a revival or transformation of the earthly body. If the text implies that Jesus pushed the stone away from the tomb and walked out, the resurrection is understood as the revival of the body.[99] But such is not a necessary implication. The stone had to be rolled aside so that the women could enter the tomb and see that Jesus was not there. The stone could just as well have been moved by the angel. At least this is how the author of Matthew seems to have understood Mark (Matt 28:2).[100] If the text does not imply that Jesus walked out of the tomb, according to Mark, his resurrection is best understood as a transformation of his earthly body.

If the risen Jesus is not pictured as walking out of the tomb, the alternative, in the language of the modern Western Christian exegete, is that he ascended to heaven immediately.[101] It has been pointed out that the ascension of Jesus, as narrated in the book of Acts, is similar to the Greco-Roman narratives of translation.[102] I am suggesting that this tradition also influenced how Mark narrated the resurrection.[103] The Christian affirmation was that a single individual, Jesus, had been raised from the dead. Apart from the usual collective context of the Jewish notion of resurrection, this affirmation seemed quite similar to the claim made in some Jewish circles that Enoch had been taken up to heaven and to the claims made in Greco-Roman circles regarding

99. Bultmann implies that the position of the stone when the women come to the tomb indicates that Jesus pushed it aside (*History*, 290 n. 3).

100. Compare the *Gospel of Peter* in which the stone rolls away by itself, presumably by divine power (*Gospel of Peter* 37; an English translation is given in David R. Cartlidge and David L. Dungan, *Documents for the Study of the Gospels* [Philadelphia: Fortress, 1980] 85).

101. Bultmann, *History*, 290 n. 3.

102. Hans Conzelmann, *Acts of the Apostles* (Hermeneia; Philadelphia: Fortress, 1987) 7 n. 26; Haenchen, *Acts*, 149 n. 5.

103. Citing a brief suggestion by F. Pfister, Pease notes that the disappearance of the body of Jesus from the tomb is like certain pagan traditions, but he does not attempt to explain the likenesses or to reconstruct the process by which they arose ("Invisibility," 29).

the translation or apotheosis of heroes, rulers, and emperors.[104] I am not claiming that the empty tomb story was created with an apologetic purpose in the narrow sense. It was not meant to *prove* to outsiders that Jesus really was raised. Rather, the narrative pattern according to which Jesus died, was buried, and then was translated to heaven was a culturally defined way for an author living in the first century to narrate the resurrection of Jesus.

One could object that it is hard to find much influence of Greco-Roman literature in Mark. The first response that must be made to such an objection is to remind the objector that the Gospel of Mark was composed in Greek. This simple fact speaks volumes about the cultural milieu in which the text was written. One does not learn and use a language without being influenced by the culture of which it is part. Similarly, one does not address people competent in a certain language without drawing upon the thought-world for which that language is a vehicle. Recent studies have supported older suggestions that there are significant similarities between Mark and Greco-Roman literature in form, content, and style.[105]

If, according to Mark, Jesus was translated from the grave to heaven, then there was no period of time during which the risen Jesus walked the earth and met with his disciples. The book of Acts states that he did so for forty days. The Gospels of John and Luke also imply that he did so, but, in the case of John at least, for a shorter period. Even Matthew recounts a scene in which the women meet the risen Jesus and take hold of his feet (28:9). If, as previously concluded, the author of Mark accepted the tradition that the risen Jesus had appeared to Peter and to the twelve, this appearance (or appearances) was probably of a more heavenly type, like the apocalyptic visions of heavenly beings. The appearance to the eleven in Galilee in Matthew (28:16-20) may

---

104. On the translation of rulers and emperors, see ibid., 16–17.
105. Hubert Cancik, "Die Gattung Evangelium. Markus im Rahmen der antiken Historiographie," *Markus-Philologie: Historische, literargeschichtliche und stilistische Untersuchungen zum zweiten Evangelium* (ed. Hubert Cancik; WUNT 33; Tübingen: Mohr/Siebeck, 1984) 85–113; idem, "Bios und Logos: Formengeschichtliche Untersuchungen zu Lukians 'Leben des Demonax,'" ibid., 115–30; Marius Reiser, "Der Alexanderroman und das Markusevangelium," ibid., 131–63; Gert Lüderitz, "Rhetorik, Poetik, Kompositionstechnik im Markusevangelium," ibid., 165–203; David E. Aune, *The New Testament in Its Literary Environment* (Philadelphia: Westminster, 1987); Vernon K. Robbins, *Jesus the Teacher: A Socio-Rhetorical Interpretation of Mark* (Philadelphia: Fortress, 1984; 1992, paperback ed. with new intro.).

be understood in this way. The appearance to Paul as it is narrated in Acts is definitely of this type.

CONCLUSION

The effect of this understanding of the resurrection of Jesus is to place the accent on the absence of Jesus more than on the presence of Jesus during the time of the readers. As noted earlier, this accent is related to apocalyptic expectation. The disciples have a mission in this world (Mark 13:9-13; 8:34-37) and they will be judged on the basis of their fulfillment or nonfulfillment of that mission (8:38). The interpretation of the resurrection of Jesus as a type of translation affects one's reading of the apocalyptic discourse of chapter 13. That discourse has its climax in the prediction of the coming of the Son of Man in clouds with great power and glory. The result of his appearance is his sending out the angels to gather the faithful "from the four winds, from the end of the earth to the end of heaven" (13:27). It is likely that this prediction refers to the same event that Paul describes in 1 Thess 4:17 and 1 Cor 15:52. As their master was translated, so will his faithful disciples be.

BIBLIOGRAPHY

Achtemeier, Paul J. "Miracles and the Historical Jesus: A Study of Mark 9:14-29," *CBQ* 37 (1975) 471–91.

Allen, Thomas W. *Homer: The Origins and the Transmission*. Oxford: Clarendon, 1924.

Attridge, Harold. "The Gospel of Truth as an Exoteric Text." In *Nag Hammadi, Gnosticism, and Early Christianity*. Ed. Charles W. Hedrick and Robert Hodgson, Jr. Peabody, Mass.: Hendrickson, 1986. Pp. 239–55.

Auerbach, E. *Mimesis: The Representation of Reality in Western Literature*. Princeton: Princeton Univ. Press, 1953.

Aune, David E. "The Apocalypse of John and the Problem of Genre." In *Early Christian Apocalypticism: Genre and Social Setting*. Ed. Adela Yarbro Collins. *Semeia* 36. Atlanta: Scholars Press, 1986. Pp. 65–96.

———. "Greco-Roman Biography." In *Greco-Roman Literature and the New Testament*. Ed. David E. Aune. Atlanta: Scholars Press, 1988. Pp. 107–26.

———. *The New Testament in Its Literary Environment*. Philadelphia: Westminster, 1987.

Bauer, Walter, William F. Arndt, and F. Wilbur Gingrich, eds. *A Greek-English Lexicon of the New Testament and Other Early Christian Literature*. 2d ed. revised and augmented by F. Wilbur Gingrich and Frederick W. Danker. Chicago: Univ. of Chicago Press, 1979.

Beasley-Murray, G. R. *Jesus and the Future: An Examination of the Criticism of the Eschatological Discourse, Mark 13, with Special Reference to the Little Apocalypse Theory*. London: Macmillan, 1954.

————. "The Rise and Fall of the Little Apocalypse Theory," *ExpTim* 64 (1953) 346–49.

————. "Second Thoughts on the Composition of Mark 13," *NTS* 29 (1983) 414–20.

Begg, Christopher. " 'Josephus's Portrayal of the Disappearances of Enoch, Elijah, and Moses': Some Observations," *JBL* 109 (1990) 691–93.

Best, Ernest. *The Temptation and the Passion: The Markan Soteriology*. 2d ed. Cambridge: Cambridge Univ. Press, 1990.

Betz, H. D., ed. *The Greek Magical Papyri in Translation: Including the Demotic Spells*. Vol. 1, *Texts*. Chicago: Univ. of Chicago Press, 1986.

Bickermann, E. "Das leere Grab," *ZNW* 23 (1924) 281–92.

Bilezikian, Gilbert G. *The Liberated Gospel: A Comparison of the Gospel of Mark and Greek Tragedy*. Grand Rapids, Mich.: Baker, 1977.

Boring, M. Eugene. "Mark 1:1-15 and the Beginning of the Gospel," *Semeia* 52 (1991) 43–81.

Brandenburger, Egon. *Markus 13 und die Apokalyptik*. Göttingen: Vandenhoeck & Ruprecht, 1984.

Brenton, Lancelot C. L. *The Septuagint with Apocrypha: Greek and English*. London: Samuel Bagster & Sons, 1851. Reprint. Peabody, Mass.: Hendrickson, 1986.

Brown, Raymond E. "The Burial of Jesus (Mark 15:42-47)," *CBQ* 50 (1988) 233–45.

Buckley, E. R. "The Sources of the Passion Narrative in St. Mark's Gospel," *JTS* 34 (1932/33) 138–44.

Budge, E. A. Wallis. *Amulets and Superstitions*. London: Oxford Univ. Press, 1930. Reprint. New York: Dover, 1978.

Bultmann, Rudolf. *The History of the Synoptic Tradition*. Trans. John Marsh. Rev. ed. New York: Harper & Row, 1968.

————. "Neues Testament und Mythologie: Das Problem der Entmythologisierung der neutestamentlichen Verkündigung." In *Offenbarung und Heilsgeschehen*. BEvT 7. Munich: A. Lempp, 1941. Reprint in *Kerygma und Mythos*, vol. 1. Ed. H. W. Bartsch. Hamburg-Volksdorf: Herbert Reich, 1948. ET: "New Testament and Mythology: The Mythological Element in the Message of the New Testament and the Problem of Its Reinterpretation." In *Kerygma and Myth: A Theological Debate*. Ed. H. W. Bartsch. Rev. ed. Reginald Fuller. New York: Harper & Row, 1961.

————. *Theology of the New Testament*. 2 vols. New York: Scribner's, 1951–55.

Burnham, Frederic B. "The Bible and Contemporary Science," *The Bible and the Intellectual Life, Religion and Intellectual Life* 6 (1989).

Cancik, Hubert, ed. *Markus-Philologie: Historische, literargeschichtliche und stilistische Untersuchungen zum zweiten Evangelium*. WUNT 33. Tübingen: Mohr/Siebeck, 1984.

Carroll, Robert P. *When Prophecy Failed: Cognitive Dissonance in the Prophetic Traditions of the Old Testament*. New York: Seabury, 1979.

Cartlidge, David R., and David L. Dungan. *Documents for the Study of the Gospels*. Philadelphia: Fortress, 1980.

Cary, M., et al., eds. *The Oxford Classical Dictionary*. Oxford: Clarendon, 1949.

Cavallin, H. C. C. *Life after Death: Paul's Argument for the Resurrection of the Dead in I Cor. 15*. Part I, *An Enquiry into the Jewish Background*. Lund: Gleerup, 1974.

Charles, R. H. *A Critical and Exegetical Commentary on the Book of Daniel*. ICC. Oxford: Clarendon, 1929.

Collins, Adela Yarbro. "Narrative, History, and Gospel: A General Response." In *Genre, Narrativity, and Theology*. Pp. 145–53. *See* Gerhart.

————. "The Origin of the Designation of Jesus as 'Son of Man,' " *HTR* 80 (1987) 391–407.

Collins, John J. *The Apocalyptic Imagination*. New York: Crossroad, 1984.

Conzelmann, Hans. *Acts of the Apostles*. Hermeneia. Philadelphia: Fortress, 1987.

————. *1 Corinthians*. Hermeneia. Philadelphia: Fortress, 1975.

Cox, A. Cleveland. *Fathers of the Third and Fourth Centuries*. Vol. 7 of *The Ante-Nicene Fathers*. Ed. Alexander Roberts and James Donaldson. 10 vols. C. 1886. Reprint. Grand Rapids: Eerdmans, 1985.

Cox, Patricia. *Biography in Late Antiquity: A Quest for the Holy Man*. Berkeley: Univ. of California Press, 1983.

Crossan, John Dominic. "Aphorism in Discourse and Narrative." In *Genre, Narrativity, and Theology*. Pp. 121–36. *See* Gerhart.

————. *The Cross That Spoke: The Origins of the Passion Narrative*. San Francisco: Harper & Row, 1988.

————. "Empty Tomb and Absent Lord (Mark 16:1-8)." In *The Passion in Mark*. Pp. 138–45. *See* Kelber.

Cumont, Franz. *Lux Perpetua*. Paris: P. Geuthner, 1949.

Dibelius, Martin. *From Tradition to Gospel*. New York: Scribner's, 1935. Originally, *Die Formgeschichte des Evangeliums* (Tübingen: Mohr/Siebeck, 1919).

Donahue, John R. *Are You the Christ? The Trial Narrative in the Gospel of Mark*. SBLDS 10. Missoula, Mont.: Scholars Press, 1973.

————. "Introduction: From Passion Traditions to Passion Narrative." In *The Passion in Mark*. Pp. 1–20. *See* Kelber.

————. "Temple, Trial, and Royal Christology (Mark 14:53-65)." In *The Passion in Mark*. Pp. 61–79. *See* Kelber.

Dormeyer, Detlev. *Die Passion Jesu als Verhaltensmodell: Literarische und theologische Analyse der Traditions- und Redaktionsgeschichte der Markuspassion*. Münster: Aschendorff, 1974.

Doty, W. G. "The Concept of Genre in Literary Analysis." In *The Genre of the Gospels: Studies in Methodology, Comparative Research and Compositional Analysis*. Missoula, Mont.: SBL, 1972. Pp. 29–64.

Dowd, Sharyn Echols. *Prayer, Power, and the Problem of Suffering: Mark 11:22-25 in the Context of Markan Theology*. Atlanta: Scholars Press, 1988.

Drury, John. "Mark." In *The Literary Guide to the Bible*. Ed. Robert Alter and Frank Kermode. Cambridge: Belknap Press of Harvard Univ. Press, 1987. Pp. 402–17.

Dubrow, H. *Genre*. New York: Methuen, 1982.

Duling, Dennis C. "Testament of Solomon." In *The Old Testament Pseudepigrapha*. Vol. 1, *Apocalyptic Literature and Testaments*. Ed. James H. Charlesworth. Garden City, N.Y.: Doubleday, 1983. Pp. 935–87.

Festinger, Leon. *A Theory of Cognitive Dissonance*. Stanford, Calif.: Stanford Univ. Press, 1957.

Festinger, Leon, et al. *When Prophecy Fails: A Social and Psychological Study of a Modern Group that Predicted the Destruction of the World*. Minneapolis: Univ. of Minnesota Press, 1956.

Finegan, Jack. *The Archaeology of the New Testament*. Princeton: Princeton Univ. Press, 1969.

Ford, Desmond. *The Abomination of Desolation in Biblical Eschatology*. Washington, D.C.: Univ. Press of America, 1982.

Forsyth, Neil. *The Old Enemy: Satan and the Combat Myth*. Princeton: Princeton Univ. Press, 1987.

Fowler, A. *Kinds of Literature: An Introduction to the Theory of Genres and Modes*. Cambridge: Harvard Univ. Press, 1982.

Frazer, James G., trans. *Apollodorus: The Library*. LCL. Cambridge: Harvard Univ. Press, 1961.

Freyne, Sean. Review of *Jesus the Magician*, by Morton Smith. *CBQ* 41 (1979) 658–61.

Fridrichsen, Anton. *The Problem of Miracle in Primitive Christianity*. Trans. R. A. Harrisville and J. S. Hanson. Minneapolis: Augsburg, 1972.

Gager, John G. *Kingdom and Community: The Social World of Early Christianity*. Englewood Cliffs, N.J.: Prentice-Hall, 1975.

Gallagher, Eugene V. Review of *Biography in Late Antiquity*, by Patricia Cox. *JBL* 104 (1985) 373–75.

Gaston, L. *No Stone on Another: Studies in the Significance of the Fall of Jerusalem in the Synoptic Gospels*. NovTSup 23. Leiden: Brill, 1970.

Gerhart, Mary, and James G. Williams, eds. *Genre, Narrativity, and Theology*. Semeia 43. Atlanta: Scholars Press, 1988.

Gnilka, Joachim. *Das Evangelium nach Markus*. 2 vols. Zurich: Benziger, 1978–79.

Goodman, Felicitas D. *Anneliese Michel und ihre Dämonen: Der Fall Klingenberg in wissenschaftlicher Sicht*. Stein am Rhein: Christiana, 1980. English edition: idem, *The Exorcism of Anneliese Michel*. New York: Doubleday, 1981.

———. *Ecstasy, Ritual and Alternate Reality: Religion in a Pluralistic World*. Bloomington, Ind.: Indiana Univ. Press, 1988.

———. "Glossolalia and Hallucination in Pentecostal Congregations," *Psychiatria Clinica* 6 (1973) 97–103.

———. "Glossolalia and Single-Limb Trance: Some Parallels," *Psychotherapy and Psychosomatics* 19 (1971) 92–103.

———. *How about Demons? Possession and Exorcism in the Modern World*. Bloomington, Ind.: Indiana Univ. Press, 1988.

———. *Speaking in Tongues: A Cross-Cultural Study of Glossolalia*. Chicago: Univ. of Chicago Press, 1972.

Green, Joel B. *The Death of Jesus: Tradition and Interpretation in the Passion Narrative*. Tübingen: Mohr/Siebeck, 1988.

Gundry, Robert H. "Recent Investigations into the Literary Genre 'Gospel.'" In *New Dimensions in New Testament Study*. Ed. R. N. Longenecker and M. C. Tenney. Grand Rapids, Mich.: Zondervan, 1974. Pp. 97–114.

Hadas, Moses, and Morton Smith. *Heroes and Gods: Spiritual Biographies in Antiquity*. New York: Harper & Row, 1965.

Haenchen, Ernst. *The Acts of the Apostles: A Commentary*. Philadelphia: Westminster, 1971.

Hall, Robert G. *Revealed Histories: Techniques for Ancient Jewish and Christian Historiography*. Journal for the Study of the Pseudepigrapha Supplement Series 6. Sheffield: JSOT Press, 1991.

Halpern, Baruch. *The First Historians: The Hebrew Bible and History*. San Francisco: Harper & Row, 1988.

Hamilton, N. Q. "Resurrection Tradition and the Composition of Mark," *JBL* 84 (1965) 415–21.

Hammond, Gerald. "English Translations of the Bible." In *The Literary Guide to the Bible*. Ed. Robert Alter and Frank Kermode. Cambridge: Harvard Univ. Press, 1987. Pp. 647–66.

Hare, D. R. A. "The Lives of the Prophets." In *The Old Testament Pseudepigrapha*. Vol. 2, *Expansions of the "Old Testament" and Legends, Wisdom and Philosophical Literature, Prayers, Psalms, and Odes, Fragments of Lost Judeo-Hellenistic Works*. Ed. James H. Charlesworth. Garden City, N.Y.: Doubleday, 1985. Pp. 379–99.

Hartman, Lars. *Prophecy Interpreted: The Formation of Some Jewish Apocalyptic Texts and of the Eschatological Discourse Mark 13 Par*. Lund: Gleerup, 1966.

Harvey, Van A. *The Historian and the Believer*. New York: Macmillan, 1966.

Hedrick, Charles W. "The Role of 'Summary Statements' in the Composition of the Gospel of Mark: A Dialog with Karl Schmidt and Norman Perrin," *NovT* 26 (1984) 289–311.

———. "What Is a Gospel? Geography, Time and Narrative Structure," *Perspectives in Religious Studies* 10 (1983) 255–68.

Henney, Jeannette H. "Spirit-Possession Belief and Trance Behavior in Two Fundamentalist Groups in St. Vincent." In *Trance, Healing and Hallucination*. Pp. 1–111. *See* Zaretsky.

Hess, David J. "Spirit Surgeons and Wounded Laws: Ideology and Spiritism in the Brazilian New Republic." Lecture at the Univ. of Notre Dame, April 20, 1989.

Holladay, Carl R. *Theios Aner in Hellenistic Judaism: A Critique of the Use of This Category in New Testament Christology.* Missoula, Mont.: Scholars Press, 1977.

Horgan, Maurya. *Pesharim: Qumran Interpretations of Biblical Books.* CBQMS 8. Washington, D.C.: Catholic Biblical Association, 1979.

Horsley, Richard A., and John S. Hanson. *Bandits, Prophets, and Messiahs: Popular Movements in the Time of Jesus.* Minneapolis: Winston, 1985.

Hull, John M. *Hellenistic Magic and the Synoptic Tradition.* Naperville, Ill.: Allenson, 1974.

Hume, David. *An Enquiry concerning Human Understanding.* In *The English Philosophers from Bacon to Mill.* Ed. Edwin A. Burtt. New York: Modern Library, 1939.

Jackson, Hugh. "The Resurrection Belief of the Earliest Church: A Response to the Failure of Prophecy?" *JR* 55 (1975) 415–25.

Jacoby, Felix. *Die Fragmente der griechischen Historiker. Geschichte von Staedten und Voelkern, C: Autoren ueber einzelne Laender.* Leiden: Brill, 1958.

Jaynes, Julian. *The Origin of Consciousness in the Breakdown of the Bicameral Mind.* Boston: Houghton Mifflin, 1976.

Jeremias, Joachim. "Die älteste Schicht der Osterüberlieferungen." In *Resurrexit: Actes du symposium international sur la résurrection de Jésus.* Ed. E. Dhanis. Rome: Libreria Editrice Vaticana, 1974. ET: J. Jeremias, *New Testament Theology: The Proclamation of Jesus.* New York: Scribner's, 1971.

Juel, Donald. *Messiah and Temple: The Trial of Jesus in the Gospel of Mark.* Missoula, Mont.: Scholars Press, 1977.

Kee, Howard Clark. "Aretalogy and Gospel," *JBL* 92 (1973) 402–22.

——. *Community of the New Age.* 2d ed. Macon, Ga.: Macon Univ. Press, 1984.

——. *Medicine, Miracle and Magic in New Testament Times.* Cambridge: Cambridge Univ. Press, 1986.

——. *Miracle in the Early Christian World: A Study in Sociohistorical Method.* New Haven: Yale Univ. Press, 1983.

Kelber, Werner. *The Kingdom in Mark: A New Place and a New Time*. Philadelphia: Fortress, 1974.

———. "Narrative and Disclosure: Mechanisms of Concealing, Revealing, and Reveiling." In *Genre, Narrativity, and Theology*. Pp. 1–20. *See* Gerhart.

———. *The Oral and the Written Gospel*. Philadelphia: Fortress, 1983.

———., ed. *The Passion in Mark: Studies on Mark 14–16*. Philadelphia: Fortress, 1976.

Kloppenborg, John. "An Analysis of the Pre-Pauline Formula in 1 Cor 15:3b-5 in Light of Some Recent Literature," *CBQ* 40 (1978) 351–52.

———. *The Formation of Q*. Philadelphia: Fortress, 1987.

Koester, Helmut. *Introduction to the New Testament*. Vol. 2, *History and Literature of Early Christianity*. Philadelphia: Fortress, 1982.

Kraemer, Ross S. *Maenads, Martyrs, Matrons, Monastics: A Sourcebook on Women's Religions in the Greco-Roman World*. Philadelphia: Fortress, 1988.

Kümmel, Werner G. *Introduction to the New Testament*. Trans. H. C. Kee. Revised and expanded English edition. Nashville: Abingdon, 1975.

Lambert, W. G. *Babylonian Wisdom Literature*. Oxford: Clarendon, 1960.

Lambrecht, J. *Die Redaktion der Markus-Apokalypse: Literarische Analyse und Strukturuntersuchung*. Analecta Biblica 28. Rome: Pontifical Biblical Institute, 1967.

Lefkowitz, Mary R. *The Lives of the Greek Poets*. Baltimore: Johns Hopkins Univ. Press, 1981.

Lewis, I. M. *Ecstatic Religion: An Anthropological Study of Spirit Possession and Shamanism*. Baltimore: Penguin, 1971.

Liddell, Henry G., Robert Scott, and Henry S. Jones, eds. *A Greek-English Lexicon*. 9th ed. Oxford: Clarendon, 1940. Reprint. 1966.

Linnemann, Eta. *Studien zur Passionsgeschichte*. Göttingen: Vandenhoeck & Ruprecht, 1970.

Lockwood, John F. "Apollodorus [6]," *Oxford Classical Dictionary*. Pp. 69–70. *See* Cary.

Lohfink, G. *Die Himmelfahrt Jesu*. SANT 26. Munich: Kösel, 1971.

Lüderitz, Gert. "Rhetorik, Poetik, Kompositionstechnik im Markusevangelium." In *Markus-Philologie*. Pp. 165–203. *See* Cancik.

McDonald, Alexander H. "Nicolaus of Damascus," *Oxford Classical Dictionary*. P. 607. *See* Cary.

Mack, Burton. *A Myth of Innocence: Mark and Christian Origins*. Philadelphia: Fortress, 1988.

Magness, J. Lee. *Sense and Absence: Structure and Suspension in the Ending of Mark's Gospel*. Atlanta: Scholars Press, 1986.

Marxsen, Willi. *Mark the Evangelist: Studies on the Redaction History of the Gospel*. Nashville: Abingdon, 1969.

May, Herbert G., and Bruce M. Metzger, eds. "English Versions of the Bible." In *The New Oxford Annotated Bible with the Apocrypha, Expanded Edition, Revised Standard Version*. New York: Oxford Univ. Press, 1977. Pp. 1551–57.

Merkur, Daniel. "The Visionary Practices of Jewish Apocalyptists," *Psychoanalytic Study of Society* 14 (1989) 119–48.

Metzger, Bruce M. *A Textual Commentary on the Greek New Testament*. New York: United Bible Societies, 1971.

Mohr, Till Arend. *Markus- und Johannespassion: Redaktions- und traditionsgeschichtliche Untersuchung der Markinischen und Johanneischen Passionstradition*. Zurich: Theologischer Verlag Zürich, 1982.

Momigliano, Arnaldo. *The Development of Greek Biography*. Cambridge: Harvard Univ. Press, 1971.

Moule, C. F. D. "Introduction (to the English Edition)." In *The Significance of the Message of the Resurrection for Faith in Jesus Christ*. Ed. C. F. D. Moule. SBT 2/8. Naperville, Ill.: Allenson, 1968. Pp. 9–10.

———. *The Origin of Christology*. Cambridge: Cambridge Univ. Press, 1977.

Murray, Oswyn. "Greek Historians." In *The Oxford History of the Classical World*. Ed. John Boardman et al. New York: Oxford Univ. Press, 1986. Pp. 186–203.

Nestle, Eberhard, and Erwin Nestle, Kurt Aland et al., eds. *Novum Testamentum Graece*. 26th ed. Stuttgart: Deutsche Bibelgesellschaft, 1979.

Nevius, J. L. *Demon Possession and Allied Themes*. Chicago: Revell, 1986.

Nickelsburg, George W. E., Jr. *Resurrection, Immortality, and Eternal Life in Intertestamental Judaism*. Cambridge: Harvard Univ. Press, 1972.

Niebuhr, Richard R. *Resurrection and Historical Reason*. New York: Scribner's, 1957.

Oesterreich, Traugott K. *Possession, Demoniacal and Other: Among Primitive Races in Antiquity, the Middle Ages, and Modern Times*. Trans. D. Ibberson. London: Kegan Paul, 1930.

Pease, Arthur S. "Some Aspects of Invisibility," *HSCP* 53 (1942) 1–36.

Perkins, Pheme. *Resurrection: New Testament Witness and Contemporary Reflection*. Garden City, N.Y.: Doubleday, 1984.

Perrin, Norman. *The Resurrection according to Matthew, Mark, and Luke*. Philadelphia: Fortress, 1977.

———. *What Is Redaction Criticism?* Philadelphia: Fortress, 1969.

Perrin, Norman, and Dennis C. Duling. *The New Testament: An Introduction*. 2d ed. New York: Harcourt Brace Jovanovich, 1982.

Perry, Ben. *Aesopica*. Urbana, Ill.: The Univ. of Illinois Press, 1952.

Pesch, Rudolf. *Das Evangelium der Urgemeinde: Wiederhergestellt und erläutert*. Freiburg/Basel/Vienna: Herder, 1979.

———. *Das Markusevangelium*. HTKNT 2. 2 vols. Freiburg/Basel/Vienna: Herder, 1976–77.

———. *Naherwartungen: Tradition und Redaktion in Mark 13*. Düsseldorf: Patmos, 1968.

Preisendanz, Karl, ed. *Papyri Graecae Magicae: Die griechischen Zauberpapyri*. Rev. ed. by Albert Henrichs. Stuttgart: Teubner, 1973.

Pressel, Esther. "Umbanda Trance and Possession in Sao Paulo, Brazil." In *Trance, Healing and Hallucination*, Pp. 113–225. *See* Zaretsky.

Priessnig, Anton. "Die literarische Form der Patriarchenbiographien des Philon von Alexandrien," *Monatschrift für Geschichte und Wissenschaft des Judentums* 37 (1929) 143–55.

Pritchard, James B., ed. *Ancient Near Eastern Texts Relating to the Old Testament*. 3d ed. Princeton: Princeton Univ. Press, 1969.

Räisänen, Heikki. *The 'Messianic Secret' in Mark*. Studies of the New Testament and Its World. Edinburgh: T. & T. Clark, 1990.

Reiser, Marius. "Der Alexanderroman und das Markusevangelium." In *Markus-Philologie*. Pp. 131–63. *See* Cancik.

Rhoads, David, and Donald Michie. *Mark as Story: An Introduction to the Narrative of a Gospel*. Philadelphia: Fortress, 1982.

Robbins, Vernon. *Jesus the Teacher: A Socio-Rhetorical Interpretation of Mark*. Philadelphia: Fortress, 1984; 1992, paperback ed. with new introduction.

Robinson, James M. "LOGOI SOPHON: On the Gattung of Q." In James M. Robinson and Helmut Koester. *Trajectories through Early Christianity*. Philadelphia: Fortress, 1971. Pp. 71–113.

————. "On the Gattung of Mark (and John)." In *Jesus and Man's Hope*. Ed. D. G. Buttrick. 2 vols. Pittsburgh: Pittsburgh Theological Seminary, 1970/71. Vol. 1, pp. 99–129.

————. *The Problem of History in Mark: And Other Marcan Studies*. Philadelphia: Fortress, 1982. Originally, *The Problem of History in Mark* (London: SCM, 1957).

Rohde, Erwin. *Psyche: The Cult of Souls and Belief in Immortality among the Greeks*. New York: Harcourt Brace Jovanovich, 1925.

Rolfe, John C. "Cornelius (2) Nepos," *Oxford Classical Dictionary*. P. 236. *See* Cary.

Ruhland, Maria. *Die Markuspassion aus der Sicht der Verleugnung*. Eilsbrunn: Ko'amar, 1987.

Saggs, H. W. F. *The Greatness That Was Babylon*. New York: Mentor, 1962.

Schenke, Ludger. *Der gekreuzigte Christus: Versuch einer literarkritischen und traditionsgeschichtlichen Bestimmung der vormarkinischen Passionsgeschichte*. Stuttgart: Katholisches Bibelwerk, 1974.

————. *Studien zur Passionsgeschichte des Markus: Tradition und Redaktion in Markus 14, 1-42*. Würzburg: Echter, 1971.

Schmidt, Karl Ludwig. "Die literarische Eigenart der Leidensgeschichte Jesu," *Die Christliche Welt* 32 (1918) 114–16. Reprint in *Redaktion und Theologie des Passionsberichtes nach den Synoptikern*. Ed. Meinrad Limbeck. Darmstadt: Wissenschaftliche Buchgesellschaft, 1981. Pp. 17–20.

————. *Der Rahmen der Geschichte Jesu: Literarkritische Untersuchungen zur ältesten Jesusüberlieferung*. 1919. Reprint. Darmstadt: Wissenschaftliche Buchgesellschaft, 1964.

————. "Die Stellung der Evangelien in der allgemeinen Literaturgeschichte." In *EUCHARISTERION: Studien zur Religion und Literatur des Alten und Neuen Testaments Hermann Gunkel zum 60. Geburtstag ... dargebracht*. Ed. Hans Schmidt. FRLANT, n.f. 19. Göttingen: Vandenhoeck & Ruprecht, 1923. Vol. 2, pp. 50–134.

Schubert, K. "Die Entwicklung der Auferstehungslehre von der nachexilischen bis zur frührabbinischen Zeit," *Biblische Zeitschrift*, n.f. 6 (1962) 177–214.

Schulz, S. "Die Bedeutung des Mk für die Theologiegeschichte des Urchristentums," *Second International Congress on New Testament Studies at Christ Church, Oxford.* Ed. F. L. Cross. Studia Evangelica 2–3. TU 87 (1964).

Schwally, Friedrich. *Das Leben nach dem Tode: Nach den Vorstellungen des alten Israel und das Judentums einschliesslich das Volksglaubens im Zeitalter Christi.* Giessen: J. Ricker, 1892.

Scroggs, Robin. "Section VIII: The Crucifixion." In W. Kelber, A. Kolenkow, and R. Scroggs, "Reflections on the Question: Was There a Pre-Markan Passion Narrative?" *SBL Seminar Papers 1971.* Pp. 505–85.

Senior, Donald. *The Passion of Jesus in the Gospel of Mark.* Wilmington, Del.: Michael Glazier, 1984.

Smith, Dennis. "Narrative Beginnings in Ancient Literature and Theory," *Semeia* 52 (1991) 1–9.

Smith, Morton. *Jesus the Magician.* San Francisco: Harper & Row, 1978.

——. "On the History of *apokalyptō* and *apokalypsis*." In *Apocalypticism in the Mediterranean World and the Near East.* Ed. David Hellholm. Tübingen: Mohr/Siebeck, 1983. Pp. 9–20.

——. "Prolegomena." In idem, *Clement of Alexandria and a Secret Gospel of Mark.* Cambridge: Harvard Univ. Press, 1973.

——. "Prolegomena to a Discussion of Aretalogies, Divine Men, the Gospels and Jesus," *JBL* 90 (1971) 174–99.

——. *The Secret Gospel: The Discovery and Interpretation of the Secret Gospel according to Mark.* New York: Harper & Row, 1973.

Soards, Marion L. "The Question of a Pre-Markan Passion Narrative," *Biblebhashyam* 11 (1985) 144–69.

Sparks, H. F. D., ed. *The Apocryphal Old Testament.* Oxford: Clarendon, 1984.

Strauss, David F. *The Life of Jesus Critically Examined.* Trans. of 4th German ed. 3 vols. London: Chapman Brothers, 1846.

Stump, Eleonore. "Visits to the Sepulcher and Biblical Exegesis," *Faith and Philosophy* 6 (1989) 353–77.

Suggs, M. Jack. "Gospel, Genre." In *Interpreter's Dictionary of the Bible, Supplementary Volume.* Ed. Keith Crim. Nashville: Abingdon, 1976. Pp. 370–72.

Sugrue, Thomas. *There Is a River: The Story of Edgar Cayce.* Rev. ed. New York: Holt, 1945.

Tabor, James D. " 'Returning to Divinity': Josephus's Portrayal of the Disappearances of Enoch, Elijah, and Moses," *JBL* 108 (1989) 225–38.

Talbert, Charles. "The Gospel and the Gospels," *Interpretation* 33 (1979) 351–62.

———. "Once Again: Gospel Genre." In *Genre, Narrativity and Theology*. Pp. 53–73. *See* Gerhart.

———. *What Is a Gospel?* Philadelphia: Fortress, 1977.

Tannehill, Robert C. "The Disciples in Mark: The Function of a Narrative Role," *JR* 57 (1977) 386–405.

———. *The Narrative Unity of Luke-Acts: A Literary Interpretation.* Vol. 1, *The Gospel According to Luke.* Philadelphia: Fortress, 1986.

Taylor, Vincent. *The Gospel According to St. Mark.* 2d ed. Grand Rapids, Mich.: Baker, 1966.

Telford, W. R. Review of *Die Markuspassion*, by Maria Ruhland. *JTS* 40 (1989) 182–85.

Thackeray, H. St. J., and Ralph Marcus, trans. *Josephus.* Vol. 5, *Jewish Antiquities, Books V–VIII.* LCL. Cambridge: Harvard Univ. Press, 1934. Reprint. 1977.

Theissen, Gerd. *Lokalkolorit und Zeitgeschichte in den Evangelien: Ein Beitrag zur Geschichte der synoptischen Tradition.* Novum Testamentum et Orbis Antiquus 8. Freiburg, Schweiz: Universitätsverlag; Göttingen: Vandenhoeck & Ruprecht, 1989.

———. *Urchristliche Wundergeschichten: Ein Beitrag zur formgeschichtlichen Erforschung der synoptischen Evangelien.* Gütersloh: Mohn, 1974. ET: *The Miracle Stories of the Early Christian Tradition.* Trans. Francis McDonagh. Philadelphia: Fortress, 1983.

Tiede, David L. *The Charismatic Figure as Miracle Worker.* Missoula, Mont.: SBL, 1972.

———. Review of *Urchristlichen Wundergeschichten*, by Gerd Theissen. *JBL* 95 (1976) 483–84.

Torrey, Charles C. *The Lives of the Prophets: Greek Text and Translation.* JBLMS 1. Philadelphia: Society of Biblical Literature and Exegesis, 1946.

Trocmé, Etienne. *The Passion as Liturgy: A Study in the Origin of the Passion Narratives in the Four Gospels.* London: SCM, 1983.

Ulansey, David. "The Heavenly Veil Torn: Mark's Cosmic *Inclusio*," *JBL* 110 (1991) 123–25.

van der Horst, P. W. *The Sentences of Pseudo-Phocylides*. Leiden: Brill, 1978.

Vermes, Geza. *The Dead Sea Scrolls in English*. 2d ed. New York: Penguin, 1975.

————. *Jesus the Jew: A Historian's Reading of the Gospels*. Philadelphia: Fortress, 1973.

Vielhauer, Philipp. *Geschichte der urchristlichen Literatur*. New York: de Gruyter, 1975.

Vorster, Willem S. "Der Ort der Gattung Evangelium in der Literaturgeschichte." In *Verkündigung und Forschung: Wissenschaft vom Neuen Testament, Beihefte zu Evangelische Theologie* 29 (1984) 2–25.

Votaw, Clyde W. *The Gospels and Contemporary Biographies in the Greco-Roman World*. Facets Books, Biblical Series 27. Philadelphia: Fortress, 1970.

Walzer, R. *Galen on Jews and Christians*. London: Oxford Univ. Press, 1949.

Weeden, Theodore J. *Mark: Traditions in Conflict*. Philadelphia: Fortress, 1971.

Wilamowitz-Moellendorff, Ulrich von, ed. *Vitae Homeri et Hesiodi*. Kleine Texte 137. Berlin: de Gruyter, 1929.

Wrede, Wilhelm. *The Messianic Secret*. Trans. J. C. G. Greig. Library of Theological Translations. Greenwood, S.C.: Attic, 1972. Originally, *Das Messiasgeheimnis in den Evangelien*. Göttingen: Vandenhoeck & Ruprecht, 1901.

Zaretsky, Irving I., ed. *Trance, Healing and Hallucination: Three Field Studies in Religious Experience*. New York: John Wiley & Sons, 1974. Reprint. Malabar, Fla.: Robert E. Krieger Publishing Company, 1982.

Zuntz, Günther. "Ein Heide las das Markusevangelium." In *Markus-Philologie*, Pp. 205–22. *See* Cancik.

INDEX OF
MODERN AUTHORS

INDEX OF MODERN AUTHORS

Mack, B., 46, 52
Marxsen, W., 8
Merkur, D., 31 n.107
Mohr, T. A., 100
Momigliano, A., 2 nn.4, 5;
12–13, 14 n.49
Moule, C. F. D., 65 n.86
Murray, O., 28 n.100

Neirynck, F., 133 n.43
Nicklesburg, G. W. E., 144
n.95
Niebuhr, R. R., 121

Pease, A. S., 146 n.103
Perkins, P., 134, 136 n.56,
141 n.79
Perrin, N., 38, 66 n.93, 99
Pesch, R., 99, 100
Pfleiderer, O., 84
Piganiol, A., 84
Priessnig, A., 19 n.72

Räisänen, H., 116 n.76

Rawlinson, A. E. J., 84
Reiser, M., 12 n.36
Robbins, V., 12, 22, 99
Robinson, J. M., 21 n.83
Rohde, E., 140
Ruhland, M., 100

Schenke, L., 98, 104, 106,
108 n.43, 109 nn.45,
47; 110, 111, 112, 113,
114–15, 116, 117
Schmidt, K. L., 93, 94, 95,
100, 102, 103
Schreiber, J., 112 n.60
Schulz, S., 8, 20
Schwartzkopff, P., 80
Smith, D., 18 n.69
Smith, M., 10–11, 44, 57
n.60
Soards, M. L., 112 n.59
Strauss, D., 42–43, 45, 52,
73
Streeter, B. H., 84

Talbert, C., 24–26, 27
Tannehill, R. C., 69 n.96
Taylor, V., 85, 90 n.47, 96
Theissen, G., 44
Tiede, D., 57 n.60
Trocmé, E., 100

Ulansey, D., 116 n.79

Vaganay, L., 81 n.19, 83
n.24
Vermes, G., 48, 53 n.49
Vielhauer, P., 6–10, 11, 20
Votaw, C. W., 10

Weeden, T., 99
Weizsäcker, C. von, 74
n.4, 79 n.14, 83
Weiss, J., 80, 85
Wellhausen, J., 83 n.28
Wilamowitz-Moellendorff,
U. von, 21

Zuntz, G., 18 n.68

164

INDEX OF ANCIENT SOURCES

NEW TESTAMENT

167

APOCRYPHA AND PSEUDEPIGRAPHA

OTHER ANCIENT SOURCES

Ancient Near Eastern Sources

Jewish Writings

Early Christian Literature

Greek and Latin Authors

170